HOSTING
WITHOUT
HASSLE

A Complete
Guide to Easy
Entertaining
at Home

Daisy King

Rutledge Hill Press
Nashville, Tennessee

This book is dedicated to all of my busy friends
who showed me the great need for a planning guide
that takes the hassle out of entertaining.

Copyright © 1996 by Daisy King

Published by Rutledge Hill Press, Inc., 211 Seventh Avenue North, Nashville, Tennessee 37219

Distributed in Canada by H. B. Fenn & Company, Ltd., 1090 Lorimar Drive, Mississauga, Ontario L5S 1R7.

Design by Harriette Bateman/Bateman Design
Typography by Trina Fulton/TF Designs

Some of the recipes included here first appeared in other cookbooks by Daisy King.

Library of Congress Cataloging-in-Publication Data
King, Daisy, 1945–
    Hosting without hassle : a complete guide to easy entertaining at home / Daisy King.
        p.   cm.
    Includes index.
    ISBN 1-55853-395-8 (pbk.)
    1. Cookery.   2. Entertaining.   3. Menus.   4. Quick and easy cookery.
I. Title.
TX714.K566   1996
642'.4—dc20   96-12797
                                                                   CIP

Printed in the United States of America

1 2 3 4 5—99 98 97 96

CONTENTS

Afternoon *123*

Evening *179*

Celebrations 257

Lighter Fare 311

INDEX 336

I'd like to thank
Amy Lyles Wilson, Keri Moser, and Linda Bristow
for helping me with this project.
And many thanks to
the Nashville Baptist Hospital Nutrition Center
for helping gather nutritional information
for the "Lighter Fare" recipes.

NOTE TO THE READER

Each recipe contains an indication of degree of difficulty and preparation time involved. Unless otherwise noted, preparation time does *not* include cooking time.

Degrees of difficulty are as follows: Easy; Moderately easy; Moderate; and Moderately difficult.

This scale ranges from recipes requiring little or no technical skill to recipes that require some care and skill in preparation.

The icon indicates items you can purchase at your local grocery or specialty store.

INTRODUCTION

A good party doesn't just happen, not even for the host or hostess who has a natural flair for entertaining. The successful party is the result of careful planning, from the menu to the invitations, the decorations to the ambiance, as well as an awareness of just what makes an occasion memorable. It is the purpose of this book to help you do just that—create culinary memories for you and your guests.

I, like so many of you, maintain a full-time job, and still must face the challenge of preparing a meal for my family at the end of a long day. My menus are brought together from what's available in my kitchen, combined with already prepared items from grocery and specialty stores. I use any shortcuts available to me in order to get out of the kitchen and into my life!

From "Breakfast in Bed" to "Oscar Night Buffet Supper," I have provided you with several hundred easy, affordable recipes. Mixed in with regional menus and celebratory themes are shopping lists; cooking, decorating, and entertaining tips; and instructional sidebars devoted to such topics as brewing coffee for a crowd and making ingredient substitutions.

As a home economist and nutritionist, I am keenly aware of today's dietary lifestyle. My cookbook *Miss Daisy Cooks Light* was my answer to keeping the taste and losing the fat in southern cooking. The book reflects the health concerns, eating habits, and shopping awareness of today's consumer, no matter the age. I focused much of the subject matter on how to maintain a healthy lifestyle while continuing to enjoy your favorite recipes. Now I have turned my attention toward maintaining a busy lifestyle while hosting great parties!

Often, as we organize our entertaining efforts, we become so preoccupied with the tasks at hand that we forget why we are doing it at all.

We overlook the real purpose of entertaining—the pleasure of hospitality. Our goal should be for our family and friends to be warmed by the memory of a happy, exciting party. We hope they will think back on an interesting discussion or recall the magic of our food and ambiance.

It's almost impossible to enhance the warmth and charm of your home for your guests if you are consumed by the demands of planning and serving the menu. The recipes in this book invite you to spend more time with your friends, and less time in the kitchen. Today, we need a straightforward, realistic approach to preparing balanced menus. *Hosting without Hassle* offers just such an approach. If entertaining is to be done with confidence and pleasure—and often if it is to be done at all—prepare some of the foods ahead of time. This will allow you to test your favorite recipes and make any necessary adjustments to conform to the lifestyles of you and your guests. It will also allow for smoother entertaining and fewer last-minute preparations.

The menus presented here revolve around the times of the day. In addition, there are chapters devoted to celebrations and healthier eating. Although I have provided you with specific menus for each party or gathering, I encourage you to adapt them in any way you like, especially to satisfy the tastes of your guests and family. Combine elements from several menus, add old favorites, or substitute something new to create a self-styled party with your own stamp of originality.

Remember, the key to successful and enjoyable entertaining is to create a feeling of relaxed hospitality. Make the event fun for yourself, and it will be fun for your guests. Pretensions and old-fashioned rules are out! Inventiveness, congeniality, and fun are always in.

Happy hosting without hassle!

MORNING

*M*orning, *with its promise of a fresh start and new* beginnings, offers a delightful time for entertaining friends and family. Meals served in the morning find guests who are hungry and anxious to be fed. Because they are also grateful for having someone else prepare their first food of the day, they will seldom notice if everything isn't perfect!

If you're serving breakfast in bed to overnight guests, make sure they know of your plans, and prepare food that can be presented simply—yet still elegantly—and that does not require a lot of effort to eat.

When serving breakfast at your dining table or on your outdoor patio for company, plan your table appointments before your guests arrive. Make sure the coffee is ready and the juices are fresh as you greet your friends.

Brunch is another option for welcoming the day. It is a perfect vehicle for appreciating an especially good morning, whether it's just the family coming together, or old friends wanting sustenance before a ball game.

Brunch is normally served between 10:00 A.M. and 12:00 P.M. But the time is flexible, and you can choose which hour is best for your situation. Drinks compatible with this time of day include Bloody Marys, screw drivers, milk punch, mimosas, and for special occasions, champagne. Of course, you will want to offer a couple of nonalcoholic selections as well.

Whether your morning get-together is a simple coffee or an ornate brunch, remember that the menu, as well as the flower arrangements and the serving dishes, can reflect a spirit that will set the pace and feeling of the day.

Breakfast in Bed

> *"If a man be sensible and one fine morning, while he is lying in bed, count at the tips of his fingers how many things in this life truly will give him enjoyment, invariably he will find food is the first one."*—LIN YUTANG

FRENCH TOAST

CAFÉ AU LAIT AND ORANGE JUICE

SERVES 2

Breakfast in bed is a treat few of us can refuse. Whether you surprise your spouse or cater to your guests, an elegantly appointed breakfast tray says "good morning" with style.

Notes

French Toast

3	eggs	¼	teaspoon salt
1	cup milk	6	slices thick white bread
2	tablespoons Grand Marnier	¼	cup vegetable oil
1	tablespoon sugar		Confectioners' sugar for topping
½	teaspoon vanilla extract		Syrup and whipped butter

Easy • Prep time: 5 minutes • Prepare ahead

In a bowl, beat eggs, milk, and flavorings. Arrange bread slices in a flat dish and pour liquid over them, making sure each slice is soaked. Cover and refrigerate overnight. In a large skillet, sauté slices in hot oil until brown on both sides, about 3 to 4 minutes per side. Sprinkle with confectioners' sugar and serve immediately with syrup and whipped butter.

Yields 2 to 4 servings

Serve this light breakfast on trays. Put a fresh flower in a small vase, even an old jelly jar will do, and bring the recipient his or her favorite daily newspaper.

Café au Lait

2 cups strong, dripped coffee (such as French or Italian roast) or 1 cup
   dripped espresso, heated to boiling
2 cups milk, heated
   Sugar to taste

Easy • Prep time: 5 minutes
Pour each oversized mug half full of milk; add an equal amount of
dripped coffee or ¼ cup espresso. Sweeten as desired.
Yields 2 servings

SHOPPING LIST

BAKERY
__ 1 loaf thickly sliced white bread

DAIRY
__ ½ dozen eggs
__ 1 quart milk
__ 1 stick butter

EXTRAS
__ 1 small bottle Grand Marnier

MISCELLANEOUS
__ 1 small bottle real maple syrup

PRODUCE
__ 6 to 8 juice oranges

STAPLES/SPICES
__ Coffee (French or Italian roast)
__ Confectioners' sugar
__ Salt
__ Sugar
__ Vanilla extract
__ Vegetable oil

Touchdown Brunch

Au Gratin Egg Bake

Herbed Tomato Halves

Green Beans with Almonds

Assorted Fresh Fruit

Football Cake

Bloody Marys

S E R V E S   1 2

Hosting your friends for a televised football game is a great excuse for catching up on old times and celebrating your current relationships. Start the festivities well in advance of the kickoff, so that you can visit beforehand and then concentrate on the field—instead of the food—when the time comes!

Au Gratin Egg Bake

2   10¾-ounce cans cream of celery soup, undiluted
¼   cup milk
1   small onion, grated
1   tablespoon prepared mustard

2   cups shredded Cheddar cheese
12   hard-boiled eggs, cut in half lengthwise
Chopped parsley
Paprika

Moderately easy • Prep time: 15 to 20 minutes
Preheat the oven to 350°. In a saucepan, combine the first 4 ingredients. Cook and stir until heated through. Remove from the heat; stir in cheese until melted. Pour 1½ cups sauce into a 3-quart baking dish. Place eggs cut side down in the sauce. Spoon the remaining sauce around eggs. Bake for about 15 minutes. Sprinkle with chopped parsley and paprika. *Yields 12 servings*

Use miniature school pennants as decorations and party favors, and incorporate team colors into your flowers and other appointments.

Herbed Tomato Halves

6	large tomatoes	2	tablespoons chopped parsley
1	tablespoon salt	2	teaspoons whole oregano
2	teaspoons Dijon mustard	1	teaspoon thyme
2	teaspoons chopped onion	2	teaspoons butter,
2	tablespoons chopped celery leaves		chopped into tiny pieces

Easy • Prep time: 10 minutes

Preheat the oven to 350°. Wash tomatoes; remove stem ends, and cut crosswise in half. Sprinkle tomatoes with salt and spread with mustard. Combine onion, celery leaves, parsley, oregano, and thyme. Sprinkle over tomatoes. Pat each half with butter. Bake for 30 minutes, or until tender.

Yields 12 servings

Fresh tomatoes keep longer when placed stem down.

———————

Tiny pearl onions make a delightful addition to green beans.

Green Beans with Almonds

1	2-pound package frozen French-style green beans
⅔	cup slivered blanched almonds
1	cup melted butter

Easy • Prep time: 5 minutes

Cook beans according to the package directions; drain. Sauté almonds in butter until golden brown. Pour over hot, drained green beans.

Yields 12 servings

Decorated cakes with your favorite team logo are available at most supermarket bakeries, where the cake decorators should be able to create something according to your specifications.

Football Cake

1   18½-ounce box any flavor cake mix, plus ingredients needed to prepare according to the package directions
1   container chocolate frosting
1   small tube white decorators' icing

Easy • Prep time: 25 minutes
Prepare the cake according to the package directions, using two 9-inch round cake pans. Cool thoroughly. Frost the top of one layer and gently place the second layer on top. Cut a 2- to 3-inch-wide strip lengthwise out of the middle of the round cake. Press the two remaining pieces of the cake together to form a football shape. Use the remaining frosting to ice the cake. Use the decorators' icing to draw the "strings" on the pigskin.
Yields 16 to 20 servings

Bloody Marys

1   jigger Vodka
2   jiggers tomato juice
    Dash of Worcestershire sauce
    Dash of Tabasco sauce

    Salt and pepper to taste
½   cup cracked or cubed ice
    Celery for garnish

Easy • Prep time: 5 minutes
Combine all ingredients, except celery, in a shaker. Shake until blended and chilled. Strain into glass. Garnish with a rib of celery.
Yields 1 serving

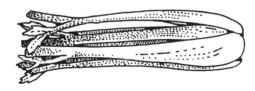

SHOPPING LIST _____

CANNED GOODS
__ 2 10¾-ounce cans cream of
   celery soup
__ 3 32-ounce cans tomato juice

DAIRY
__ 2 dozen eggs
__ ½ pint milk
__ ½ pound Cheddar cheese
__ 1 pound butter

EXTRAS
__ 1 large bottle vodka

MISCELLANEOUS
__ 1 small package slivered
   blanched almonds
__ 1 small jar Dijon mustard
__ 1 2-pound package frozen
   French-style green beans
__ 1 bag ice
__ 1 18½-ounce box any flavor
   cake mix
__ 1 container chocolate frosting
__ 1 small tube decorators' white
   icing

PRODUCE
__ 3 or 4 apples
__ 3 oranges
__ 1 bunch grapes
__ 1 bunch bananas
__ 2 small onions
__ 6 large tomatoes
__ 1 small bunch parsley
__ 1 stalk celery

STAPLES/SPICES
__ Coffee
__ Paprika
__ Pepper
__ Prepared mustard
__ Salt
__ Sugar
__ Thyme
__ Tabasco sauce
__ Whole oregano
__ Worcestershire sauce

On the Green

"Golf is a game whose aim is to hit a very small ball into an even smaller hole, with weapons singularly ill-designed for the purpose."
—Sir Winston Churchill

Notes

_____

_____

_____

_____

_____

_____

_____

_____

_____

To celebrate the Masters or a local golf tournament, decorate the buffet table with green felt to resemble a golfing green. Use several small containers of azalea or dogwood around the green.

FRUIT BROCHETTES

COUNTRY BAKED HAM

BAKED EGGS IN TOMATO SHELLS

WINNERS BISCUITS

BLUEBERRY CAKE

BLOODY MARYS (see p. 6)

SERVES 8 TO 10

It's no surprise that golf is one of the more popular sports today. You get to spend quality time with your playing partners, and you're usually surrounded by gorgeous scenery. Before your next round, treat your fellow golfers to this substantial menu. It will give you the energy you need for that hole in one.

Fruit Brochettes

Fruit suggestions:

Pineapple chunks	*Spiced figs*
Grapes	*Canned apricots*
Banana slices	*Canned pears*
Canned peaches	*Maraschino cherries*
Lime juice	*Maple syrup*

Easy • Prep time: 10 minutes

Preheat the broiler. Thread a combination of small fruits on bamboo skewers. Coat with lime juice and maple syrup. Just before serving, heat through under the broiler. Can be used as a garnish for ham.

Yields as many servings as needed

Baked Eggs in Tomato Shells

10   firm medium tomatoes
1⅓ cups butter, melted
      Salt and pepper to taste
10   eggs

1   cup grated Parmesan cheese
      Fresh minced chives
      Fresh parsley for garnish

Moderately easy • Prep time: 20 minutes

Preheat the oven to 400°. Cut tops off of tomatoes and reserve. Scoop out tomatoes, leaving ⅓- to ½-inch shells. Discard the pulp. Brush insides of shells with butter. Season with salt and pepper. Place in a baking dish with a small amount of water added. Bake shells with tops on for 12 minutes. Remove from the oven. Remove baked tops and set aside. Place an egg in each shell, and top with an equal distribution of cheese and chives. Return to the oven for 12 to 15 minutes, or until eggs are desired doneness. Place a baked tomato top on or beside each portion before serving. Garnish with sprig of fresh parsley.

Yields 10 servings

Winners Biscuits

2   cups all-purpose flour
3   teaspoons baking powder
1   teaspoon salt

¼   cup shortening
¾   cup milk

Moderately easy • Prep time: 10 to 15 minutes

Preheat the oven to 450°. In a large bowl, sift the dry ingredients together and cut in shortening. Add milk, stirring until all flour is moistened. Turn out onto a lightly floured board. Knead the dough for about 20 seconds, then roll out to about ½-inch thickness. Cut the biscuits with a 1-inch biscuit cutter and place on an ungreased baking sheet. Bake for 10 to 12 minutes.

Yields 24 one-inch biscuits

Shortening can be cut in or mixed with flour with a pastry blender or by using two knives.

Kneading is the process by which dough is made pliable by working with one's hands in an over and under method for a short period of time, about 5 to 7 minutes.

Blueberry Cake

1	cup butter, softened		¼	teaspoon mace
2	cups sugar		½	cup milk
3	eggs		2	teaspoons sugar
3	cups all-purpose flour		2	teaspoons all-purpose flour
1½	teaspoons baking powder		2	cups blueberries
⅛	teaspoon salt			

Moderately easy • Prep time: 15 to 20 minutes

Preheat the oven to 350°. In a large bowl of an electric mixer, cream butter and sugar until light and fluffy. Add eggs, one at a time, beating well after each addition. In a separate bowl, combine the next 4 ingredients and then add to the creamed mixture alternately with milk. Coat berries with remaining sugar and flour. Fold into the batter. Pour into a greased and floured tube or bundt pan. Bake for 70 to 80 minutes.

Yields 1 large cake of 12 to 14 slices

Toss a few golf balls and tees around the serving tables.

Have a blackboard near the serving area listing the players and their standings in the tournament.

SHOPPING LIST

BUTCHER
__ 1 4- or 5-pound country ham

CANNED GOODS
__ 1 16-ounce can each: pears, pineapple chunks, apricots, peaches, maraschino cherries (can combine with some fresh fruit)
__ 4 32-ounce cans tomato juice

DAIRY
__ 1 pound butter
__ 1½ dozen eggs
__ 1 4-ounce block Parmesan cheese
__ 1 pint milk

EXTRAS
__ 1 bottle vodka
__ Wooden skewers

MISCELLANEOUS
__ 1 small bottle lime juice
__ 1 small bottle maple syrup
__ 1 jar spiced figs

PRODUCE
__ 10 firm medium tomatoes
__ 1 bunch fresh chives
__ 1 bunch fresh parsley
__ 1 pint fresh blueberries
__ 1 stalk celery
__ 1 small bunch bananas
__ 1 small bunch grapes

STAPLES
__ All-purpose flour
__ Baking powder
__ Coffee
__ Mace
__ Pepper
__ Salt
__ Sugar
__ Tabasco sauce
__ Vegetable shortening
__ Worcestershire sauce

FRESH SHRIMP WITH DIPPING SAUCE

DERBY PÂTÉ

BACON WRAPPED WATER CHESTNUTS

BAKED HAM WITH RAISIN SAUCE

EGGPLANT CASSEROLE

MISS DAISY'S FRIED CHICKEN

RICE-POTATO SALAD

BUTTERMILK BISCUITS

DERBY PIE

MINT JULEPS

SERVES 16 TO 20

This brunch menu honors the Bluegrass State, which gives us the best of horse racing in the form of the Kentucky Derby. No doubt these foods will appeal to horse lovers and the uninitiated alike. So place your bets and saddle up.

Fresh Shrimp with Dipping Sauce

2   cups chili sauce
1   cup finely chopped celery
3   tablespoons lemon juice
3   tablespoons horseradish
1   teaspoon salt
5 to 6   pounds cooked shrimp

Easy • Prep time: 5 minutes
In a bowl, combine all ingredients, except shrimp, and mix well. Serve with shrimp for dipping.
Yields about 4 cups sauce

When boiling shrimp, drop fresh celery leaves into the pot. This destroys the shrimp odor and leaves a pleasing aroma in its place.

Derby Pâté

8 to 10	ounces raw chicken livers	1	tablespoon chopped fresh tarragon
1	cup butter, softened	1	teaspoon salt
⅓	cup chicken broth		Fresh parsley for garnish
4	eggs		Baby jerkins for garnish
			Cherry tomatoes for garnish

Easy • Prep time: 10 minutes
Preheat the oven to 350°. In a food processor or blender, combine all ingredients, except those used for garnish. Mix on high for 2 minutes or less. Layer a 9x5x3-inch loaf pan with aluminum foil that has been buttered. Place the mixture in the pan. Set that pan in a pan of water. Bake for 30 to 40 minutes, or until firm. Refrigerate until ready to serve. Garnish with fresh parsley. Surround the platter with baby jerkins and cherry tomato halves.
Yields 12 to 15 servings

Bacon Wrapped Water Chestnuts

2	8-ounce cans water chestnuts, drained and halved		Brown sugar
	Soy sauce	10	slices bacon, each cut into 4 pieces

Moderately easy • Prep time: 20 to 30 minutes • Prepare ahead
Preheat the oven to 400°. In a bowl, marinate water chestnuts in soy sauce for 30 minutes. Roll in brown sugar and wrap in bacon pieces. Bake for 20 to 25 minutes in a broiler pan so that water chestnuts will not sit in the grease. Serve with toothpicks. These can be prepared ahead and reheated for 5 minutes in a 350° oven before serving.
Yields 16 servings

Have a replica of a betting ticket printed or use a postcard for your invitations. Put horses, roses, jockeys, juleps, and horseshoes around the edges. Call your horse-loving friends for inspiration.

Baked Ham with Raisin Sauce

1	tablespoon butter	1	teaspoon salt
3	tablespoons brown sugar	2	tablespoons molasses
3	tablespoons all-purpose flour	2	cups water
2	teaspoons prepared mustard	¼	cup sugar
1	teaspoon ground cinnamon	5	tablespoons cider vinegar
1	teaspoon ground cloves	1	cup seedless raisins
⅛	teaspoon paprika		Baked ham slices for 16 guests

Easy • Prep time: 10 minutes
In a large bowl of an electric mixer, cream butter, brown sugar, flour, mustard, spices, paprika, salt, and molasses. In a saucepan, combine water, sugar, and vinegar and bring to a boil. Add the creamed mixture. Stir in raisins and cook for 10 minutes over low heat. Serve sauce over warmed ham slices.
Yields 16 servings

Eggplant Casserole

3	eggplants, peeled, diced, soaked in salted water for 30 minutes, and drained	½	cup grated American cheese
		3	slices bacon
¾	cup chicken broth	1	medium onion, chopped
3	slices whole-wheat bread processed into soft crumbs		Salt and pepper to taste
			Tabasco sauce to taste
2	eggs, beaten	¾	cup grated Parmesan cheese

Moderately easy • Prep time: 20 minutes • Prepare ahead and freeze
Preheat the oven to 350°. In a saucepan, cook soaked eggplant in salted water until tender, about 12 to 15 minutes. Drain well. Add chicken broth, bread crumbs, eggs, and cheese. Sauté bacon until crisp, then crumble. Reserve the drippings. Sauté onion in bacon grease. Add onion and bacon to the eggplant mixture. Season with salt, pepper, and Tabasco. Pour into 1 large or 2 medium casserole dishes. Top with Parmesan cheese. Bake for 45 to 50 minutes.
Yields 16 to 18 servings

Miss Daisy's Fried Chicken

Salt and pepper to taste
16 chicken breasts, split
6 cups all-purpose flour
1 tablespoon paprika

1 tablespoon chili powder
4 eggs, slightly beaten
2 cups milk
Vegetable oil

Easy • Prep time: 10 minutes
Salt and pepper chicken breasts. Combine flour, paprika, and chili powder; set aside. In a large bowl, combine egg and milk. Dip chicken in the egg mixture, then dredge in the flour mixture. Heat oil in a large skillet. Place 6 to 8 pieces of chicken in a skillet; cover. Cook over medium heat for about 30 minutes, or until golden brown, turning occasionally.
Yields 16 servings

Rice-Potato Salad

6 hard-boiled eggs, chopped
¾ cup finely chopped celery
½ cup finely chopped stuffed green olives
½ cup finely chopped green bell pepper
½ cup finely chopped dill pickles
½ cup minced green onion tops
½ cup minced parsley
2 teaspoons minced onion
2 teaspoons salt

½ teaspoon ground black pepper
½ teaspoon chili powder
1 cup mayonnaise
3 cups hot, cooked rice
1 large baking potato, peeled, boiled, and cut into bite-size pieces
Paprika for garnish
Freshly chopped parsley for garnish

Moderately easy • Prep time: 20 to 30 minutes
In a large bowl, combine all ingredients, except rice and potato. Mix well. Add rice and potato; mix thoroughly. Refrigerate until ready to serve. Garnish with paprika and freshly chopped parsley.
Yields 14 to 16 servings

Buttermilk Biscuits

4   cups self-rising flour
½   teaspoon baking soda

1   cup vegetable shortening
2   cups buttermilk

Easy • Prep time: 10 minutes
Preheat the oven to 400°. In a mixing bowl, combine flour and soda. Cut in shortening with a pastry blender or 2 knives until the mixture resembles coarse cornmeal. Add buttermilk. Stir until the dough clings together. Turn the dough onto a lightly floured surface; knead lightly for about 15 seconds. Roll or pat the dough to ½-inch thickness. Cut into rounds with a 2-inch biscuit cutter. Place on a greased baking sheet. Brush tops with additional buttermilk, if desired. Bake for 12 minutes.
Yields 24 to 30 biscuits

Derby Pie

2   unbaked 9-inch pie crusts
1   cup pecan halves
1   12-ounce package
    semisweet chocolate chips
4   eggs, beaten

2   tablespoons bourbon,
    optional
1   cup sugar
1   cup light corn syrup
½   cup butter, melted

Easy • Prep time: 10 minutes
Preheat the oven to 350°. Divide pecans and chocolate chips equally in the bottoms of the pie crusts. In a bowl, combine the other ingredients and pour over nuts and chips. Bake for 10 minutes; reduce the oven temperature to 325° and bake for an additional 30 minutes.
Yields 2 pies of 8 servings each

Decorate the buffet table with red roses, statues of horses, riding hats, and colorful silks.

Mint Juleps

4	cups sugar	Fresh mint leaves
1⅓	cups water	Confectioners' sugar
	Kentucky bourbon	Fresh mint leaves for garnish

Easy • Prep time: 5 minutes • Prepare ahead

In a 2-quart saucepan, combine sugar, water, and mint leaves. Boil for 5 minutes, or until green. Strain into a glass pitcher and chill for 24 hours. For each julep, fill a 10-ounce glass with crushed ice and add 3 ounces bourbon and 1 ounce sugar, and mint syrup. Garnish with mint leaves that have been moistened and dipped in confectioners' sugar.
Yields 40 servings

SHOPPING LIST

BAKERY
__ 1 small loaf whole-wheat bread

BUTCHER/DELI
__ 8 pounds chicken breasts
__ 8 to 10 ounces raw chicken livers
__ 5 to 6 pounds fresh shrimp
__ 1 pound bacon
__ 4 pounds sliced baked ham

CANNED GOODS
__ 1 16-ounce can chicken broth
__ 2 8-ounce cans water chestnuts

DAIRY
__ 1 pound butter
__ 2 dozen eggs
__ 1 pint milk
__ 1 4-ounce block American cheese
__ 1 4-ounce block Parmesan cheese
__ 1 pint buttermilk

EXTRAS
__ 1 bottle Kentucky bourbon
__ 1 box toothpicks

MISCELLANEOUS
__ 1 small jar baby jerkins
__ 1 small jar molasses
__ 1 small box seedless raisins
__ 1 small bottle stuffed green olives
__ 1 small jar dill pickles or dill pickle relish
__ 2 9-inch unbaked pie crusts
__ 2 small packages pecan halves
__ 1 16-ounce bottle chili sauce
__ 1 small jar horseradish
__ 1 12-ounce package semisweet chocolate chips
__ 1 bottle light corn syrup

PRODUCE
__ 1 bunch fresh mint
__ 1 bunch fresh tarragon
__ 1 bunch fresh parsley
__ 1 pint cherry tomatoes
__ 2 medium onions
__ 1 bunch green onions
__ 1 green bell pepper
__ 1 large baking potato
__ 1 stalk celery
__ 3 medium eggplants
__ 2 lemons

STAPLES/SPICES
__ All-purpose flour
__ Baking soda
__ Brown sugar
__ Chili powder
__ Cider vinegar
__ Cinnamon
__ Cloves
__ Confectioners' sugar
__ Mayonnaise
__ Paprika
__ Pepper
__ Prepared mustard
__ Salt
__ Self-rising flour
__ Soy sauce
__ Sugar
__ Tabasco sauce
__ Vegetable oil
__ Vegetable shortening
__ White rice

MINT

Retirement Brunch

RICE RING

ORANGE WALNUT CHICKEN

STEAMED BROCCOLI

JELLY MUFFINS

COCONUT PECAN BARS

MIMOSAS (see p. 29),

NONALCOHOLIC MIMOSA PUNCH, AND KIR

SERVES 18

For the special friend who deserves more than a gold watch, consider throwing a party when retirement time rolls around. Invite the person's closest friends and co-workers, and prepare a sketch of "This Is Your Life" to pay homage to the honoree.

One cup raw rice becomes 3 cups when cooked.

_____

Use only enough water to create steam and prevent sticking when cooking vegetables. This will cause them to retain more vitamins, taste less bitter, and require less energy for cooking.

Rice Ring

2 cups white rice cooked in 4 cups chicken broth	⅓ cup golden raisins
¼ cup butter, melted	⅓ cup chopped walnuts
2 teaspoons celery salt	1 tablespoon Worcestershire sauce
⅔ cup chopped chives	

Easy • Prep time: 10 minutes
In a saucepan, heat rice with butter and add the remaining ingredients. Pack into a greased 3-quart ring mold. Place the mold in a pan of hot water and keep warm in the oven until serving time. To unmold, run a spatula around the edges and invert onto a heated platter.
Yields 18 servings

Orange Walnut Chicken

9	pounds boneless chicken breasts	1	cup walnut pieces
	Salt and pepper to taste	1	cup raisins
3	tablespoons curry powder	½	teaspoon ground cinnamon
1	cup melted butter	6	navel oranges, peeled, sliced, and cut to center on one side
1	tablespoon grated orange peel		
2	cups orange juice	½	cup warm water
1	20-ounce can pineapple tidbits with juice	3	tablespoons all-purpose flour
		1	tablespoon soy sauce

Moderately easy • Prep time: 20 to 30 minutes

Preheat the oven to 400°. Sprinkle chicken on all sides with salt, pepper, and curry powder; dip in butter. In a large shallow baking pan, place chicken pieces skin side down. Bake for 10 minutes. Turn pieces and return to the oven for 10 minutes. Heat to boiling orange peel, juice, pineapple, nuts, raisins, and cinnamon. Pour the hot mixture over chicken and reduce the oven temperature to 350°. Bake for 35 to 40 minutes. Remove chicken to a warm serving platter, reserving pan with drippings. Twist orange slices and arrange over chicken. In a saucepan, gradually add water to flour, stirring constantly. Add soy sauce and pour all into the baking pan. Simmer over low heat for 1 to 2 minutes, scraping constantly. When well mixed with drippings, pour the mixture over orange-garnished chicken.

Yields 18 servings

Fill vases with the honoree's favorite flowers.

Steamed Broccoli

3	bunches broccoli, cut into serving-size pieces	2	tablespoons sugar
		2	tablespoons salt
1	quart water or less	½ to 1	cup butter, melted

Easy • Prep time: 5 minutes

If you have a steamer, use it to steam broccoli until tender. If not, place broccoli, water, sugar, and salt in a large pot, making sure broccoli has enough water to create a steam effect when brought to a boil. Steam or boil for 5 minutes, or until crisp-tender. Remove from the heat and drain. Arrange on a platter and drizzle with butter.

Yields 18 servings

Jelly Muffins

2	cups sifted all-purpose flour	2	eggs, beaten
2	cups cornmeal	2	cups milk
2 ½	tablespoons baking powder	½	cup vegetable oil
¼	cup sugar	½	cup jelly (any flavor)
2	teaspoons salt		

Easy • Prep time: 15 minutes

Preheat the oven to 425°. In a large mixing bowl, sift the dry ingredients together. Combine eggs, milk, and oil in a separate bowl. Stir into the dry ingredients, mixing only until moist. Fill greased muffin cups half full. Spoon 1 teaspoon jelly onto the center of each unbaked muffin. Bake for 20 minutes.

Yields 24 muffins

Coconut Pecan Bars

1	cup butter, softened	2	tablespoons all-purpose flour
1	cup dark brown sugar	1 ½	cups chopped pecans
2	cups all-purpose flour	¼	teaspoon salt
4	eggs	2	teaspoons vanilla extract
2	cups light brown sugar		Confectioners' sugar
1	cup grated coconut		

Easy • Prep time: 15 minutes

Preheat the oven to 350°. In a large bowl of an electric mixer, cream butter and dark brown sugar. Add 2 cups flour and mix well. Divide the dough and press into two 9-inch square pans. Bake for 20 minutes. In a bowl, beat eggs until frothy and pale yellow. Gradually add light brown sugar and beat until thick. Toss coconut in 2 tablespoons flour and stir into the mixture. Add pecans, salt, and vanilla. Mix well. Spread over the baked crusts and bake for 20 minutes more, or until browned. When cool, dust with confectioners' sugar and cut into 1½-inch squares.

Yields 70 to 72 bars

Nonalcoholic Mimosa Punch

2	64-ounce jars orange juice
2	large containers frozen lemonade concentrate
1	2-liter bottle ginger ale
2	naval oranges, sliced

Easy • Prep time: 10 minutes

Combine all ingredients in a large punch bowl and mix well. The orange slices should float to the top for decoration. Serve cold.

Yields approximately 32 servings

Ask one of the honoree's family members to put together a scrapbook of the person's working life, or to bring a few pictures that represent the person's professional accomplishments.

Kir

1 cup crème de cassis
1 gallon white wine, preferably chardonnay

Easy • Prep time: 5 minutes
Add crème de cassis to wine. Chill.
Yields 36 four-ounce servings

SHOPPING LIST

BUTCHER
__ 18 whole chicken breasts

CANNED GOODS
__ 1 20-ounce can pineapple tidbits
__ 1 7-ounce can flaked coconut
__ 2 16-ounce cans chicken broth

DAIRY
__ 2 pounds butter
__ ½ dozen eggs
__ 1 pint milk

EXTRAS
__ 1 small bottle crème de cassis
__ 1 gallon chardonnay
__ ½ case champagne

MISCELLANEOUS
__ 4 64-ounce jars orange juice
__ 2 large containers frozen
   lemonade concentrate
__ 1 2-liter bottle ginger ale
__ 1 6-ounce package chopped
   pecans
__ 1 6-ounce package chopped
   walnuts
__ 1 small box raisins
__ 1 small box golden raisins
__ 1 jar any flavor jelly

PRODUCE
__ 8 navel oranges
__ 3 bunches fresh broccoli
__ 1 bunch fresh chives

STAPLES/SPICES
__ All-purpose flour
__ Baking powder
__ Celery salt
__ Confectioners' sugar
__ Curry powder
__ Dark brown sugar
__ Ground cinnamon
__ Light brown sugar
__ Pepper
__ Salt
__ Soy sauce
__ Sugar
__ Vanilla extract
__ Vegetable oil
__ White rice
__ Worcestershire sauce
__ Yellow cornmeal

HONEYDEW BOWL OF FRESH FRUIT

TOMATOES STUFFED WITH WALNUT SPINACH

CREAMED CHICKEN IN PASTRY SHELLS

SPICED PECAN TORTE

FRESH ORANGE SPRITZER AND COFFEE

S E R V E S 6 T O 8

Some of us can't spend as much time with our families as we would like. (Others, of course, think they have too much "quality time" with their relatives!) When the opportunity arrives to gather your family around you, be it once a week or once a year, take advantage of it.

Tomatoes Stuffed with Walnut Spinach

6 to 8   *medium ripe tomatoes*
10   *ounces frozen chopped spinach, thawed and drained*
½   *cup crushed walnut pieces*
½   *cup freshly grated Parmesan cheese*

Dash of cayenne pepper
1   *tablespoon spicy brown mustard*
Buttered bread crumbs

Easy • Prep time: 10 minutes
Preheat the oven to 325°. Cut off tomato stems and scoop out small amount of tomato. Season lightly with salt and pepper. Combine the spinach, walnuts, Parmesan, cayenne, and mustard and mix well. Mound the spinach mixture into scooped out tomatoes and place on a greased baking sheet. Top with buttered bread crumbs. Bake for 5 minutes, or until heated through.
Yields 6 to 8 servings

If you haven't seen your family in a while, have photos ready that represent some of the things that have happened to you since your family last got together.

For those family members who are lucky enough to see each other on a regular basis, try to do one new thing when you have your family over for brunch. Use a different place setting, rearrange something in your dining room, put a special touch on the table—anything that says you're not in a dull routine!

Creamed Chicken in Pastry Shells

3 cups cooked chicken, diced	1 tablespoon Worcestershire sauce
1½ cups Medium White Sauce	½ teaspoon salt or to taste
1 cup mushroom pieces and stems, drained	¼ teaspoon ground black pepper
½ cup diced celery	1 10-ounce box frozen pastry shells, baked
3 tablespoons chopped pimiento	Fresh parsley sprigs for garnish

Moderately easy • Prep time: 20 minutes
Combine all ingredients, except pastry shells, and heat thoroughly in the top of a double boiler or heavy saucepan. Serve in prebaked pastry shells garnished with a large sprig of parsley.
Yields 8 servings

Medium White Sauce

¼ cup butter	1½ cups chicken stock
¼ cup all-purpose flour	½ cup light cream
⅛ teaspoon paprika	

Easy • Prep time: 10 minutes
In a heavy saucepan, melt butter; add flour and paprika. Cook over low heat for 5 minutes. Stirring frequently, add stock and cream and cook over medium heat until thickened, about 10 to 15 minutes.
Yields 1½ to 2 cups sauce

Spiced Pecan Torte

1 cup prune pulp,
   plus 2 tablespoons
   (about ½ pound prunes)
1¾ cups sugar
2⅓ cups cake flour
1 teaspoon baking soda
1 teaspoon grated nutmeg
1 teaspoon ground cinnamon

1 teaspoon salt
3 eggs
1 cup vegetable oil,
   plus 2 tablespoons
1 cup buttermilk,
   plus 1 tablespoon
1 teaspoon vanilla extract
¾ cup chopped pecans

Moderately easy • Prep time: 20 minutes • Prepare ahead
The day before baking the torte, soak, cook, and pit ½ pound prunes.
Chop. This should yield the desired amount of prune pulp.

   Preheat the oven to 350°. Sift together the dry ingredients. Beat
eggs, oil, buttermilk, and vanilla together in a small mixing bowl. Add
to the dry ingredients and mix until smooth. Stir in pecans and prune
pulp. Bake in two greased, floured 9-inch layer cake pans for 45 minutes. Let cool.
Yields 16 servings

Topping

½ cup butter
½ teaspoon baking soda

⅔ cup buttermilk
1 cup sugar

In a saucepan, combine all ingredients and bring to a rolling boil. Pour,
hot, over torte. Chill torte in the refrigerator. Keeps well for several
days.
Yields topping for 1 torte

Fresh Orange Spritzer

2   6-ounce cans frozen
    orange juice concentrate
1   28-ounce bottle club
    soda, chilled

3   tablespoons lemon juice
2   cups ice cubes

Easy • Prep time: 5 minutes
In a large pitcher, combine orange juice concentrate and 1 cup cold
water. Stir until orange juice is thawed. Add soda, lemon juice, and
ice cubes.
Yields 6 to 8 servings

SHOPPING LIST

BUTCHER
__ 2 pounds boneless, skinless
   chicken breasts

CANNED GOODS
__ 1 10-ounce can mushroom stems
   and pieces
__ 1 16-ounce can chicken broth

DAIRY
__ 1 pint buttermilk
__ ½ pint light cream
__ 2 sticks butter
__ 1 4-ounce block Parmesan
   cheese
__ ½ dozen eggs

MISCELLANEOUS
__ 2 6-ounce containers frozen
   orange juice concentrate
__ 1 small canister buttered bread
   crumbs

__ 1 28-ounce bottle club soda
__ 1 8-ounce package prunes
__ 1 4-ounce jar chopped pimiento
__ 1 small package crushed walnut
   pieces
__ 1 small package chopped pecans
__ 1 10-ounce package frozen
   chopped spinach
__ 1 box frozen tart or pastry shells
__ 1 small jar spicy brown mustard

PRODUCE
__ 6 to 8 medium, ripe tomatoes
__ 1 stalk celery
__ 1 bunch fresh parsley
__ 2 lemons
__ 1 honeydew melon
__ Grapes, strawberries,
   blueberries, and any other fruit
   your family enjoys

STAPLES/SPICES
__ All-purpose flour
__ Baking soda
__ Cake flour
__ Cayenne pepper
__ Cinnamon
__ Coffee
__ Nutmeg
__ Paprika
__ Pepper
__ Salt
__ Sugar
__ Vanilla extract
__ Vegetable oil
__ Worcestershire sauce

DILLED HAM TRIANGLES

MARINATED ASPARAGUS

HEAVENLY CHEESE SOUFFLÉ

FROZEN STRAWBERRY SALAD

MIMOSAS AND CINNAMON COFFEE

SERVES 8

Cleaning out your closets is not the only way to
celebrate the arrival of spring, as this light and airy
menu shows. Following these recipes will be a lot
easier—and a lot more fun—than wiping your
baseboards. After you've eaten with friends, if you still
have the urge to organize something, then go for it.
But don't say I didn't warn you!

*"I love spring anywhere,
but if I could choose I would
always greet it in a garden."*
—RUTH STOUT

Notes

Dilled Ham Triangles

8	slices white bread	1	3-ounce package cream cheese, softened
½	pound thinly sliced baked ham	1	teaspoon minced fresh dill weed
¼	cup unsalted butter, softened	¼	teaspoon dry mustard
			Sprigs of fresh dill for garnish

Moderately easy • Prep time: 20 to 25 minutes
Remove crust from bread; cut each slice in half diagonally. Toast bread
triangles and set aside. In a food processor or blender, combine ham
(all but 1 slice), butter, cream cheese, minced dill, and mustard. Process or blend until smooth. Spread the ham mixture on toast points.
Garnish with a bit of ham and fresh dill.
Yields 8 servings

Canned deviled ham
mixed with a small amount
of cream cheese and dill
may be used as a spread
for toast points.

Weather permitting, set your table in a flower garden or on your patio or screened-in porch. Wicker furniture is great for an outdoor setting.

Have a basket of seed packets by the front door. Allow guests to pick one or two as they leave.

Marinated Asparagus

2	pounds fresh asparagus	¼	cup olive oil
8	green onions, diagonally sliced	¼	teaspoon white pepper
		½	teaspoon dried basil
4	radishes, thinly sliced	¼	teaspoon salt
¼	cup white wine vinegar	2	sprigs fresh dill for garnish

Easy • Prep time: 10 minutes
Cut or break off ends of asparagus. Remove any scales from stalks and then cook, covered, in a small amount of boiling water for 5 minutes, or until crisp-tender. Drain. Place asparagus in a large bowl; cover and chill thoroughly. Add green onions and radishes to asparagus; set aside. In a jar, combine vinegar and remaining ingredients, except dill. Cover tightly and shake until combined. Pour over vegetables and toss just before serving. Garnish with dill.
Yields 8 servings

Heavenly Cheese Soufflé

7	slices white bread, crusts removed	⅛	teaspoon cayenne pepper
		1	teaspoon Worcestershire sauce
2½	cups milk	8	ounces sharp Cheddar cheese, grated
1	teaspoon salt		
⅛	teaspoon garlic powder	3	eggs, separated

Moderately easy • Prep time: 30 minutes
In a bowl, soak bread in milk and break into tiny pieces. Add salt, garlic powder, cayenne, Worcestershire, and cheese. Beat egg yolks and whites separately; fold both into the bread-cheese mixture. Pour into a 2-quart buttered casserole dish. Start in a cold oven; then turn the oven temperature to 350° and bake for 50 to 60 minutes.
Yields 8 servings

Frozen Strawberry Salad

1	10-ounce package frozen strawberries, thawed and drained, reserving juice	24	large marshmallows	
1	8-ounce can crushed pineapple, drained, reserving juice	1	3-ounce package cream cheese, softened	
		¼	cup mayonnaise	
		1	cup frozen whipped topping	
		½	cup chopped nuts	

Easy • Prep time: 10 minutes • Prepare ahead and freeze
In a saucepan, heat reserved fruit juices with marshmallows until melted. Cool. Fold in fruits and remaining ingredients. Pour the mixture into an 8x8-inch square pan and freeze for 3 to 4 hours.
Yields 8 servings

Mimosas

Orange juice
Champagne

Easy • Prep time: 2 minutes
Combine equal parts orange juice and champagne in tall glasses.
Yields as many servings as needed

Sprinkle a little ground cinnamon in your coffee before brewing. It will reduce the bitterness and add a little hint of something special to the taste. For an especially festive touch, dollop whipped topping on brewed coffee after pouring into mugs.

SHOPPING LIST _____

BAKERY
__ 1 loaf sliced white bread

BUTCHER/DELI
__ ½ pound thinly sliced baked ham

CANNED GOODS
__ 1 8-ounce can crushed pineapple

DAIRY
__ 1 stick unsalted butter
__ 2 3-ounce packages cream cheese
__ 8 ounces sharp Cheddar cheese
__ ½ dozen eggs
__ 1 quart milk

EXTRAS
__ 4 bottles champagne

MISCELLANEOUS
__ 1 10-ounce package frozen strawberries
__ 1 small container frozen whipped topping
__ 1 small package chopped nuts
__ 1 bag large marshmallows
__ 1 bottle white wine vinegar
__ 2 64-ounce bottles orange juice

PRODUCE
__ 2 pounds fresh asparagus
__ 1 bunch green onions
__ 1 small package thinly sliced radishes
__ 1 bunch fresh dill

STAPLES/SPICES
__ Cayenne pepper
__ Cinnamon
__ Coffee
__ Dried basil
__ Dried whole thyme
__ Dry mustard
__ Garlic powder
__ Mayonnaise
__ Olive oil
__ Salt
__ White pepper
__ Worcestershire sauce

Arrange as many natural flowers as are available in your part of the country. Small baskets or jars overflowing with regional wildflowers on each table are a nice touch. If none are accessible, use soft spring colors in the fabrics you select for your napkins and table appointments.

Wedding Brunch for Out-of-Towners

MANDARIN ORANGE, WALNUT, AND CRANBERRY SALAD

HONEY LIME CHICKEN

BROWN RICE PILAF

LEEK AND MUSHROOM QUICHE

LEMON SPARKLERS

TEA, COFFEE, AND CHAMPAGNE

SERVES 24

What better way to honor the bride and groom than by hosting their friends and family on their wedding day? By preparing this substantial menu, you can provide nourishment and entertainment for friends and strangers who have gathered to rejoice with the two people they have in common.

Notes

Mandarin Orange, Walnut, and Cranberry Salad

2	16-ounce packages fresh raw cranberries, rinsed and drained	4	cups walnut pieces
		6	16-ounce cans mandarin oranges, drained
2 to 2½	cups sugar	2 to 3	heads Red Boston lettuce
½	cup champagne		Mint leaves for garnish

Easy • Prep time: 10 minutes
Combine cranberries, sugar, and champagne in a food processor. Pulse until the pieces of berry are small but still chunky. Pour the mixture into a large bowl. Add more sugar if needed. Mix in walnuts. Gently add mandarin oranges. Place ½ to ¾ cup on 2 or 3 leaves of lettuce for each serving. Garnish with mint leaves.
Yields 24 servings

Decorations can include white flowers, doves, and silver.

Honey Lime Chicken

12 boneless, skinless
    chicken breasts,
    split in half
    Salt and pepper to taste
¼ cup olive oil
1 ½ tablespoons minced garlic

2 cups chicken broth
1 ½ teaspoons cornstarch
    dissolved in 1 tablespoon
    water
1 cup honey
¾ cup lime juice

Moderately easy • Prep time: 30 minutes
Preheat the broiler to 500°. Carefully wash and dry chicken and season both sides of the breasts with salt and pepper. Arrange the breasts on broiling racks placed in baking dishes. Broil for 10 to 15 minutes on each side. Keep warm.

Meanwhile, heat olive oil in a large skillet over medium-high heat. Sauté garlic in the olive oil. Add chicken broth and cornstarch and stir continuously until the mixture starts to thicken. Remove from the heat and stir in honey and lime juice. Serve over chicken breasts.
Yields 24 servings

Brown Rice Pilaf

3 cups chopped onion
3 cups chopped celery
1 cup chopped carrot
1 pound mushrooms, sliced
3 cups chicken broth
3 cups water

3 teaspoons salt
3 teaspoons poultry seasoning
1 teaspoon pepper
3 cups long-grain brown rice
3 cups chopped parsley

Easy • Prep time: 20 minutes
Combine vegetables, broth, water, and seasonings in a large pot and bring to a boil. Stir in rice. Cover, reduce the heat to simmer, and cook for 45 to 50 minutes, or until rice is tender and liquid is absorbed. Stir in parsley. Serve immediately.
Yields 20 to 24 servings

Leek and Mushroom Quiche

2	cups shredded Swiss Gruyère cheese	1	cup chopped asparagus
1	cup shredded sharp Cheddar cheese	24	eggs
⅔	cup chopped leeks	2	cups milk
2	cups sliced mushrooms	2	cups heavy cream
			Salt and pepper to taste
			Grated nutmeg to taste

Moderately easy • Prep time: 30 minutes

Preheat the oven to 375°. Grease two 10x12-inch baking pans. Divide and spread cheese between the pans. Distribute cheese evenly along the bottom of each pan. In a large mixing bowl, combine leeks, mushrooms, and asparagus. Divide between the pans and spread on top of cheese. Whisk together eggs, milk, cream, and seasonings. Divide and pour over cheese and vegetables. Sprinkle lightly with nutmeg. Bake for 40 to 45 minutes. Serve warm.

Yields 24 servings

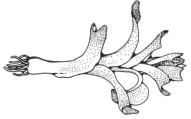

Lemon Sparklers

Lemon sorbet or sherbet	Whipped cream
Vanilla ice cream	Mint leaves for garnish
Lemon-flavored sparkling water	

Easy • Prep time: 5 minutes

For each sparkler, alternate scoops of sorbet and ice cream in a parfait glass. Pour flavored sparkling water over to fill up glass. Top with whipped cream. Garnish with fresh mint leaves.

Yields as many servings as needed

Sparklers can be made in a variety of flavors (orange, raspberry, kiwi), as long as you match the flavor of the sorbet and the sparkling water.

SHOPPING LIST _____

BUTCHER
__ 12 whole boneless, skinless chicken breasts

CANNED GOODS
__ 6 16-ounce cans mandarin oranges
__ 3 16-ounce cans chicken broth

DAIRY
__ 8 ounces Gruyère cheese
__ 4 ounces sharp Cheddar cheese
__ 1 quart milk
__ 2 dozen eggs
__ 2 pints heavy cream
__ 2 quarts vanilla ice cream

EXTRAS
__ 1 or 2 cases champagne

MISCELLANEOUS
__ 1 16-ounce bag walnut pieces
__ 1 12-ounce jar honey
__ 1 8-ounce bottle lime juice
__ 2 14-ounce packages long-grain brown rice
__ 2 quarts lemon sorbet or sherbet
__ 3 64-ounce bottles lemon-flavored sparkling water

PRODUCE
__ 2 16-ounce packages fresh raw cranberries
__ 2 or 3 heads Boston Red lettuce
__ 2 bunches fresh mint leaves
__ 1 head garlic
__ 1 stalk celery
__ 1 bag carrots
__ 2 pounds mushrooms
__ 1 bunch fresh parsley
__ 1 or 2 large leeks
__ 1 bunch fresh asparagus
__ 2 large onions

STAPLES/SPICES
__ Coffee
__ Cornstarch
__ Family-size tea bags
__ Nutmeg
__ Olive oil
__ Pepper
__ Poultry seasoning
__ Salt
__ Sugar

FRESH FRUIT WITH GINGER YOGURT DIP

SAUSAGE BALLS

HAM TARTS

CARAMEL NUT RING

RUM CAKE

FROSTED COFFEES AND ORANGE-PINEAPPLE TEA

SERVES 25

Moving into a new city, or even into a new neighborhood, can be traumatic. Not only do you have to learn your way around, you also have to make new friends. Help your new neighbors adjust by having them over for coffee. Just don't forget to invite the other neighbors!

Fresh Fruit with Ginger Yogurt Dip

1¾ cups plain, nonfat yogurt
⅓ cup ginger marmalade or
     chopped crystallized ginger
¼ cup firmly packed
     brown sugar

1 tablespoon lemon juice
1 teaspoon grated lemon rind
    Assorted fresh fruit,
    cut into chunks for dipping

Easy • Prep time: 5 minutes
Combine all ingredients and mix until smooth and blended. Serve with fresh fruit.
Yields 2 cups dip

Sausage Balls

1	pound hot, ground pork sausage	1½	cups all-purpose flour
¾	cup dry bread crumbs	¼	teaspoon salt
⅓	cup chicken broth	1	teaspoon paprika
⅛	teaspoon grated nutmeg	2	cups shredded sharp Cheddar cheese
¼	teaspoon poultry seasoning	½	cup butter, softened

Moderately easy • Prep time: 25 minutes • Prepare ahead
In a bowl, combine the first 5 ingredients. Mix well. Shape into 1-inch balls. Cook in a skillet over low heat until done. Drain on paper towels. Combine flour, salt, paprika, and cheese. Cut in butter. Mix by hand until the dough is smooth. Shape 1 tablespoon of dough around each sausage ball, covering sausage completely. Sausage balls may be frozen at this point. Thaw before baking. To bake, preheat the oven to 350°. Place balls on greased baking sheets. Bake for 15 to 20 minutes.
Yields 48 pieces

Ham Tarts

1	cup dry biscuit mix (such as Bisquick)	⅛	teaspoon garlic powder
1⅔	cups whole milk	½	cup chopped onion
1½	cups grated Cheddar cheese	1	cup sliced fresh mushrooms
5	eggs, beaten	1	10-ounce package frozen chopped spinach, thawed and drained well
½	teaspoon salt		
½	teaspoon sage	1½	cups finely diced baked ham
¼	teaspoon crushed basil		

Easy • Prep time: 10 minutes
Preheat the oven to 375°. In a bowl, mix all ingredients and fill greased miniature muffin tins two-thirds full with mixture. Bake for 25 to 30 minutes, or until the edges begin to pull away from the tins.
Yields about 50 tarts

Caramel Nut Ring

½ cup butter
½ cup chopped pecans
 1 cup firmly packed dark
    brown sugar

2 tablespoons water
2 8-ounce cans crescent
   dinner rolls

Moderately easy • Prep time: 20 minutes • Prepare ahead and freeze

Preheat the oven to 350°. In a small saucepan, melt butter. Use 2 tablespoons to coat the bottom and sides of a 12-cup bundt pan. Sprinkle the pan with 3 tablespoons chopped pecans. Add remaining nuts, brown sugar, and water to remaining butter. Heat to boiling, stirring occasionally. Remove dinner rolls from can but do not unroll. Cut each can of rolls into 16 slices. Arrange 16 slices, cut side up, in the bottom of the pan, overlapping slices. Separate each slightly to allow the sauce to cover completely. Spoon half the caramel nut sauce over slices. Repeat next layer with second can of rolls and top with remaining caramel sauce. Bake for 25 to 30 minutes, or until golden brown. Cool for 3 minutes. Turn onto a serving dish and slice.

Yields 8 to 10 servings

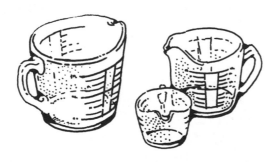

For frosted coffees, brew your favorite coffee and offer an extra topping, such as whipped cream, froth (from steamed milk), or liqueurs. For amaretto coffee, stir 1 to 2 tablespoons amaretto liqueur into a cup of strong coffee. Top with whipped cream and toasted almonds. For Belgian coffee, fold beaten egg whites into whipped cream and put a large dollop in the bottom of a coffee cup. Pour in the coffee until the froth comes to the top, and garnish with grated semisweet chocolate.

Rum Cake

1	cup butter, softened	1	teaspoon vanilla extract
1½	cups sugar	1	teaspoon almond extract
4	eggs, separated	¼	cup rum
1½	cups cake flour, sifted	½	cup crushed pecans
1¼	teaspoons baking powder	⅛	teaspoon salt

Moderately easy • Prep time: 15 minutes
Preheat the oven to 325°. In a large bowl of an electric mixer, cream butter and sugar. Add egg yolks, one at a time, beating well. Sift flour with baking powder. Combine flavorings. Add flour and flavorings alternately to the sugar-egg mixture. Mix well. Beat egg whites to form stiff peaks. Fold in stiffly beaten egg whites. Grease and flour a tube or 12-cup bundt pan. Toss pecans with salt and cover the bottom of the pan. Spoon in the batter. Bake for 55 to 60 minutes, or until a knife inserted in the center comes out clean. Cool in the pan for 10 to 15 minutes before turning out.
Yields 14 to 16 slices

Orange-Pineapple Tea

1	gallon water	2	tablespoons whole cloves
8	family-size tea bags	1	46-ounce can pineapple juice
2½	cups sugar	1	46-ounce can orange juice

Easy • Prep time: 5 minutes • Prepare ahead • Tea will keep in refrigerator for 1 week
Place 1 gallon water in a large pot and bring to a boil. Add tea bags. Remove from the heat and let steep for 3 minutes. In a saucepan, combine sugar with 2 cups water and bring to a boil. Add cloves and boil for 10 minutes, stirring often, until syrupy. Add syrup to steeped tea. Mix in juices. Strain and refrigerate for at least 4 hours. Serve cold or hot.
Yields 2 gallons

Welcome your new neighbor with an address book complete with names, addresses, and telephone numbers of new neighbors (ask for permission, of course), as well as doctors and babysitters. Include a list of reliable banks, dry cleaners, and repair services in your area, or give them personalized stationary imprinted with their new address (make sure you know exactly how the name should appear).

SHOPPING LIST _____

BUTCHER/DELI
__ 1 pound hot, ground pork
    sausage
__ ¾ pound sliced baked ham

CANNED GOODS
__ 1 46-ounce can pineapple juice
__ 1 46-ounce can orange juice
__ 1 16-ounce can chicken broth

DAIRY
__ 1 16-ounce container plain,
    nonfat yogurt
__ 1 quart milk
__ ½ pint whipping cream
__ 16 ounces sharp Cheddar
    cheese
__ 1 pound butter
__ 1 dozen eggs

EXTRAS
__ 1 small bottle rum

MISCELLANEOUS
__ 1 small jar ginger marmalade
__ 1 canister dry bread crumbs
__ 1 10-ounce package frozen
    chopped spinach
__ 1 6-ounce package chopped
    pecans
__ 1 small box dry biscuit mix
__ 2 8-ounce cans crescent dinner
    rolls

PRODUCE
__ 4 or 5 apples
__ 1 quart strawberries
__ 1 bunch grapes
__ 3 or 4 oranges
__ 1 10-ounce package mushrooms
__ 1 onion
__ 1 large lemon

STAPLES/SPICES
__ All-purpose flour
__ Almond extract
__ Baking powder
__ Basil
__ Cake flour
__ Coffee
__ Dark brown sugar
__ Family-size tea bags
__ Garlic powder
__ Paprika
__ Poultry seasoning
__ Sage
__ Salt
__ Sugar
__ Vanilla extract
__ Whole cloves

Rainy Day Repast

Notes

APPLE OAT SQUARES

EGGS IN BRIOCHE CUPS

SMOKED SALMON

CINNAMON-LACED HOT CHOCOLATE

SERVES 6

Inspired by the Pacific Northwest,
this menu offers the best of that region.
So on those rainy days that remind you of Seattle,
serve up a taste of that great city. And if you've
never been, what are you waiting for?

Apple Oat Squares

4	cups thinly sliced, peeled apples	1	cup rolled oats
2	tablespoons lemon juice	½	cup light brown sugar
2	tablespoons lemon zest	1	cup chopped pecans
¼	cup sugar	1	teaspoon ground cinnamon
⅓	cup all-purpose flour	½	teaspoon salt
		½	cup melted butter

Easy • Prep time: 20 minutes

Preheat the oven to 375°. In a bowl, combine apples, lemon juice, zest, and sugar. Turn into a buttered 9-inch square baking pan. In a mixing bowl, combine flour, oats, brown sugar, pecans, and seasonings. Stir in melted butter. Distribute evenly over apples. Bake for 30 to 35 minutes.

Yields 9 three-inch squares

Eggs in Brioche Cups

Brioche Cups
- 6 large individual brioches
- 1 clove garlic, finely minced
- ½ cup butter, melted

Cheese Sauce
- 3 tablespoons butter
- 3 tablespoons all-purpose flour
- 1 teaspoon dry mustard
-    Salt to taste
- ⅛ teaspoon ground white pepper
- 1 cup scalded milk
- 1 cup shredded sharp Cheddar cheese

Assembly
- 6 eggs, poached
-    Pimiento, finely chopped
-    Dill weed, finely chopped

Moderate • Prep time: 30 minutes

Preheat the oven to 250°. Slice tops off brioche to make "lids." Hollow out the centers, leaving the shells intact. Combine garlic and butter in a small bowl. Working with a small pastry brush, brush the brioche shells (inside and out) and lids (top and bottom) with garlic butter and place on a baking sheet. Bake for 25 to 30 minutes, or until light brown.

To make the sauce: Melt butter in a saucepan over medium-low heat. Stir in flour; cook and stir for 1 minute (do not allow to brown). Remove from the heat. Stir in seasonings. Return to the heat and slowly add milk, stirring constantly. Cook and stir the sauce until it is thick and bubbly. Stir in cheese and remove from the heat. Cover and set aside. Poach the eggs (if you haven't already done so).

To assemble: Place a tablespoon of the warm cheese sauce in the bottom of each brioche shell. Place a poached egg down inside each shell. Cover eggs with as much additional cheese sauce as each brioche shell will hold. Garnish with pimiento and dill. Stand the brioche "lid" up against the side of the brioche shell. Serve warm.

Yields 6 servings

When a recipe calls for a double boiler, you may use a heavy, durable saucepan instead.

Cinnamon-Laced Hot Chocolate

3 1-ounce squares
    semisweet chocolate
⅓ cup sugar
½ teaspoon salt
2 cups boiling water

8 cups scalded milk
1 teaspoon vanilla extract
2 teaspoons ground cinnamon
    Chocolate shavings for garnish

Easy • Prep time: 10 to 12 minutes

In the top of a double boiler, melt chocolate. Slowly add sugar and salt. Add boiling water, a little at a time, stirring constantly to combine. Add scalded milk and beat thoroughly for 1 to 2 minutes. Stir in vanilla and cinnamon. Beat again until the mixture obtains a frothy consistency. Pour into individual mugs and top with chocolate shavings.

Yields 8 to 10 servings

SHOPPING LIST

BAKERY
__ 6 brioches

BUTCHER
__ 1 pound smoked salmon

DAIRY
__ 1 pound butter
__ 1 gallon milk
__ 4 ounces sharp Cheddar cheese
__ ½ dozen eggs

MISCELLANEOUS
__ 1 4-ounce jar pimiento
__ 1 canister rolled oats
__ 1 6-ounce package chopped
   pecans
__ 1 8-ounce box bittersweet
   chocolate squares

PRODUCE
__ 1 head garlic
__ 1 bunch dill weed
__ 3 to 4 apples
__ 1 large lemon

STAPLES/SPICES
__ All-purpose flour
__ Sugar
__ Light brown sugar
__ Dry mustard
__ Salt
__ White pepper
__ Ground cinnamon
__ Vanilla extract

FESTIVE CRANBERRY PEARS

WILD RICE AND ARTICHOKE HEART BREAKFAST PIE

TOASTED BAGELS

COFFEE AND ORANGE JUICE

S E R V E S   6

Here's a menu meant to bring to mind strains of "amber waves of grain." The food, from basic bagel to pungent pie, is sure to make you feel like part of the heartland, no matter where you are. Prepare these foods when you're hungry for home.

Festive Cranberry Pears

1	cup orange juice	1½	cups raw cranberries, washed and drained
½	cup sugar		
6	whole cloves	6	firm pears, peeled, cored, and halved
2	cinnamon sticks		
		¾	cup heavy cream

Easy • Prep time: 15 minutes

Combine orange juice and sugar in a saucepan over medium-low heat. Cook and stir until sugar melts. Add remaining ingredients, except cream, and simmer gently until pears are tender, about 12 to 15 minutes. Turn pears carefully once or twice while cooking so that they color evenly.

To serve, place 2 pear halves in each bowl and spoon some of the cooking sauce and cranberries over the top. Drizzle 2 tablespoons heavy cream over each portion and serve warm.

Yields 6 servings

Notes

Heavy cream doubles and sometimes triples when whipped.

Wild Rice and Artichoke Heart Breakfast Pie

1	cup chopped marinated artichoke hearts	6	eggs, lightly beaten
1	cup cooked brown rice, cooled	¾	cup milk
¾	cup cooked wild rice, cooled	½	teaspoon dry mustard
1½	cups shredded Monterey Jack cheese	⅛	teaspoon black pepper
			Paprika for garnish

Moderately easy • Prep time: 20 minutes •Prepare ahead
Preheat the oven to 350°. In a large mixing bowl, combine artichoke hearts, rice, and cheese. Place the mixture into a greased 9-inch deep-dish pie plate. Whisk together eggs, milk, mustard, and pepper. Pour over the rice mixture. Sprinkle the top with paprika. (Recipe can be made in advance to this point and refrigerated overnight.) Bake for 50 minutes.
Yields 6 servings

SHOPPING LIST

BAKERY
__ 6 bagels

CANNED GOODS
__ 1 46-ounce can orange juice

DAIRY
__ 1 stick butter
__ 10 ounces Monterey Jack cheese
__ ½ dozen eggs
__ ½ pint milk
__ ½ pint heavy cream

MISCELLANEOUS
__ 1 13-ounce jar marinated artichoke hearts
__ 1 14-ounce bag brown rice
__ 1 small box wild rice

PRODUCE
__ 1 16-ounce bag cranberries
__ 6 firm pears

STAPLES/SPICES
__ Cinnamon sticks
__ Coffee
__ Dry mustard
__ Paprika
__ Pepper
__ Sugar
__ Whole cloves

Times Square New Year's Day Brunch

TOMATOES AND CREAM

CAVIAR PIE

TOP HAT HAM

MELON BALLS IN CHAMPAGNE

CHAMPAGNE

SERVES 6

Not many occasions call for caviar and champagne, but surely the dawn of the new year merits such decadence. Treat your closest friends to these delicacies as a way to get off on the right foot. And who knows, maybe next year they'll do the same for you.

Tomatoes and Cream

5	tomatoes		*Herbes de Provence to taste*
¼	cup butter		*(available in spice section of*
	Salt and pepper		*grocery or gourmet store)*
	to taste	5 to 10	*tablespoons heavy cream*

Easy • Prep time: 10 minutes

Slice tomatoes into ¼-inch-thick slices. Sprinkle one side of each tomato slice with salt, pepper, and herbes de Provence. Melt butter in a large skillet over medium heat. Working in batches, sauté tomato slices in butter; turning once. Do not overcook. Pour 1 to 2 tablespoons heavy cream per tomato over slices. Simmer for 1 minute to allow cream to thicken slightly. Serve warm.

Yields 6 servings

Caviar Pie

Nonstick vegetable oil spray
¼ cup finely chopped onion
¼ teaspoon sugar
4 hard-boiled eggs, peeled and coarsely chopped
⅛ cup mayonnaise
1 teaspoon chopped dill weed
1 tablespoon pickle relish
1 3-ounce package cream cheese, softened
1 tablespoon milk
4 ounces caviar (several colors)
1 lemon slice
Dill weed for garnish
Assorted crackers

Moderately easy• Prep time: 25 to 30 minutes • Prepare ahead
Spray a 4-inch diameter tart pan with a removable bottom with vegetable oil spray. Combine onion, sugar, eggs, mayonnaise, dill, and pickle relish; mix well. Turn the egg mixture into the tart pan and press down to compact. Refrigerate for 15 to 20 minutes. Combine cream cheese and milk in a small bowl. Using an electric mixer, mix to blend well. Drop the cream cheese mixture by the spoonful onto top of chilled eggs; using a flat blade knife, spread to cover. Refrigerate, covered, for at least 1 hour, and up to 1 day ahead of time. When ready to serve, spoon caviar in rows on top of cream cheese; alternate colors. Decorate with lemon slices. Press the bottom of pan up to release the pie from the outer ring. Plate and garnish with sprigs of dill weed. Serve with assorted crackers.
Yields 6 servings

DILL

Top Hat Ham

3 tablespoons butter	1 10-ounce package frozen spinach; cooked, drained, and squeezed dry
1 onion, chopped	
20 mushrooms, sliced	
½ teaspoon savory	2 tablespoons finely chopped walnuts
Salt and pepper to taste	
1 tablespoon all-purpose flour	6 ham slices, ¼-inch thick
½ cup milk	6 Swiss cheese slices
½ teaspoon instant chicken bouillon granules	6 egg whites
	Pinch of salt

Moderate • Prep time: 25 to 30 minutes

Preheat the oven to 500°. In a large skillet, melt 1 tablespoon butter. Sauté onions and mushrooms until limp. Add savory, salt, and pepper. Add remaining 2 tablespoons butter and stir until melted. Sprinkle in flour; blend. Add milk, cooking and stirring to make a sauce. Mix in chicken bouillon granules. Add spinach; cook and stir for 1 minute longer. Remove from the heat and mix in walnuts. Cool slightly.

To assemble: Arrange ham slices on a baking sheet, leaving ample space between each piece. Divide and distribute the spinach mixture evenly over each slice, spreading right to the edge of each and mounding slightly in the center. Lay a slice of cheese on top of the spinach. Trim the cheese, if necessary, so it does not hang over the edges.

In a small mixing bowl, beat the egg whites with the salt until stiff peaks form. Evenly divide and pile the egg meringue over each ham-cheese slice to cover completely. Bake for 10 to 12 minutes, or until the meringue is nicely browned. Serve immediately.

Yields 6 servings

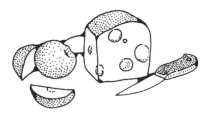

The most appropriate temperature for serving sparkling wines and champagne is 40°.

Melon Balls in Champagne

1 honeydew melon, chilled
1 cantaloupe, chilled

1 bottle champagne, chilled

Easy • Prep time: 10 minutes

Halve the melons and discard seeds. Use a melon baller to scoop alternating melon balls into champagne flutes. Pour chilled champagne over all. Serve cold with dainty skewers or forks long enough to reach the bottom of the flute.

Yields 6 servings

SHOPPING LIST

BUTCHER/DELI
__ 6¼-inch ham slices

EXTRAS
__ 3 or 4 bottles champagne

DAIRY
__ 1 stick butter
__ ½ pint milk
__ ½ pound thickly sliced Swiss cheese
__ 1 dozen eggs
__ ½ pint heavy cream
__ 1 3-ounce package cream cheese

MISCELLANEOUS
__ 1 10-ounce package frozen spinach
__ 1 2-ounce package chopped walnuts
__ 1 small jar pickle relish
__ 4 ounces caviar, various colors
__ Assorted crackers

PRODUCE
__ 1 honeydew melon
__ 1 cantaloupe
__ 2 onions
__ 20 mushrooms
__ 5 tomatoes
__ 1 bunch dill weed
__ 1 lemon

STAPLES/SPICES
__ All-purpose flour
__ Chicken bouillon granules
__ Herbes de Provence
__ Mayonnaise
__ Nonstick vegetable oil spray
__ Pepper
__ Salt
__ Savory
__ Sugar

CRISPY CHEESE WAFERS

CHICKEN SALAD ROUNDS

PUMPKIN MUFFINS

CINNAMON CRISPS

APPEALING APPLE CAKE

FRESH STRAWBERRIES WITH BROWN SUGAR DIP

CRANBERRY PUNCH AND COFFEE

S E R V E S   1 2

Offering a variety of foods that are easy to eat is the very best of hospitality. This menu allows you to prepare several kinds of treats without having to make too much or having to devise complicated serving techniques. Just fill up the platters, pour the coffee, and enjoy your friends.

"The morning cup of coffee has an exhilaration about it which the cheering influence of the afternoon or evening cup of tea cannot be expected to reproduce."
—DR. OLIVER WENDELL HOLMES

Notes

Crispy Cheese Wafers

1	cup grated sharp Cheddar cheese	1	cup puffed rice cereal
½	cup butter		Cayenne pepper to taste
1	cup all-purpose flour	1	teaspoon paprika

Moderately easy • Prep time: 20 to 30 minutes
Preheat the oven to 400°. In a large bowl of an electric mixer, cream Cheddar cheese and butter. Add flour and mix. Add remaining ingredients and mix well. Make ½-inch balls; place on a sheet pan and press with a wet fork to flatten. Bake for 10 minutes.
Yields 48 wafers

Chicken Salad Rounds

½ pound cooked chicken breast, minced
1 rib celery, minced
1 tablespoon finely minced red onion
½ teaspoon curry powder
Salt to taste

Freshly ground black pepper to taste
¼ cup mayonnaise, plus additional
12 thin slices whole-wheat bread
¾ cup sliced almonds, toasted and finely chopped

Moderately easy • Prep time: 30 minutes
Combine chicken, celery, onion, curry powder, salt, pepper, and mayonnaise. Blend well and add more mayonnaise if needed. Cut bread into 2-inch rounds and make sandwiches. Spread the sides of each sandwich all around with additional mayonnaise and roll in nuts. Chill and serve.
Yields 24 sandwiches

Pumpkin Muffins

1 16-ounce can pumpkin pie filling or plain pumpkin
1 cup vegetable oil
1 cup water
3 cups sugar
3 eggs, lightly beaten
1 cup chopped black walnuts
1½ cups chopped dates

3½ cups self-rising flour
2 teaspoons baking soda
2 teaspoons ground cinnamon
1 teaspoon each grated nutmeg, ginger, and salt
½ teaspoon ground cloves
½ teaspoon baking powder

Moderately easy • Prep time: 20 minutes
Preheat the oven to 325°. In a large bowl of an electric mixer, combine the first 7 ingredients. Sift together remaining ingredients in a separate bowl. Combine with the pumpkin mixture. Mix well. Divide batter between 2 greased muffin pans, filling tins half full. Bake for 15 to 20 minutes.
Yields 24 muffins

Breads baked in a microwave will not brown or crust on top, but you can use a topping or icing to provide color. Suggested toppings for breads are graham cracker crumbs, nuts, cinnamon sugar, or wheat germ.

Cinnamon Crisps

1	cup butter, softened	1½	teaspoons ground cinnamon
1	cup sugar	1	egg, divided
2	cups all-purpose flour	1	teaspoon vanilla extract
½	teaspoon grated nutmeg	½	cup chopped pecans

Easy • Prep time: 15 minutes • Prepare ahead and freeze
Preheat the oven to 275°. In a large bowl of an electric mixer, cream butter and sugar. Then add remaining ingredients, except egg white. Mix well. The dough will be very stiff. Press into a large ungreased cookie pan. Pour unbeaten egg white on top of the dough and spread evenly with your fingertips. Pour off any excess egg white. Sprinkle with chopped nuts. Press nuts into the dough. Bake for 60 minutes. Remove from the oven and immediately cut into 2-inch squares.
Yields 36 squares

Appealing Apple Cake

1½	cups vegetable oil	1	teaspoon grated nutmeg
2	cups sugar	1	teaspoon ground cloves
2	eggs	1	teaspoon vanilla extract
3	cups all-purpose flour	4	large Winesap or Jonathan
1½	teaspoons baking soda		apples, peeled and chopped
1	teaspoon salt	1	cup chopped pecans
1	teaspoon ground cinnamon	½	cup chopped dates

Easy • Prep time: 10 minutes • Great for cupcakes
Preheat the oven to 325°. In a large bowl of an electric mixer, mix oil and sugar; beat in eggs. Add remaining ingredients, mixing thoroughly. Pour into a tube or bundt cake pan that has been well greased with butter. Bake for 1½ hours.
Yields 18 to 20 servings

Line baskets with linen tea towels to keep breads warm during serving.

Fresh Strawberries with Brown Sugar Dip

1	16-ounce container plain, nonfat yogurt	½	teaspoon grated nutmeg
¾ to 1	cup brown sugar	2 to 3	pints fresh strawberries, rinsed and stems removed

Easy • Prep time: 30 minutes
Combine yogurt, brown sugar, and nutmeg in a large container and mix well. Serve with strawberries for dipping.
Yields 2 to 2½ cups dip

Cranberry Punch

2	quarts ginger ale	1	6-ounce can frozen lemonade, thawed
1	pint cranberry juice		
1	quart pineapple juice	1	quart Tom Collins mix

Easy • Prep time: 5 minutes
Freeze 1 quart ginger ale in ice cube trays. Mix together juices and Tom Collins mix and chill. Just before serving, combine the chilled mixture with remaining ginger ale and ginger ale ice cubes.
Yields 10 servings

For delicious iced coffee, you must first make good coffee and it must remain fresh. Sweeten if you choose, cover, and refrigerate to cool. When ready to serve, fill your glass with either one-half coffee and one-half ice complimented with lemon peel, or try a scoop of coffee, chocolate, or vanilla ice cream. This easy recipe will take you only about 5 minutes of prep time.

SHOPPING LIST _____

BAKERY
__ 1 loaf whole-wheat bread

BUTCHER/DELI
__ ½ pound boneless, skinless chicken breasts

CANNED GOODS
__ 1 32-ounce can pineapple juice
__ 1 16-ounce can pumpkin pie filling

DAIRY
__ 1 16-ounce container plain, nonfat yogurt
__ ½ dozen eggs
__ 1 pound butter
__ 4 ounces sharp Cheddar cheese

EXTRAS
__ 1 32-ounce bottle Tom Collins mix

MISCELLANEOUS
__ 2 32-ounce bottles ginger ale
__ 1 16-ounce bottle cranberry juice
__ 1 6-ounce package sliced almonds
__ 1 6-ounce package black walnut pieces
__ 1 6-ounce package chopped pecans
__ 1 8-ounce package chopped dates
__ 1 small box puffed rice cereal
__ 1 6-ounce container frozen lemonade concentrate

PRODUCE
__ 2 or 3 quarts strawberries
__ 1 stalk celery
__ 1 small red onion
__ 4 large Winesap or Jonathan apples

STAPLES/SPICES
__ All-purpose flour
__ Baking powder
__ Baking soda
__ Cayenne pepper
__ Cinnamon
__ Coffee
__ Curry powder
__ Ginger
__ Ground cloves
__ Light brown sugar
__ Mayonnaise
__ Nutmeg
__ Paprika
__ Pepper
__ Salt
__ Self-rising flour
__ Sugar
__ Vanilla extract
__ Vegetable oil

Harvest Coffee

SAUSAGE BALLS IN APPLE BUTTER

TINY MEAT PIES

HARVEST YAM BREAD

HONEY BANANA BREAD

STRAWBERRY BREAD

STRAWBERRY BUTTER

APRICOT DAINTIES

APPLE CIDER, COFFEE, AND HOT BUTTERED RUM

SERVES 30 TO 35

Although most of us haven't "harvested" in the literal sense, we do know what it's like to rejoice in the changing of the seasons. As autumn approaches, use this menu to celebrate fresh produce and crisp days.

Sausage Balls in Apple Butter

1   pound mild, ground pork sausage
1   large jar apple butter

Easy • Prep time: 10 minutes • Recipe doubles easily
Make sausage balls the size of a nickel. Sauté in a skillet until well done. Drain on paper towels. When ready to serve, heat apple butter in a saucepan or chafing dish and add sausage balls. Keep warm during serving.
Yields approximately 30 sausage balls

Tiny Meat Pies

¾ cup cream cheese, softened
1 cup butter, softened
2 to 3 cups all-purpose flour
1 pound ground chuck, browned and drained
1 6-ounce package spaghetti sauce mix
¼ cup tomato sauce
¾ teaspoon chili powder
⅓ cup chopped ripe olives
1 jalapeño pepper, seeded and chopped fine

Moderately easy • Prep time: 25 to 30 minutes • Prepare ahead
In a large bowl of an electric mixer, combine cream cheese, butter, and flour. Gather the dough into a ball; cover, refrigerate, and chill thoroughly. In another bowl, mix the remaining ingredients. Cover and chill for several hours, or overnight. Roll the dough thin between lightly floured sheets of wax paper. Use a biscuit cutter, about 2¼ inches wide, to cut circles. Put 1 teaspoon meat mixture on each circle, fold over, and pinch edges together. Prick tops with a fork. Freeze on cookie sheets for several hours. When ready to serve, bake, frozen, in a 425° oven for 12 to 15 minutes, or until pastry is golden brown.
Yields 72 to 75 pies

The most successful parties are those where the hosts welcome each guest by name, so that each person is made to feel special with meaningful introductions one to another.

Harvest Yam Bread

4½ cups all-purpose flour	6 eggs, beaten lightly
1½ teaspoons salt	¾ teaspoon grated nutmeg
3 cups sugar	¾ teaspoon ground cinnamon
1 tablespoon baking soda	¾ teaspoon allspice
3 cups cooked puréed yams	3 cups peeled, chopped apples
1½ cups vegetable oil	2 cups chopped pecans

Easy • Prep time: 20 minutes

Preheat the oven to 350°. Sift together flour, salt, sugar, and baking soda in a large bowl. Mix in puréed yams, oil, eggs, and spices. Combine just until mixed with the dry ingredients. Do not overmix. Stir in apples and pecans. Divide the batter among 3 well-greased 9x5x3-inch loaf pans. Bake for 60 to 70 minutes, or until a knife inserted in the center comes out clean. Reheat after slicing, just before serving.

Yields 3 loaves of 14 to 16 slices per loaf

Honey Banana Bread

1 cup butter, softened	2 cups all-purpose flour
¾ cup honey	1 teaspoon baking soda
2 eggs, lightly beaten	¼ teaspoon salt
1 cup mashed, overripe bananas	1 cup pecans, chopped
	1 8-ounce package chopped dates

Easy • Prep time: 20 minutes

Preheat the oven to 350°. Cream butter and honey. Add eggs, then mashed bananas. Blend well. Add flour, soda, and salt and mix well. Stir in pecans and dates. Pour the mixture into a greased and floured 9x5x3-inch loaf pan. Bake for 30 minutes, or until a knife inserted in the center comes out clean.

Yields 1 loaf of 14 to 16 slices

Strawberry Bread

3	cups all-purpose flour	4	eggs, lightly beaten
1	teaspoon baking soda	2	cups sliced frozen
1	teaspoon salt		strawberries, thawed
1	teaspoon ground cinnamon	1½	cups vegetable oil
2	cups sugar	1¼	cups chopped pecans

Easy • Prep time: 20 minutes • Prepare ahead and freeze

Preheat the oven to 325°. Sift the dry ingredients together. Combine eggs, strawberries, and oil in a large bowl of an electric mixer. Add the sifted dry ingredients slowly. Mix well. Stir in pecans. Pour into a greased 9x5x3-inch loaf pan. Bake for 60 minutes, or until a knife inserted in the center comes out clean. Cool before slicing.

Yields 1 loaf of 14 to 16 slices

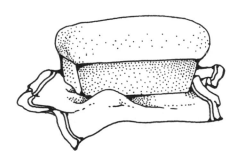

Strawberry Butter

½	cup butter, softened	½	teaspoon lemon juice
⅓	cup strawberry jam	½	teaspoon confectioners' sugar

Easy • Prep time: 5 minutes

In a mixing bowl, combine all ingredients until thoroughly blended. Refrigerate until ready to use.

Yields ¾ cup

Sweet butters are made by combining butter, jam, lemon juice, and confectioners' sugar. Follow the Strawberry Butter recipe and substitute your jam of choice. These make a delightful spread for various breads.

Apricot Dainties

1   6-ounce package dried
    apricots, chopped
1   cup sugar

3   tablespoons orange juice
1   cup finely chopped pecans
    Confectioners' sugar

Moderately easy • Prep time: 30 minutes

In the top of a double boiler, cook apricots, sugar, and orange juice until sugar dissolves and apricots soften. Cool the mixture and shape fruit into balls with a pinch of pecans in the center of each. Roll balls in remaining pecans, then in confectioners' sugar.

Yields approximately 50 balls

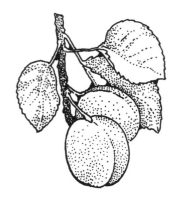

Apple Cider

3   gallons apple cider
2   ounces whole cloves

12   cinnamon sticks
    Mint sprigs for garnish

Easy • Prep time: 10 minutes

In a large pot, bring all ingredients, except mint, to a boil. Remove from the heat. Allow to sit for 60 minutes. Remove spices and chill. Add a sprig of mint to each serving. Serve cold.

Yields 64 six-ounce servings

Have shakers of cocoa, cinnamon, and nutmeg available for guests to top off their coffees.

Hot Buttered Rum

1 gallon apple cider
2 cups dark rum
35 cinnamon sticks

1 ounce whole cloves
1 cup butter

Easy • Prep time: 10 minutes • Recipe doubles easily

In a large pot, combine cider and rum and heat to boiling. Heat serving mugs and into each place 1 cinnamon stick and 3 cloves. Fill with the hot rum mixture. Top with ½ tablespoon butter.

Yields 35 four-ounce servings

COFFEE

Good coffee depends on good preparation. Be sure to use the correct grind, measured amounts, and appropriate brewing time. Follow these guidelines when making coffee for a group.

Number of Guests	Number of 5 ½-ounce Servings	Pounds of Coffee	Gallons of Water
25	40	1	2
50	80	2	4
75	120	3	6
100	160	4	8
125	200	5	10
150	240	6	12

SHOPPING LIST _____

BUTCHER
__ 1 pound ground chuck
__ 1 pound mild, ground pork
  sausage

CANNED GOODS
__ 1 small can chopped black olives
__ 1 8-ounce can tomato sauce
__ 2 16-ounce cans yams

DAIRY
__ 1 8-ounce package cream cheese
__ 2 pounds butter
__ 1 dozen eggs

EXTRAS
__ 1 bottle dark rum

MISCELLANEOUS
__ Various flavored coffees
__ 1 16-ounce package frozen sliced
  strawberries
__ 1 6-ounce package spaghetti
  sauce mix
__ 1 24-ounce package chopped
  pecans
__ 1 small jar honey
__ 1 8-ounce package chopped dates
__ 1 large jar apple butter
__ 1 small jar strawberry jam
__ 1 6-ounce package dried apricots
__ 4 gallons apple cider

PRODUCE
__ 1 jalapeño pepper
__ 3 to 4 apples
__ 2 or 3 overripe bananas
__ 1 lemon
__ 1 orange
__ 1 bunch fresh mint

STAPLES/SPICES
__ All-purpose flour
__ Baking soda
__ Chili powder
__ Cinnamon sticks
__ Coffee
__ Confectioners' sugar
__ Ground cinnamon
__ Nutmeg
__ Salt
__ Sugar
__ Vegetable oil
__ Whole cloves

MIDDAY

Between breakfast and dinner there's so much that can happen. These hours offer great opportunities for hosting your friends and family with lots of flair and little fuss.

The ladies luncheon still survives in some communities, especially among women who enjoy bridge, gardening, or some other afternoon activity. Lunchtime is also a good time to get together a group of men and women to plan a community project. At this type of working session you will want to keep things moving so you can get down to the business at hand.

If you know the drinking habits of your guests, plan accordingly. If you don't, have on hand the makings of a Bloody Mary or a small selection of wine that can be sampled beforehand. As always, be sure to provide nonalcoholic drinks as well.

Whatever the purpose, business or pleasure, remember that few people in today's health conscious world like to eat heavy food in the middle of the day. In hot weather, you might serve gazpacho or another cold soup, followed by a chicken salad. Fresh fruit or frozen desserts are a welcome treat during the dog days of summer. On a chilly day, homemade soups or casseroles can be complemented by delicious cookies and plenty of hot coffee.

If you're hosting a sit-down luncheon, set the table the night before the guests are to arrive. Buffet service is expedient when serving a seated lunch. Occasions that favor lunch in a basket or box, like a "grab-and-go" sandwich sampler, are becoming popular with today's busy lifestyles.

The menus here are easy to prepare, and many can be prepared ahead of time and frozen until needed. Supplement your menus with already prepared foods from local bakeries and supermarkets.

Poolside Luncheon

Notes

_____

_____

_____

_____

_____

_____

_____

_____

_____

_____

_____

_____

_____

_____

_____

_____

_____

_____

GAZPACHO

SALMON MOUSSE

CALICO BEAN SALAD

TINY HERB BISCUITS

PLATTER OF FRESH FRUIT

YUMMY CHOCOLATE COOKIES

SOUR CREAM COFFEE CAKE

ICED TEA AND SOFT DRINKS

SERVES 8 TO 10

You don't have to go swimming to enjoy your backyard pool. Use it as a setting for a casual luncheon when the weather's just right—not too hot.

Gazpacho

1	cup finely chopped, peeled tomatoes	1	teaspoon freshly chopped basil
1	cup finely chopped green bell pepper	⅛	teaspoon garlic powder
1	cup diced celery	¼	cup red wine vinegar
1	cup diced cucumber	¼	cup olive oil
¼	cup minced green onion	1	teaspoon salt
2	tablespoons parsley flakes	1	teaspoon pepper
1	teaspoon freshly chopped chives	1	teaspoon Worcestershire sauce
		2	cups tomato juice
			Sour cream

Easy • Prep time: 15 to 20 minutes • Prepare ahead
In a large bowl, mix all ingredients, except sour cream, and chill. Top individual portions with sour cream when ready to serve.
Yields 8 to 10 servings

Serve gazpacho in mugs for easy eating.

Salmon Mousse

2	envelopes unflavored gelatin	½	teaspoon salt
½	cup cold water	1	tablespoon Worcestershire
1	cup boiling water		sauce
1	tablespoon white vinegar	1	medium onion, grated
3	tablespoons lemon juice	1	cup diced celery
1	16-ounce can salmon, flaked	1	cup finely chopped cucumber
1	cup mayonnaise		Leaf or Romaine lettuce
1	cup heavy cream, whipped		

Easy • Prep time: 15 minutes • Prepare ahead
Soak gelatin in cold water, then dissolve in hot water. Add vinegar and lemon juice and refrigerate to thicken. Combine salmon, mayonnaise, and whipped cream. Then add all remaining ingredients, except lettuce. Mix well. Pour the mixture into 10 oiled individual molds or 1 large 8- to 10-cup fish mold. Chill until firm. Unmold and serve over lettuce.
Yields 8 to 10 servings

Mousse is better if prepared a day before serving.

Calico Bean Salad

1	16-ounce can green beans, drained	¾	cup sugar
1	16-ounce can cut wax beans, drained	⅔	cup white vinegar
		⅓	cup vegetable oil
1	16-ounce can kidney beans, drained	1	teaspoon salt
		1	teaspoon black pepper
		3	green onions, sliced
½	cup chopped green bell pepper	1	cup sugar peas, optional

Easy • Prep time: 10 minutes • Prepare ahead
In a large bowl, combine all ingredients. Toss lightly. Refrigerate overnight. Drain before serving. Great for picnics or outside buffets in hot weather.
Yields 8 to 10 servings

To make canned green beans taste fresh, add a small amount of onion or lemon juice.

Tiny Herb Biscuits

2	cups biscuit mix (such as Bisquick)	1	teaspoon parsley flakes
¼	teaspoon dry mustard	1 ½	teaspoons caraway seeds
		⅔	cup buttermilk

Easy • Prep time: 10 to 15 minutes
Preheat the oven to 450°. In a large bowl combine all dry ingredients. Add buttermilk and mix lightly. Turn onto a lightly floured board and knead 10 times. Roll dough to ½-inch thickness. Cut out biscuits with a small cutter and bake on an ungreased cookie sheet for 10 to 12 minutes or until golden.
Yields 24 small biscuits

Yummy Chocolate Cookies

8	ounces semisweet chocolate	2	cups chopped pecans
1	14-ounce can sweetened condensed milk	1	teaspoon vanilla extract
1	3½-ounce can flaked coconut		

Easy • Prep time: 15 minutes
Preheat the oven to 350°. In the top of a double boiler or heavy saucepan, melt chocolate in milk. Add coconut, pecans, and vanilla. Drop by teaspoonsfuls onto greased cookie sheets. Bake for 8 to 10 minutes.
Yields 4 to 5 dozen cookies

Sour Cream Coffee Cake

Crumb Mixture
- ¾ cup chopped pecans
- 3 tablespoons sugar
- 1 teaspoon ground cinnamon

Cake
- 1 cup butter, softened
- 2 cups sugar
- 2 eggs
- 2 cups all-purpose flour
- 1 teaspoon baking powder
- ¼ teaspoon salt
- 1 cup sour cream
- ½ teaspoon vanilla extract

Easy • Prep time: 10 minutes

Preheat the oven to 350°. Grease a bundt pan and set it aside. Combine all ingredients for the crumb mixture and set aside.

In a large mixing bowl, cream butter and sugar. Add eggs one at a time and beat well after each addition. Sift flour, baking powder, and salt together and add them to the butter mixture alternately with sour cream, starting and ending with flour. Add vanilla. Pour half of the batter into the greased bundt pan. Sprinkle three-fourths of the crumb mixture over top, then pour on the remaining batter. Bake for 50 to 60 minutes, or until a knife inserted in the center of the cake comes out clean. Allow the cake to cool in the pan on a rack for 5 to 10 minutes, then turn out onto a serving platter and sprinkle with the remaining crumb mixture.

Yields 12 to 14 servings

Ice down cold drinks in colorful plastic sand buckets.

SHOPPING LIST _____

CANNED GOODS
__ 1 16-ounce can pink salmon
__ 1 16-ounce can green beans
__ 1 16-ounce can wax beans
__ 1 16-ounce can kidney beans
__ 1 can sugarpeas (optional)
__ 1 14-ounce can sweetened
    condensed milk
__ 1 3 ½-ounce can flaked coconut
__ 1 16-ounce can tomato juice

DAIRY
__ ½ dozen eggs
__ 1 16-ounce carton sour cream
__ ½ pint heavy cream
__ 1 pound butter
__ 1 pint buttermilk

MISCELLANEOUS
__ 2 6-ounce boxes semisweet
    chocolate squares
__ 1 small box biscuit mix
__ 1 box unflavored gelatin
__ 1 16-ounce bag chopped pecans
__ 2 or 3 six-packs soft drinks

PRODUCE
__ 3 large Granny Smith apples
__ 3 large Red Delicious apples
__ 3 oranges
__ 1 bunch grapes
__ 1 pint strawberries
__ 4 kiwi fruit
__ 2 large green bell peppers
__ 1 stalk celery
__ 2 large cucumbers
__ 2 large tomatoes
__ 1 medium onion
__ 1 small bunch green onions
__ 1 bunch fresh chives
__ 1 bunch fresh basil

STAPLES/SPICES
__ All-purpose flour
__ Apple cider vinegar
__ Baking powder
__ Caraway seeds
__ Cinnamon
__ Dry mustard
__ Family-size tea bags
__ Garlic powder
__ Lemon juice
__ Mayonnaise
__ Olive oil
__ Parsley flakes
__ Pepper
__ Red wine vinegar
__ Salt
__ Sugar
__ Vanilla extract
__ Vegetable oil
__ White vinegar
__ Worcestershire sauce

TUNA SALAD

CURRIED CHICKEN SALAD

EGG SALAD

ASSORTED ROLLS AND BREADS

MARINATED MUSHROOM SALAD

RATATOUILLE SALAD

FRESH FRUIT SALAD WITH POPPY SEED DRESSING

BLONDE BROWNIES

ICED TEA

SERVES 8

Offering a variety of salads for making sandwiches is an easy way to feed a group of people without much fuss. This buffet is great for working lunches, when you're planning an event or organizing a committee.

Tuna Salad

2 9-ounce cans solid light tuna, drained
¼ cup mayonnaise
1 teaspoon dill weed
1 teaspoon garlic salt
1 teaspoon prepared horseradish
½ cup minced sweet onion (such as Vidalia)

Easy • Prep time: 10 minutes • Prepare ahead
Combine all ingredients thoroughly and chill until ready to serve.
Yields 6 to 8 servings

Curried Chicken Salad

½ cup mayonnaise	3 ½ cups cold cooked chicken, chopped into ½-inch chunks
½ teaspoon garlic salt	
1 teaspoon curry powder	⅔ cup diced celery
⅛ teaspoon cayenne pepper	½ cup sliced green onions
½ teaspoon prepared mustard	1 small apple, diced
2 teaspoons fresh lemon juice	3 tablespoons toasted, sliced almonds
2 tablespoons finely chopped mango chutney	

Easy • Prep time: 15 minutes • Prepare ahead
In a bowl, combine mayonnaise, garlic salt, curry powder, cayenne, mustard, lemon juice, and chutney. Add remaining ingredients and stir to blend. Chill.
Yields 8 to 10 servings

Egg Salad

8 hard-boiled eggs, chopped	1 tablespoon spicy brown mustard, optional
½ cup mayonnaise	
½ teaspoon salt	1 teaspoon chopped fresh chives, optional
1 teaspoon pepper	

Easy • Prep time: 15 minutes • Prepare ahead
Combine all ingredients thoroughly and chill until serving time.
Yields 8 servings

Marinated Mushroom Salad

1¼ pounds small mushrooms,
     washed and ends trimmed
     Salted water
¼   cup olive oil
2   tablespoons fresh lemon juice
⅛   teaspoon garlic powder

½   teaspoon each: black pepper,
     coriander seed, and
     mustard seed
½   cup chopped onions
½   cup chopped parsley
     Salt to taste

Easy • Prep time: 10 minutes • Prepare ahead

In a large saucepan, place mushrooms in enough boiling salted water to cover. Simmer, uncovered, for 5 minutes. Drain and let cool. Combine olive oil, lemon juice, garlic powder, pepper, coriander seed, and mustard seed. Add mushrooms, onions, parsley, and salt to taste. Stir. Cover and marinate at room temperature for at least 2 hours, stirring occasionally.

Yields 10 to 12 servings

Ratatouille Salad

½ cup chopped onions
⅛ teaspoon garlic powder
¼ cup olive oil
1 eggplant (¾ pound),
   cut into 1-inch cubes
1 medium zucchini,
   cut into ½-inch-thick slices
1 medium green bell pepper,
   cut into ¼-inch strips

¼ cup chopped fresh parsley
1 14½-ounce can pear-shaped
   tomatoes, including liquid
1 teaspoon dry basil
1 teaspoon salt
⅓ cup grated Parmesan cheese

Easy • Prep time: 20 minutes • Can prepare ahead
In a large frying pan over medium heat, cook onions and garlic powder in olive oil, stirring, until limp. Add eggplant, zucchini, green pepper, parsley, tomatoes and liquid, basil, and salt. Cover and simmer, stirring occasionally, until all vegetables are tender, about 25 minutes. Cook, uncovered, stirring occasionally, over high heat until most liquid has evaporated. Remove from the heat. Cool, cover, and chill. Serve at room temperature with Parmesan cheese for topping individual servings.
Yields 8 half-cup servings

Twice as much fresh herbs as dried herbs should be used when cooking.

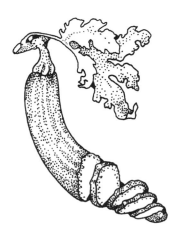

Fresh Fruit Salad with Poppy Seed Dressing

2	Granny Smith apples, cored and cubed	1	cup pineapple chunks
2	Red Delicious apples, cored and cubed	¼	cup raisins
		¼	cup chopped walnuts
1 ½	cups halved green seedless grapes	2	tablespoons fresh lemon juice
1	seedless orange, peeled and cubed	¾	cup poppy seed dressing (storebought, or see recipe p. 328)

Easy • Prep time: 20 minutes
Gently toss together all of the ingredients. Cover and chill until ready to serve.
Yields 8 to 10 servings

Blonde Brownies

¼	cup butter or margarine	1	cup all-purpose flour
1	cup brown sugar	1	teaspoon baking powder
1	egg, beaten	1	6-ounce package semisweet chocolate chips
1	teaspoon vanilla extract		Confectioners' sugar
⅛	teaspoon salt		

Easy • Prep time: 20 minutes
Preheat the oven to 350°. In a saucepan, melt butter; combine with brown sugar, egg, vanilla, and salt. Stir in flour and baking powder; add chocolate chips. Mix well. Bake for 30 minutes in a greased and floured 8-inch square pan. Cool. Cut into squares. Sprinkle with confectioners' sugar.
Yields 18 to 20 squares

SHOPPING LIST

BAKERY
__ Assorted rolls and bread for sandwiches

BUTCHER/DELI
__ Approximately 1½ pounds boneless, skinless chicken breasts

CANNED GOODS
__ 2 9-ounce cans solid light tuna
__ 1 14½-ounce can pear shaped tomatoes
__ 1 15¼-ounce can pineapple chunks
__ 1 small can grated Parmesan cheese

DAIRY
__ 1 dozen eggs
__ 1 stick butter

MISCELLANEOUS
__ 1 small jar mango chutney
__ 1 small package chopped walnuts
__ 1 small package sliced almonds
__ 1 6-ounce package chocolate chips
__ 1 small bottle poppy seed salad dressing
__ 1 small jar prepared horseradish

PRODUCE
__ 1 bunch parsley
__ 2 large lemons
__ 1 stalk celery
__ 1 bunch green onions
__ 3 Red Delicious apples (one small)
__ 2 Granny Smith apples
__ 1 bunch white seedless grapes
__ 1 seedless orange
__ 1¼ pounds small mushrooms
__ 1 bunch fresh chives
__ 1 small sweet onion
__ 1 large white onion
__ 1 (¾-pound) eggplant
__ 1 medium zucchini
__ 1 medium green bell pepper

STAPLES/SPICES
__ All-purpose flour
__ Baking powder
__ Brown sugar
__ Cayenne pepper
__ Confectioners' sugar
__ Coriander seed
__ Curry powder
__ Dill weed
__ Dried basil
__ Family-size tea bags
__ Garlic powder
__ Garlic salt
__ Mayonnaise
__ Mustard seed
__ Olive oil
__ Pepper
__ Prepared mustard
__ Salt
__ Spicy brown mustard
__ Vanilla extract

Mediterranean Lunch

SALAD NIÇOISE

PITAS TOASTED WITH HERB BUTTER

FUDGE PIE

SAUVIGNON BLANC

SERVES 4

Serve this menu when you want to offer a taste of the
Mediterranean.

Salad Niçoise

3	cups combination greens	1	2-ounce can anchovy fillets
2	7-ounce cans white tuna	4	artichoke hearts, halved
2	tomatoes, cut in eighths	¾	cup cooked (very crisp) French green beans
1	small sweet onion (such as Vidalia or purple), thinly sliced	2	cups cooked new potato halves
2	tablespoons capers, drained	¼	cup Greek olives
			Dressing

Easy • Prep time: 15 minutes

Arrange greens on 4 plates; divide remaining ingredients evenly among
the plates. Just before serving, drizzle with dressing.

Yields 4 servings

Dressing

½	cup olive oil	1	teaspoon sugar
¼	cup vegetable oil	¾	teaspoon salt
¼	cup red wine vinegar	¼	teaspoon cracked black pepper

Combine all ingredients in a jar with a tight-fitting lid. Shake well.

Yields 1 cup dressing

Notes

Pitas Toasted with Herb Butter

1 tablespoon chopped basil, dill, or oregano
1 small tub whipped butter, softened
6 pitas

Easy • Prep time: 10 minutes
Preheat the oven to 400°. Thoroughly stir dried herbs into softened butter. Lightly spread butter onto pitas. Toast in the oven until crisped on the outside. Cut into quarters and serve.
Yields 24 pita pieces

Fudge Pie

½ cup butter
2 squares unsweetened chocolate
2 eggs, beaten
1 cup sugar
¼ cup all-purpose flour

⅛ teaspoon salt
1 teaspoon vanilla extract
½ cup chopped pecans, optional
Whipped topping or vanilla ice cream, optional

Easy • Prep time: 10 minutes • Prepare ahead and freeze
Preheat the oven to 350°. In a heavy saucepan or double boiler, melt butter and unsweetened chocolate. Combine eggs, sugar, flour, salt, and stir into the chocolate mixture. Mix in vanilla and pecans. Grease an 8-inch pie plate and pour in filling (no crust needed). Bake for 20 to 25 minutes. Top with whipped topping or ice cream, if desired.
Yields 6 servings

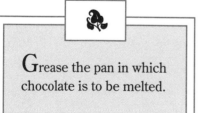
Grease the pan in which chocolate is to be melted.

SHOPPING LIST _____

BAKERY
__ 1 package pita bread

CANNED GOODS
__ 2 7-ounce cans solid packed
   white tuna
__ 1 2-ounce can anchovy fillets
__ 1 16-ounce can new potatoes
__ 1 small can artichoke hearts

DAIRY
__ 1 stick butter
__ ½ dozen eggs
__ 1 small carton whipped butter

EXTRAS
__ 2 bottles Sauvignon Blanc

MISCELLANEOUS
__ 1 small jar capers
__ 1 small box unsweetened
   chocolate squares
__ 1 small jar Greek olives
__ 1 10-ounce package frozen
   French green beans

PRODUCE
__ 2 large tomatoes
__ 1 small sweet onion (such as
   Vidalia or purple)
__ Combination of greens:
   Romaine, Boston, Iceberg,
   Spinach
__ 1 bunch fresh basil, dill, or
   oregano

STAPLES/SPICES
__ All-purpose flour
__ Cracked black pepper
__ Olive oil
__ Red wine vinegar
__ Salt
__ Sugar
__ Vanilla extract
__ Vegetable oil

Summertime Bridge Luncheon

CHICKEN AND CARROT SALAD

LIME-GRAPE GELATIN MOLDS

POPPY SEED CRESCENTS

RUM CREAM DESSERT

ICED TEA AND COFFEE

SERVES 4

People who love to play bridge really love to play bridge. So the next time it's your turn to host the players, offer them something good to eat.

Chicken and Carrot Salad

1 tablespoon freshly squeezed lemon juice
1 cup mayonnaise
2 cups diced, cooked chicken
1 cup shredded carrots
¾ cup diced celery
½ cup slivered blanched almonds
2 tablespoons finely chopped onion
Salt and pepper to taste
Romaine lettuce

Easy • Prep time: 15 minutes
In a bowl, stir lemon juice into mayonnaise. Toss with chicken, carrots, celery, almonds, onion, salt, and pepper. Chill and serve over lettuce.
Yields 4 servings

Rub your hands with the cut end of a celery rib or with lemon juice when peeling onions. Your hands will smell sweeter (although you still might shed a few tears).

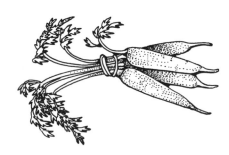

Lime-Grape Gelatin Molds

1	3-ounce package lime-flavored gelatin	1	cup small green seedless grapes
¼	cup freshly squeezed lime juice		Lettuce or watercress
			Dressing

Easy • Prep time: 10 minutes
Prepare gelatin according to the package directions, substituting lime juice for part of water. When partially set, fold in grapes and pour into 4 individual molds. Chill until set; unmold on a bed of lettuce or watercress. Top with dressing.
Yields 4 servings

Dressing

2½	tablespoons mayonnaise	Salt and sugar to taste
⅓	cup sour cream	

Blend all ingredients in a bowl and refrigerate until ready to serve.
Yields about 1½ cups dressing

Poppy Seed Crescents

1	8-ounce container instant crescent rolls
¼	cup butter
¼	cup poppy seeds

Easy • Prep time: 5 minutes
Spread crescents on a baking sheet. Melt butter and brush lightly over crescents. Sprinkle with poppy seeds. Roll up and bake according to package directions.
Yields 8 crescents

"When the human passions are ebbing, bridge takes their place."—ANNE SHAW

Rum Cream Dessert

18	ladyfingers	5	tablespoons rum
72	large marshmallows	2	pints heavy cream
¼	cup milk		

Easy • Prep time: 20 minutes • Prepare ahead

Line a 9-inch springform pan with ladyfingers. Crumble remaining ladyfingers in the bottom of the pan. Heat marshmallows and milk in a heavy saucepan or double boiler. When marshmallows have melted, remove from the heat and let cool. Add rum. Whip cream until it peaks. Fold the marshmallow mixture into cream. Pour into the pan. Freeze for 30 minutes. Remove and refrigerate overnight.

Yields 8 servings

SHOPPING LIST

BAKERY
__ 1 package ladyfingers

BUTCHER
__ Approximately 1 pound boneless, skinless chicken breasts

DAIRY
__ 1 quart heavy cream
__ 1 pint milk
__ 1 stick butter
__ 1 8-ounce carton sour cream

EXTRAS
__ 1 small bottle dark rum

MISCELLANEOUS
__ 1 3-ounce package lime-flavored gelatin
__ 1 6-ounce package slivered blanched almonds
__ 1 8-ounce container instant crescent rolls
__ 2 bags large marshmallows
__ 1 small jar poppy seeds

PRODUCE
__ 1 small bunch green seedless grapes
__ 2 large limes
__ 1 lemon
__ 2 large carrots (or 1 small bunch)
__ 1 small onion
__ 1 small stalk celery
__ 1 head Romaine lettuce

STAPLES/SPICES
__ Coffee
__ Mayonnaise
__ Pepper
__ Salt
__ Sugar
__ Tea bags

BRUSSELS SPROUTS WITH LEMON-PEPPER

MEDITERRANEAN TART

FALL FRUIT SALAD

PUMPKIN CHEESECAKE

COFFEE AND HOT TEA

S E R V E S   1 0

What better way to welcome the fall season than by having a few friends over for lunch? Use the crisp weather as an excuse to whip up these tasty recipes.

"Delicious autumn! My very soul is wedded to it, and if I were a bird I would fly about the earth seeking the successive autumns."
—GEORGE ELIOT

Notes

Brussels Sprouts with Lemon-Pepper

40 to 50	Brussels sprouts	¼	cup lemon juice
1	teaspoon salt	1	tablespoon pepper
6	tablespoons butter		

Easy • Prep time: 10 minutes
Wash Brussels sprouts and cut off tough bottoms. Cut each sprout in half. Place in a large saucepan and barely cover with boiling water. Add salt; cover and cook for 8 to 10 minutes. Drain; add butter, lemon juice, and pepper. Serve hot.
Yields 10 to 12 servings

Mediterranean Tart

3	tablespoons butter	½	pound baked ham,
1	onion, chopped fine		cut into small pieces
1	cup sliced mushrooms	½	cup chopped black olives
¼	teaspoon thyme		Salt and pepper to taste
2	tablespoons all-purpose flour	¾	cup unsalted butter, melted
1	cup chicken broth	16	16x12-inch sheets phyllo
2	tomatoes, peeled,		dough
	seeded, and chopped	½	cup freshly grated Parmesan
6	cups cooked, cubed chicken		cheese

Moderately easy • Prep time: 25 to 30 minutes

Preheat the oven to 300°. In a large skillet, melt butter. Add onions and sauté until transparent. Add mushrooms and thyme and cook for 5 minutes. Blend in flour and cook for 2 to 3 more minutes, stirring frequently. Add chicken broth and tomatoes and cook until thickened, stirring constantly. Reduce heat; add chicken, ham, and olives and simmer for 5 minutes. Add salt and pepper. Remove from the heat. Let cool. Brush the bottom and sides of a 16x12-inch casserole dish with melted butter. Line the dish with 1 sheet phyllo, pressing firmly into corners and sides of dish. Brush with melted butter, being sure to reach into the corners and sides. Repeat until 8 sheets of phyllo are stacked in the dish. Spoon filling over phyllo, spreading into the corners. Sprinkle with all the cheese. Top with a sheet of phyllo and brush with butter. Repeat with remaining phyllo. Using scissors, trim excess phyllo from the edges of the dish. Brush the top with remaining butter. Bake, brushing the top with butter several times, until the pastry is crisp and golden, about 60 minutes. Cut into squares and serve immediately.

Yields 10 to 12 servings

Fall Fruit Salad

3 Granny Smith apples, chilled
3 Red Delicious apples, chilled
⅔ cup sherry vinegar
1 ½ cups chopped celery
½ cup walnut halves
¼ cup golden raisins
½ cup green seedless grapes
3 green onions, chopped
¼ cup walnut oil

Easy • Prep time: 10 minutes
Wash apples and dry well. Core and chop them, but do not peel. Toss apples in a bowl with sherry vinegar. Add celery, walnut halves, raisins, grapes, and onions; drizzle with walnut oil. Toss again. Taste and adjust seasonings, adding more vinegar and oil as necessary. Serve immediately.
Yields 8 to 10 servings

Pumpkin Cheesecake

1 cup uncooked rolled oats
⅓ cup light brown sugar
¼ cup butter, melted
½ teaspoon ground cinnamon
⅓ cup chopped pecans
4 8-ounce packages cream cheese, softened
4 cups sugar
5 eggs
1 18-ounce can pumpkin pie mix
3 tablespoons pumpkin pie spice
1 cup heavy cream, whipped
2 tablespoons confectioners' sugar

Easy • Prep time: 15 minutes • Prepare ahead
Preheat the oven to 475°. Mix the first 5 ingredients in a bowl. Press into a greased 9-inch springform pan and bake for 8 to 10 minutes, or until golden. Reduce the oven temperature to 325°. In a large bowl of an electric mixer, beat cream cheese until smooth and fluffy. Add sugar and continue beating. Add eggs, one at a time, beating well after each addition. Add pumpkin pie mix and spice; mix well. Pour the mixture into the prebaked crust and bake for 1 hour and 45 minutes. Remove from the oven and let cool. Refrigerate for at least 12 hours. Top with whipped cream and sprinkle with confectioners' sugar.
Yields 12 to 15 servings

Recipes are written for regular or large eggs.

SHOPPING LIST _____

_____
_____
_____
_____
_____
_____
_____
_____
_____
_____
_____
_____
_____
_____
_____
_____
_____
_____
_____
_____
_____
_____
_____
_____
_____
_____
_____
_____
_____
_____
_____
_____
_____

BUTCHER/DELI
__ Approximately 2 pounds
   boneless, skinless chicken
   breasts
__ ½ pound lean ham

CANNED GOODS
__ 1 small can pitted and chopped
   black olives
__ 1 18-ounce can pumpkin pie
   filling
__ 1 16-ounce can chicken broth

DAIRY
__ 2 sticks unsalted butter
__ 2 sticks regular butter
__ 4 8-ounce packages cream
   cheese
__ ½ pint heavy cream
__ 1 4-ounce block Parmesan cheese
__ ½ dozen eggs

MISCELLANEOUS
__ 1 bottle sherry vinegar
__ 1 16-ounce box phyllo dough (in
   the frozen section)
__ 1 small bottle lemon juice
__ 1 small bottle walnut oil
__ 1 container rolled oats
__ 1 small package chopped pecans
__ 1 small package walnut halves

PRODUCE
__ 1 small box golden raisins
__ 3 Granny Smith apples
__ 3 Red Delicious apples
__ 1 stalk celery
__ 1 bunch green onions
__ ½ pound green seedless grapes
__ 2 large tomatoes
__ 1 large onion
__ ½ pound fresh mushrooms
__ 40 to 50 Brussels sprouts

STAPLES/SPICES
__ All-purpose flour
__ Cinnamon
__ Coffee
__ Confectioners' sugar
__ Light brown sugar
__ Pepper
__ Pumpkin pie spice
__ Salt
__ Sugar
__ Tea bags
__ Thyme

CHEESE WAFERS

COLD CUCUMBER SOUP

COURTSIDE PASTA

ICE CREAM PIE

WIMBLEDON DAIQUIRIS AND MINT TEA

S E R V E S   1 0   T O   1 2

Even if your serve is lacking, *what* you serve doesn't have to be. When you and your friends are off the court, this menu offers something for everyone.

Cheese Wafers

1	cup grated Swiss cheese
8	slices bacon, cooked and crumbled
3	tablespoons mayonnaise

1	tablespoon chopped onion
½	teaspoon celery seeds
30	rounds rye or pumpernickel bread

Easy • Prep time: 15 minutes • Prepare cheese spread ahead and freeze
Preheat the broiler. In a blender, combine the first 5 ingredients; blend well. Spread the cheese mixture on each round of bread. Broil until the mixture is hot and bubbly. Serve hot or cold.
Yields 30 wafers

Cold Cucumber Soup

Decorate the serving table with a simple bowl or basket filled with tennis balls.

¼	cup butter
2	tablespoons grated onion
4	cucumbers, peeled, seeded, and sliced
¼	cup all-purpose flour
2	cups chicken broth

1	cup whole milk, heated just to boiling
1	cup heavy cream
1½	teaspoons salt
¼	teaspoon white pepper
10 to 12	slices cucumber, skin on and cut paper thin

Moderately easy • Prep time: 30 minutes • Prepare ahead

In a saucepan, cook butter, onion, and cucumbers over medium heat for 10 minutes. Add flour and continue to cook and stir for 5 minutes; pour purée in a blender. Add chicken broth and milk and cook over low heat for 10 minutes. Remove from the heat. Add cream, salt, and pepper. Stir to blend and chill in the refrigerator. When ready to serve, garnish each serving with a paper-thin slice of cucumber.

Yields 10 to 12 servings

Courtside Pasta

½ cup butter
½ cup milk
2½ pounds uncooked fettucine or linguine
8 ounces fresh Parmesan cheese, grated
1 teaspoon garlic salt
1 teaspoon freshly ground black pepper
12 Roma tomatoes, cut into ½-inch dice
½ pound sliced prosciutto ham, cut into small pieces
½ cup snipped parsley for garnish

Easy • Prep time: 30 minutes
Allow butter and milk to sit out for 1 or 2 hours, or until room temperature. Cook pasta according to the package directions; drain, and immediately toss with butter and milk until butter has melted. Toss in remaining ingredients, except for parsley. Sprinkle parsley over each serving.
Yields 12 servings

Ice Cream Pie

2 cups crushed Oreo cookies
¼ cup butter, melted
1 5-ounce can evaporated milk
2 tablespoons butter
½ cup sugar
2 ounces semisweet chocolate
½ teaspoon vanilla extract
1 quart vanilla ice cream, softened
8 ounces frozen whipped topping
Chocolate shavings for garnish

Easy • Prep time: 20 minutes • Prepare ahead and freeze
In a bowl, combine cookie crumbs and melted butter; divide and press into two 8-inch pie plates. Heat milk, butter, sugar, and chocolate; stir until thickened. Remove from the heat. Add vanilla; stir and let cool. Spread softened ice cream over crust. Spoon the chocolate sauce over ice cream. Place the pie in the freezer until ready to serve. Remove and ice with whipped topping. Garnish with chocolate shavings.
Yields 2 eight-inch pies

To crush Oreos, place cookies in a large resealable bag. Cover the head of a hammer or meat tenderizer with a dish cloth and gently use it to crush the cookies in the bag.

All of the ingredients for the daiquiris may not fit in the blender at one time. Try working in batches; then mix the batches together in a freezeable container.

Wimbledon Daiquiris

3	6-ounce cans frozen limeade concentrate	1	pint frozen strawberries
3	juice cans water	½	fifth light rum
1	6-ounce can frozen orange juice concentrate		

Easy • Prep time: 5 minutes • Prepare ahead and freeze
Place all ingredients in a blender; blend well. Transfer to a container, preferably a clean juice or milk carton, and freeze. Thaw slightly to serve. Spoon into glasses.
Yields 10 to 12 servings

Mint Tea

2	family-size tea bags	2	lemons, halved
8 to 10	mint leaves	1	cup sugar
1	6-ounce can frozen orange juice concentrate		Fresh mint leaves for garnish

Easy • Prep time: 10 minutes
Put tea bags in boiling water. Steep. Twist and squeeze mint to extract flavor and drop in tea. Let stand for 15 to 20 minutes. Add undiluted orange juice. Add juice, pulp and peel of lemons, and sugar. Add enough water to make 2 quarts. Strain. Pour over ice and serve. Garnish with mint leaves.
Yields 2 quarts tea

SHOPPING LIST _____

BAKERY
__ 2 small, thin loaves rye or
     pumpernickel bread (for 30
     rounds)

BUTCHER/DELI
__ ½ pound sliced prosciutto ham

CANNED GOODS
__ 1 16-ounce can chicken broth
__ 1 5-ounce can evaporated milk

DAIRY
__ ½ pint heavy cream
__ 4 ounces Swiss cheese
__ 1 pint whole milk
__ 1 pound butter
__ 1 8-ounce block fresh Parmesan
     cheese
__ 1 quart vanilla ice cream
__ 1 8-ounce carton frozen whipped
     topping

EXTRAS
__ ½ fifth light rum

MISCELLANEOUS
__ 1 6-ounce box semisweet
     chocolate squares
__ 3 6-ounce cans frozen limeade
     concentrate
__ 2 6-ounce cans frozen orange
     juice concentrate
__ 1 16-ounce package frozen
     strawberries
__ 3 16-ounce packages fettucine or
     linguine
__ 1 small package Oreo cookies

PRODUCE
__ 5 large cucumbers
__ 2 large lemons
__ 12 Roma tomatoes
__ 1 small onion
__ 1 bunch fresh parsley
__ 1 bunch fresh mint leaves

STAPLES/SPICES
__ All-purpose flour
__ Celery seed
__ Family-size tea bags
__ Garlic salt
__ Mayonnaise
__ Peppercorns
__ Salt
__ Sugar
__ Vanilla extract
__ White pepper

PARSLEY

Bridesmaids Luncheon

Notes

_____

ICY WATERMELON SOUP

POTATO BITES

SPRING VEGETABLE CRÊPES

WHITE SANGRIA

POACHED PEACHES WITH CRÉME ANGLAISE

LEMON SPARKLING WATER

SERVES 10 TO 12

Entertaining the bridesmaids during the week of the wedding is a great way to honor the bride. Some women today are opting for fewer attendants, or choosing other ways to include their closest friends, without labeling them "bridesmaids." No matter how your friend is handling her wedding, an elegant lunch will complement the other wedding festivities.

Icy Watermelon Soup

8   cups seedless
    watermelon cubes
6   tablespoons super
    fine sugar

Raspberry-flavored
sparkling water
Fresh mint leaves for garnish

Easy • Prep time: 20 minutes • Prepare ahead and freeze
Working in batches, purée watermelon with sugar in a blender or food processor until smooth. Drain excess liquid through a fine mesh sieve. Cover and freeze until firm, about 4 hours (or overnight). Remove the purée from the freezer about 30 minutes before use. Let soften to slightly slushy consistency. Divide the purée among individual serving dishes and pour about ¼ to ⅓ cup sparkling water over each serving. Garnish with fresh mint. Serve immediately.
Yields 10 to 12 servings

Potato Bites

18 to 20 tiny new potatoes,
boiled with skins until
firm-tender and cooled
Garlic salt to taste

Freshly ground black
pepper to taste
1 cup grated sharp
Cheddar cheese
¼ cup chopped fresh parsley

Easy • Prep time: 30 minutes

Preheat the oven to 375°. Cut potatoes in half and use a spoon to scoop out a shallow indentation in the cut side of potatoes. Carefully arrange potatoes cut side up on shallow baking trays. Sprinkle garlic salt and pepper lightly over all. Sprinkle grated cheese and parsley over each potato. Bake until cheese melts.

Yields 12 servings

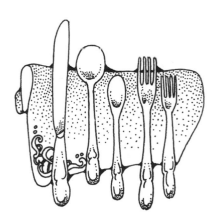

Spring Vegetable Crêpes

Batter

4	eggs		2¼	cups milk
¼	teaspoon salt		¼	cup butter, melted
2	cups flour		⅓	cup snipped fresh dill

Filling

4	cups diced zucchini		⅔	cup diced water chestnuts
1	10-ounce package frozen peas, thawed		½	cup chopped onion
			2	cloves garlic, minced or pressed
1	10-ounce package frozen snow peas, thawed		½	cup butter, melted
1	pound fresh mushrooms, sliced			Salt to taste

Assembly

⅔   cup grated Parmesan cheese

Sauce

¼	cup butter		1	tablespoon cornstarch dissolved in 2 tablespoons broth
4	cloves garlic, minced			
4	cups vegetable or chicken broth		½	cup fresh snipped parsley

Moderate • Prep time: 30 to 40 minutes • Prepare ahead

To make the crêpe batter: Combine all ingredients, except dill, in a blender container. Pulse to mix thoroughly. Scrape down the sides of the blender container and pulse again. Refrigerate the batter for at least 1 hour or overnight. Before using, mix the batter thoroughly and stir in snipped dill. Cook crêpes on preheated, lightly buttered crêpe griddle or in a nonstick skillet. Use about ¼ cup batter for each crêpe. If using a skillet, tilt and rotate the pan as you pour in the batter to form a thin, even circle. Cook each crêpe for 30 to 40 seconds, or until the underside is lightly browned. Carefully turn and cook the other side.

Remove to a platter. Repeat the process until all the batter is used up; as necessary, lightly brush the pan with additional butter. Stack

Garnishes that complement, not compete with, food add a festive touch. Make sure yours enhance your dishes without seeming overwhelming. Some to consider include herbs, edible flowers, leaves, and colorful vegetables or fruits.

cooled crêpes between sheets of waxed paper; wrap in plastic and store in the refrigerator (1 to 2 days) or freeze until ready to use.

To make the crêpe filling: Sauté vegetables in butter until tender. Stir in salt.

To make the sauce: In a large skillet, melt the butter over medium-high heat. Sauté the garlic. Add the broth and bring to a slow boil. Stir in the cornstarch and parsley. Lower heat and stir until slightly thickened.

To assemble: Fill the crêpes and fold into tubes. Place on baking sheets and sprinkle with Parmesan cheese. Bake at 350° for 10 to 12 minutes. Pour warm sauce over individual servings.

Yields about 30 crêpes

White Sangria

4	cups dry white wine	1	orange, sliced
¾	cup Cointreau	1	lemon, sliced
½	cup sugar	1	lime, sliced
1	10-ounce bottle club soda or 10 ounces champagne, chilled	1	small bunch green grapes
		2	Granny Smith apples, cored, sliced, and dipped in lemon juice

Easy • Prep time: 5 minutes • Prepare ahead

Combine the first 3 ingredients. Chill. Just before serving, add chilled soda or champagne. Garnish with oranges, lemons, limes, and grapes. Put an apple wedge on each serving glass.

Yields 1½ quarts sangria

Ask the bride if she would like to use the attendants' gifts as placecards at the table.

Poached Peaches with Crème Anglaise

Crème Anglaise

- 9 egg yolks
- 6 tablespoons sugar
- 3 cups milk

- 3 1-inch pieces vanilla bean, split lengthwise

Poached Peaches

- ¾ cup Grand Marnier
- 3 tablespoons lemon juice
- 3 teaspoons vanilla extract

- 12 large peaches, peeled, halved, and pitted

Moderately easy • Prep time: 25 to 30 minutes • Prepare ahead
To make the Crème Anglaise: Mix egg yolks and sugar; set aside. Measure milk into a saucepan. Scrape seeds from vanilla beans into milk; add beans. Bring milk to a boil. Remove from heat and strain through a fine mesh sieve. Discard vanilla beans and seeds. Gradually whisk hot milk into egg yolk mixture; return to saucepan. Cook, stirring constantly, until mixture thickens. Remove from heat and let cool slightly. Put a sheet of plastic wrap directly over the surface of crème to prevent a skin from forming; refrigerate. (Can make ahead and refrigerate up to 2 days in advance.)

To poach the peaches: Heat the first 3 ingredients in a large pan. Add peach halves; simmer, covered, until tender. Remove from the heat and let cool.

To serve: Arrange 2 peach halves on each plate. Spoon Crème Anglaise around the peaches and top with a little extra cooking liquid.
Yields 12 servings

SHOPPING LIST _____

CANNED FOODS
__ 2 16-ounce cans vegetable or chicken broth
__ 1 small can water chestnuts

DAIRY
__ 1 dozen eggs
__ 1 quart milk
__ 1 pound butter
__ 1 4-ounce block Parmesan cheese
__ 1 4-ounce block Cheddar cheese

EXTRAS
__ 1 small bottle Grand Marnier
__ 2 bottles dry white wine
__ 1 small bottle Cointreau

MISCELLANEOUS
__ 1 2-liter bottle lemon sparkling water
__ 1 liter bottle raspberry sparkling water
__ 1 10-ounce bottle club soda
__ 1 10-ounce package frozen peas
__ 1 10-ounce package frozen snow peas

PRODUCE
__ 1 watermelon
__ 1 orange
__ 2 lemons
__ 1 lime
__ 1 small bunch green seedless grapes
__ 2 Granny Smith apples
__ 12 large peaches
__ 1 bunch fresh mint leaves
__ 1 bunch parsley
__ 1 bunch fresh dill weed
__ 5 zucchini
__ 1 pound mushrooms
__ 1 small onion
__ 18 to 20 tiny new potatoes
__ 1 head garlic

STAPLES/SPICES
__ All purpose flour
__ Cornstarch
__ Garlic salt
__ Peppercorns
__ Salt
__ Sugar
__ Super-fine granulated sugar
__ Vanilla beans
__ Vanilla extract

Wedding Luncheon

HOT CHEESE-BALL APPETIZER

BREAST OF CHICKEN IN WINE SAUCE

MARINATED ASPARAGUS SALAD

HOT BUTTERED ROLLS

RASPBERRY SHERBET MOLD

WEDDING CAKE

COFFEE AND CHAMPAGNE

SERVES 20 TO 25

Hosting the wedding luncheon is a gracious way to honor the bride and groom. Make sure the guests meet one another and acknowledge their connection to the couple. In many cases the guests may not know one another well, and the honorees will have enough to worry about!

Hot Cheese-Ball Appetizer

1   pound Parmesan cheese, grated
1   pound cream cheese, softened
4   eggs, slightly beaten
1   teaspoon salt
⅛   teaspoon cayenne pepper
2   cups fresh white-bread crumbs
    Vegetable oil for deep frying

Moderately easy • Prep time: 30 minutes • Prepare ahead
In a large bowl, combine both cheeses, eggs, salt, and cayenne. Beat with a wooden spoon until smooth. Refrigerate, covered, for 1 hour. Form into 1-inch balls. Roll each ball lightly in bread crumbs. Refrigerate. In a deep skillet or deep-fat fryer, slowly heat oil (about 2 inches) to 350° on a deep-frying thermometer. Fry cheese balls, turning once, for 1 minute, or until golden brown. Drain on paper towels. Serve hot.
Yields 60 balls

Remember the rule—something old, something new, something borrowed, and something blue.

Breast of Chicken in Wine Sauce

1	cup butter	1	teaspoon salt
½	cup vegetable oil	1	teaspoon black pepper
25	small whole chicken breasts or large halves, skinned and boned	1	tablespoon dried thyme leaves
		2	bay leaves, crushed
3	cups sliced onions	2	cups dry white wine
2	pounds small, fresh mushrooms	2	13¾-ounce cans chicken broth Watercress or fresh parsley for garnish

Sauce

¼	cup dry white wine	2	tablespoons all-purpose flour

Moderately easy • Prep time: 30 minutes

Preheat the oven to 350°. In a large skillet, heat ¾ cup butter and ¼ cup oil. Add chicken breasts and sauté until golden, about 10 minutes. Remove to a large roasting pan. Overlap the browned breasts. Heat remaining butter and oil in the skillet. Add onions and mushrooms; sauté, stirring until golden, about 5 minutes. Pour the onion-mushroom mixture over chicken breasts. Combine salt, pepper, thyme, and bay leaves with drippings left in the skillet. Add wine and chicken broth; bring to a boil. Pour over chicken. Bake, covered, for 1 hour, basting several times. Remove the cooked breasts and the onion-mushroom mixture. Keep warm. Strain juices remaining in the roasting pan into a large saucepan. Bring to a boil and boil, uncovered, to reduce to 2 cups for sauce.

To make the sauce: Combine wine and flour. Add to drippings mixture in the saucepan. Bring back to boiling and then simmer for 2 minutes. Keep warm.

Just before serving, spoon the sauce over chicken breasts with onions and mushrooms. Garnish with watercress or fresh parsley.

Yields 25 servings

For something old, use antique lace and linens in your table decorations. For something new, arrange gifts from guests on a table near the entrance to the party. For something borrowed, collect recipes from the bride's close friends and present them to the honoree. For something blue, incorporate blue ribbons into the flowers used throughout the party site. And don't forget a lucky sixpence for the bride's shoe!

Marinated Asparagus Salad

4   15-ounce cans green
    asparagus spears
4   15-ounce cans white
    asparagus spears

2   heads Boston lettuce
1   bunch watercress

Lemon Vinaigrette

1   8-ounce bottle herb-garlic
    salad dressing
½   cup lemon juice

2   tablespoons chopped chives
¼   teaspoon white pepper

Easy • Prep time: 5 minutes • Prepare ahead
Drain asparagus spears. Prepare the vinaigrette by combining all ingredients in a small bowl. In a shallow dish, layer asparagus and pour dressing over. Refrigerate for several hours.

To serve, arrange clean, crisp lettuce leaves and watercress on a serving platter. Alternate marinated asparagus (green and white) in sections. Place watercress in the center. Spoon the vinaigrette over all.
Yields 25 servings

Raspberry Sherbet Mold

1½   quarts raspberry sherbet
½   pint heavy cream, whipped stiff

Crème de cassis

Easy • Prep time: 5 minutes • Prepare ahead and freeze
Line a 3-quart, heart-shaped mold with plastic wrap. Remove sherbet from the freezer and let soften, about 20 minutes. Pack into the mold. Smooth top and freeze overnight.

To unmold: Grasp the plastic wrap edges that overhang the mold and pull firmly to invert onto a chilled serving tray. Remove plastic wrap. Decorate the outside of the mold with whipped cream. If using a pastry bag, make rosettes with whipped cream.

Pass crème de cassis to serve over sherbet.
Yields 25 servings

SHOPPING LIST _____

BAKERY
__ 1 loaf white bread
__ 50 to 60 assorted rolls
__ Wedding cake

BUTCHER
__ 25 small whole chicken breasts

CANNED GOODS
__ 4 15-ounce cans green asparagus spears
__ 4 15-ounce cans white asparagus spears
__ 2 16-ounce cans chicken broth

DAIRY
__ ½ dozen eggs
__ 1 pound block Parmesan cheese
__ 2 8-ounce packages cream cheese
__ 1 pound butter
__ ½ pint heavy cream

EXTRAS
__ 1 small bottle crème de cassis
__ 1 bottle dry white wine
__ 1 case champagne

MISCELLANEOUS
__ 1 8-ounce bottle herb-garlic salad dressing
__ 1 small bottle lemon juice
__ 6 pints frozen raspberry sherbet

PRODUCE
__ 2 heads Boston lettuce
__ 1 bunch fresh watercress
__ 1 bunch fresh chives
__ 2 pounds small fresh mushrooms
__ 3 large onions

STAPLES/SPICES
__ All-purpose flour
__ Bay leaves
__ Black pepper
__ Cayenne pepper
__ Coffee
__ Salt
__ Thyme
__ Vegetable oil
__ White pepper

Lunch in a Basket

Notes

_____

_____

_____

_____

_____

_____

_____

_____

_____

_____

_____

_____

_____

_____

_____

_____

_____

_____

_____

WATER CHESTNUT DIP

PITA SANDWICHES

DUBLIN POTATO SALAD

APPLES, GRAPES, AND WEDGES OF BRIE

BOURBON BROWNIES

ICED TEA AND WINE

SERVES 8

Serving lunch in individual boxes or baskets is a
quick, easy way to feed your friends who are on the
go. This menu provides a twist to the traditional box
lunch. On a nice day, invite your guests to eat outside.
Cleaning up is a breeze!

Water Chestnut Dip

1   8-ounce can chopped
    water chestnuts, drained
½   cup chopped parsley
2   green onions, chopped
1   cup sour cream

1   cup mayonnaise
2   teaspoons Tabasco sauce
2   teaspoons soy sauce
    Chips

Easy • Prep time: 5 minutes
In a large bowl, combine and mix all ingredients. Chill. Serve in individual plastic cups with chips.
Yields 2 cups

Pita Sandwiches

8   pocket pita rounds
2   pounds thinly sliced
     smoked or maple turkey
     Alfalfa sprouts

Boston lettuce
Chopped tomatoes
Mayonnaise
Dijon mustard

Easy • Prep time: 5 minutes
Cut pita rounds in half and stuff with turkey and sandwich fixings.
Yields 16 sandwiches

Dublin Potato Salad

2   tablespoons white vinegar
1   teaspoon celery seed
1   teaspoon mustard seed
3   large baking potatoes, cubed
2   teaspoons sugar
½   teaspoon salt

3   cups finely shredded cabbage
12 ounces corned beef, diced
¼   cup finely chopped dill pickles
¼   cup chopped green onions
     Cabbage leaves for serving

Dressing

1   cup mayonnaise
¼   cup milk

½   teaspoon salt

Easy • Prep time: 25 to 30 minutes • Can prepare the day before serving
Combine vinegar, celery seed, and mustard seed; set aside. Cook potatoes and drain. While potato cubes are still warm, drizzle with the vinegar mixture. Sprinkle with sugar and salt; chill thoroughly. Add
cabbage, corned beef, pickle, and onion. Mix the dressing ingredients
and pour over salad; toss lightly. Use a cabbage leaf as a serving piece
to hold the potato salad in a basket or box.
Yields 8 servings

Hulled sunflower seeds are a crunchy addition to salads, toppings, sandwiches, and casseroles.

Bourbon Brownies

1 23-ounce package
  brownie mix
3 eggs, lightly beaten
1 cup chopped walnuts
6 tablespoons bourbon
½ cup butter, softened

2 cups confectioners' sugar
3 tablespoons rum
6 ounces semisweet
  chocolate chips
¼ cup butter

Moderately easy • Prep time: 30 minutes • Prepare ahead
In a bowl, combine brownie mix, eggs, and walnuts; omit water. Bake according to the package directions. Remove from the oven and sprinkle with bourbon. Cool thoroughly. Combine butter, confectioners' sugar, and rum. Spread evenly over the brownies. Chill for about 1 hour. Melt chocolate and butter in a saucepan. Drizzle over the brownies. Chill for an additional hour, or until chocolate hardens. Cut into squares.
Yields 48 brownies

SHOPPING LIST

BAKERY
__ 2 packages pocket pita bread

BUTCHER/DELI
__ 2 pounds thinly sliced smoked
    or maple turkey
__ 12 ounces corned beef

CANNED GOODS
__ 1½ pint chopped water chestnuts

DAIRY
__ ½ dozen eggs
__ ½ pint sour cream
__ ½ pint milk
__ 1 pound butter
__ ½ pound Brie

EXTRAS
__ 1 small bottle bourbon
__ 1 small bottle dark rum
__ 3 to 4 bottles white wine

MISCELLANEOUS
__ 1 small jar Dijon mustard
__ 1 small jar chopped dill pickles
__ 1 23-ounce box brownie mix
__ 2 2-ounce packages chopped
    walnuts
__ 1 6-ounce package semisweet
    chocolate chips
__ 1 large bag chips for dipping

PRODUCE
__ 1 small bunch green onions
__ 1 large head cabbage
__ 3 large baking potatoes
__ 1 container alfalfa sprouts
__ 1 head Boston lettuce
__ 2 ripe tomatoes
__ 1 bunch parsley
__ 4 apples
__ 1 large bunch grapes

STAPLES/SPICES
__ Celery seed
__ Confectioners' sugar
__ Family-size tea bags
__ Mayonnaise
__ Mustard seed
__ Salt
__ Soy sauce
__ Sugar
__ Tabasco sauce
__ White vinegar

Red, White, and Blue Lunch

Notes
_____
_____
_____
_____
_____
_____
_____
_____
_____
_____
_____
_____
_____

RED PEPPER SOUR CREAM DIP

RED & WHITE SHISH KABOB

BUTTERMILK BLUE CORN CAKES

WATERMELON SLICES

EASY PATRIOT CAKE

SHIRLEY TEMPLE PUNCH AND BEER

S E R V E S   1 0

This patriotic menu invites you to show off your true colors come the Fourth of July. It's easy to prepare, so you'll have plenty of time for the fireworks.

Red Pepper Sour Cream Dip

1	pint sour cream
1	tablespoon freshly chopped chives
2	tablespoons chili powder
1 to 2	teaspoons garlic salt

½ cup minced red bell pepper
Blue corn tortilla chips (available at grocery or specialty stores)

Easy • Prep time: 15 minutes • Prepare a day ahead
Combine all ingredients, except chips, in a resealable container and mix well. Cover and chill overnight. Serve with blue corn tortilla chips.
Yields 2½ cups dip

Cover the tables with red-and-white striped cloths. Use large blue paper dinner napkins. The centerpiece can be red, white, and blue balloons, red and white roses in a blue vase, or miniature arrangements of tiny American flags.

Red & White Shish Kabob

5 medium sweet onions (such as Vidalia)
5 red bell peppers
5 pounds boneless, skinless chicken breasts, cut into 1½-inch pieces
1 pint cherry tomatoes
Olive oil
Garlic salt
Pepper

Hang an American flag at the entrance to the party.

Easy • Prep time: 25 minutes
Cut each onion in half horizontally, then cut each half into 4 quarters. Do the same with bell peppers, discarding seeds. Skewer the ingredients in the following order: onion, pepper, chicken, tomato, chicken, pepper, onion. Repeat with more skewers until all the ingredients have been used. Brush all with olive oil and season generously with garlic salt and pepper. Grill the kabobs until the chicken is thoroughly cooked.
Yields about 20 kabobs

Buttermilk Blue Corn Cakes

2 cups all-purpose flour
2 cups blue cornmeal
¼ cup sugar
1 tablespoon baking powder
1 teaspoon salt
4 eggs
2 cups buttermilk
½ cup vegetable oil, plus more for cooking
1 teaspoon blue food coloring, optional

Moderate • Prep time: 25 minutes
In a large mixing bowl, combine all the dry ingredients. In another mixing bowl, beat the remaining ingredients. Add the wet ingredients to the dry ingredients and stir just until smooth. Do not overmix. Heat oil in a skillet. Pour the batter into the skillet in disks. Flip the cakes when bubbles appear on top. Serve warm.
Yields 20 to 24 cakes

Store beer in a cool, dark area with the bottles in an upright position.

After beer has been refrigerated, don't let it get warm. It will lose its flavor if warmed and then re-frigerated again.

Serve beer in large glasses. Hold the glass at a 45° angle and pour into the bottom of the glass to produce a small amount of froth. Continue pouring slowly along the side. When full, straighten the glass to an upright position to add the head.

Pair heavy food with spicy sauces with full-bodied beer.

Offer dry, light beer with grilled seafood or poultry.

Put beer in ice-filled tubs for easy serving.

Easy Patriot Cake

1 box white or yellow cake mix, plus ingredients required to follow package baking directions
1 container white icing
1 cup fresh blueberries
½ cup miniature marshmallows
1 pint fresh strawberries, cleaned, stems removed, and sliced lengthwise
3 fresh ripe bananas, peeled, sliced into disks, and tossed with 2 tablespoons lemon juice

Easy • Prep time: 30 minutes
Prepare cake according to the package directions, using a 13x9x2-inch pan. After the cake has cooled, place it on a serving dish and spread the icing over the top and sides. Arrange blueberries and marshmallows in the upper left corner of the cake to resemble the stars on the American flag. Use strawberries and bananas to form the stripes of the flag. Serve immediately.
Yields 12 servings

Shirley Temple Punch

2 2-liter bottles lemon-lime soda
8 to 12 ounces Grenadine
1 large jar maraschino cherries, with juice reserved
2 to 3 limes, cut into wedges

Easy • Prep time: 10 minutes
Pour soda, Grenadine, and maraschino cherry juice into a large punch bowl and mix well. Serve over ice and garnish with maraschino cherries and lime wedges.
Yields 16 to 18 servings

SHOPPING LIST _____

BUTCHER
__ 5 pounds boneless, skinless
   chicken breasts

DAIRY
__ 1 pint sour cream
__ ½ dozen eggs
__ 1 pint buttermilk

EXTRAS
__ 2 cases beer
__ 1 12-ounce bottle Grenadine

MISCELLANEOUS
__ 2 bags blue corn tortilla chips
__ 1 16-ounce bag blue cornmeal
__ 1 small bottle blue food coloring
   (optional)
__ 1 box white or yellow cake mix
__ 1 container white cake frosting
__ 1 small bag miniature
   marshmallows
__ 1 large jar maraschino cherries
__ 2 2-liter bottles lemon-lime soda
__ 2 bags ice

PRODUCE
__ 1 large watermelon
__ 1 small bunch chives
__ 6 red bell peppers
__ 5 medium sweet onions (such as
   Vidalia)
__ 1 pint cherry tomatoes
__ ½ pint fresh blueberries
__ 1 pint fresh strawberries
__ 3 ripe bananas
__ 1 lemon
__ 2 or 3 limes

STAPLES/SPICES
__ Chili powder
__ Garlic salt
__ Olive oil
__ Pepper
__ All-purpose flour
__ Sugar
__ Baking powder
__ Salt
__ Vegetable oil

Southwestern Sampler

SPINACH QUESO DIP

BLACK BEAN AND SALMON BURRITOS

WITH COOL PEPPER SALSA

TORTILLA CHILI SOUP

FLAN WITH FRUIT

SANGRIA

SERVES 8

Rustle up a taste of the Old West with this updated menu. A far cry from heavy food with too much spice, these recipes offer just the right combination of flavor and heft.

Spinach Queso Dip

1 small onion, finely diced
2 tablespoons olive oil
1 2-pound box Velveeta
   Mexican-style cheese, cubed
1 8-ounce can evaporated milk

1 10-ounce package frozen
   chopped spinach, thawed,
   rinsed, and well drained
   Tortilla chips

Easy • Prep time: 25 minutes
Sauté onion in olive oil. Meanwhile, heat cheese in the top of a double boiler. Once cheese has melted, add onion, evaporated milk, and spinach. Heat thoroughly. Serve with tortilla chips.
Yields about 6 cups dip

Black Bean and Salmon Burritos with Cool Pepper Salsa

1	pound boneless salmon fillets	1	orange bell pepper, diced
1	lemon, halved	1	yellow bell pepper, diced
3	16-ounce cans black beans	2	teaspoons balsamic vinegar
2	tablespoons butter, melted	1	tablespoon red wine vinegar
¼	cup chopped fresh cilantro	1	teaspoon black pepper
8	8-inch flour tortillas	1	tablespoon chopped fresh basil
1	firm, ripe tomato, diced	½	teaspoon red pepper flakes, optional
1	red bell pepper, diced		

Easy • Prep time: 30 minutes

Preheat the broiler. Arrange the fillets on a broiling rack and squeeze one half of the lemon over the top of the salmon. Broil at 500° for 15 to 25 minutes, or until the salmon is cooked through. Be careful not to overcook. Allow to cool, then flake the salmon with a fork. In a colander, rinse and drain beans. Warm beans in a saucepan over medium-high heat. Squeeze the remaining lemon half into melted butter and add cilantro. In a large bowl, gently toss salmon and beans with the butter mixture until lightly coated.

Prepare the salsa by combining tomato, peppers, vinegars, black pepper, basil, and red pepper in a bowl.

Fill each tortilla with the bean-and-salmon mixture and spoon salsa overtop.

Yields 8 servings

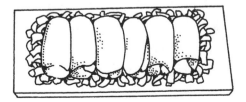

Read each recipe carefully before starting. Check to be sure that you have all the necessary ingredients and utensils.

Tortilla Chili Soup

½ small onion, chopped
2 cloves garlic, minced
2 tablespoons olive oil
1 pound ground turkey
   or beef
1 tablespoon Worcestershire
   sauce
1 16-ounce can tomatoes,
   cut into pieces and with juice
2 16-ounce cans light kidney
   beans, rinsed and drained

1 tablespoon dried basil
1½ tablespoons chili powder
1 teaspoon dried cumin
½ teaspoon salt
1 teaspoon pepper
2 13¼-ounce cans chicken,
   turkey, or beef broth
2 cups crushed tortilla chips

Easy • Prep time: 30 minutes • Prepare ahead
Sauté onion and garlic in olive oil in a large stock pot. Add ground turkey and cook until brown. Drain the fat, then stir in Worcestershire. Add tomatoes with their juice, kidney beans, and seasonings. Add the broth and bring to a boil. Remove from the heat. Serve with ¼ cup crushed tortilla chips sprinkled over each serving.
Yields 8 to 10 servings

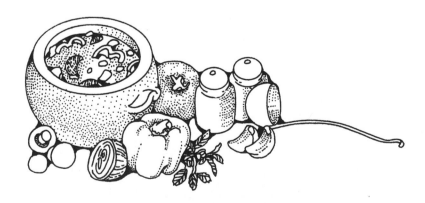

Flan with Fruit

⅓ cup sugar
4 eggs
½ cup sugar
2 cups milk

½ teaspoon ground cinnamon
1 teaspoon vanilla extract
Sliced apples, oranges,
strawberries, and papaya

Moderately difficult • Prep time: 45 minutes • Prepare ahead

Preheat the oven to 325°. Heat ⅓ cup sugar in a small, heavy saucepan over medium heat. Do not stir sugar until it begins to melt. Continue cooking and stirring until sugar turns a rich brown color. Remove from the heat immediately and pour into a 9-inch round glass baking dish. Quickly rotate the dish so sugar coats the bottom and sides evenly. Set the dish in a 14x10x2-inch baking dish and allow it to cool.

In a large mixing bowl, beat eggs until smooth, gradually adding the remaining ½ cup sugar. In a saucepan, heat milk with cinnamon over medium heat, stirring frequently, until bubbly. Slowly add milk to the egg mixture, stirring constantly. Stir in vanilla and pour the mixture into the sugar-coated pan.

Pour hot water into the larger dish to a depth of about 1 inch. Bake for 30 to 35 minutes, or until a knife inserted between the center and the edge of the dish comes out clean. Remove the pan from the baking dish and cool on a wire rack. Cover and refrigerate until ready to use.

Unmold the flan onto a serving dish by running a knife around the edge and carefully separating the flan from the side of the pan. Arrange the fruit around the flan and serve as you would cheese and crackers.

Yields 12 servings

Sangria

4 cups brandy
½ cup Triple Sec
½ cup brown sugar
2 tablespoons ground cinnamon

2 teaspoons grated nutmeg
4 cups lemon-lime soda
8 cups red wine
   Orange slices

Easy • Prep time: 10 minutes
Combine the brandy, Triple Sec, brown sugar, cinnamon, and nutmeg and set aside, stirring occasionally, until the sugar dissolves. Before serving, add the soda and wine. Garnish with orange slices.
Yields 16 servings

SHOPPING LIST

BAKERY
__ 1 package 8-inch flour tortillas

BUTCHER
__ 1 pound boneless, skinless salmon fillets
__ 1 pound ground turkey or beef

CANNED GOODS
__ 1 8-ounce can evaporated milk
__ 3 16-ounce cans black beans
__ 1 16-ounce can tomatoes
__ 2 16-ounce cans light kidney beans
__ 2 13¼-ounce cans chicken, turkey, or beef broth

DAIRY
__ 1 2-pound box Velveeta Mexican-style cheese
__ 1 stick butter
__ ½ dozen eggs
__ 1 pint milk

EXTRAS
__ 1 large bottle brandy
__ 1 small bottle Triple Sec
__ 3 bottles red wine

MISCELLANEOUS
__ 1 10-ounce package frozen chopped spinach
__ 1 bottle balsamic vinegar
__ 1 medium bag corn tortilla chips
__ 1 32-ounce bottle lemon-lime soda

PRODUCE
__ 2 small onions
__ 1 lemon
__ 1 bunch fresh cilantro
__ 1 large tomato
__ 1 red bell pepper
__ 1 orange bell pepper
__ 1 yellow bell pepper
__ 1 bunch fresh basil
__ 1 head garlic

__ 3 Granny Smith apples
__ 3 Red Delicious apples
__ 6 naval oranges
__ 1 pint strawberries
__ 1 large papaya

STAPLES/SPICES
__ Brown sugar
__ Chili powder
__ Cinnamon
__ Cumin
__ Dried basil
__ Nutmeg
__ Olive oil
__ Pepper
__ Red pepper flakes
__ Red wine vinegar
__ Salt
__ Sugar
__ Vanilla extract
__ Worcestershire sauce

Marinated Cherry Tomato Salad

Curried Tuna Melt

Mini Pumpkin Muffins

Tea Punch

S E R V E S   4

This is a great menu to use the day after Thanksgiving, or any other time when friends get together for a full day of bargain-hunting. Most of the preparation can be finished quickly the day before, leaving only a few easy steps to a tasty warm lunch that beats mall food any day.

Marinated Cherry Tomato Salad

1   pint cherry tomatoes, rinsed, drained, and halved
3   mild pepperoncini peppers, seeded and minced
1   tablespoon olive oil
3   tablespoons red wine vinegar
1   teaspoon Worcestershire sauce
½   teaspoon black pepper
½   teaspoon garlic salt
2   tablespoons minced fresh basil

Easy • Prep time: 15 minutes • Prepare ahead
Gently toss all ingredients. Refrigerate until ready to serve.
Yields 4 to 6 servings

Curried Tuna Melt

1	medium purple onion, chopped	½	teaspoon dill weed
2	tablespoons olive oil	½	teaspoon garlic salt
3	7-ounce cans white tuna, drained	1	teaspoon black pepper
¼	cup mayonnaise	½	cup freshly grated Parmesan cheese
1	tablespoon spicy brown mustard	¼	cup walnut pieces, optional
½	teaspoon curry powder	8	slices whole-wheat bread Olive oil for brushing
1	teaspoon dried basil	8	slices Mozzarella or Provolone cheese
1	teaspoon dried oregano		

Moderate • Prep time: 25 minutes • Prepare ahead

Sauté onion in 2 tablespoons olive oil. In a large bowl, combine onion, tuna, mayonnaise, mustard, curry powder, basil, oregano, dill weed, garlic salt, black pepper, Parmesan cheese, and walnuts. (This mixture can be prepared and refrigerated 1 day ahead.)

Just before serving, move the oven rack to the center position and preheat the oven to broil at 500°. Place a roasting rack on a baking sheet. Brush one side of each piece of bread with olive oil. Arrange 4 slices of bread, olive oil down, on the rack. Place 1 slice of Mozzarella or Provolone on top of the bread. Spread a generous amount of the tuna mixture over the cheese. Top with another slice of cheese and another slice of bread with the olive oil facing up.

Broil the sandwiches with the oven door cracked open. Watch carefully; as soon as the top slice of bread toasts and the cheese melts, flip the sandwiches with a metal spatula and toast the other side, about 3 to 5 minutes per side.

Yields 4 sandwiches

Mini Pumpkin Muffins

Nonstick cooking spray
¾ cup brown sugar
¼ cup molasses
½ cup butter, softened
1 egg, lightly beaten

1 cup cooked, mashed pumpkin
1¾ cups all-purpose flour
1 teaspoon baking soda
¼ teaspoon salt

Easy • Prep time: 25 minutes • Prepare ahead
Preheat the oven to 350°. Spray 2 miniature muffin tins with nonstick cooking spray. Cream brown sugar, molasses, and butter. Add egg and pumpkin. Mix well. Sift the dry ingredients together and add them to the batter slowly, beating well after each addition. Pour the batter into the muffin cups halfway up the sides. Bake for 10 to 15 minutes.
Yields about 32 muffins

Tea Punch

7 tea bags
Water
2 cups sugar
2 6-ounce cans frozen orange juice concentrate

2 6-ounce cans frozen lemonade concentrate
Sprigs of mint

Easy • Prep time: 15 minutes • Prepare ahead
Brew tea bags in 6 cups of boiling water. Remove tea bags and add the remaining ingredients. Pour into a gallon container and fill with water to make 1 gallon. Refrigerate until ready to serve.
Yields 1 gallon

Add the juice of a fresh lemon to frozen orange juice to make it taste like fresh squeezed.

_____
_____
_____
_____
_____
_____
_____
_____
_____
_____
_____
_____
_____
_____
_____
_____
_____
_____
_____
_____
_____
_____
_____
_____
_____
_____
_____
_____
_____
_____
_____
_____

SHOPPING LIST _____

BAKERY
__ 1 loaf whole-wheat bread

CANNED GOODS
__ 3 7-ounce cans white tuna
__ 1 16-ounce can cooked pumpkin

DAIRY
__ 1 6-ounce block Parmesan
cheese
__ ½ pound thinly sliced Mozzarella
or Provolone cheese
__ 1 stick butter
__ 1 egg

MISCELLANEOUS
__ 1 small jar spicy brown mustard
__ 1 small package walnut pieces
__ 1 small jar pepperoncini
__ 1 small jar molasses
__ 2 6-ounce cans frozen orange
juice concentrate
__ 2 6-ounce cans frozen lemonade
concentrate

PRODUCE
__ 1 medium purple onion
__ 1 pint cherry tomatoes
__ 1 bunch fresh basil

STAPLES/SPICES
__ All-purpose flour
__ Baking soda
__ Brown sugar
__ Curry powder
__ Dried basil
__ Dried dill weed
__ Dried oregano
__ Garlic salt
__ Mayonnaise
__ Nonstick cooking spray
__ Olive oil
__ Pepper
__ Red wine vinegar
__ Salt
__ Sugar
__ Tea bags
__ Worcestershire sauce

"Barefoot in the Park" Living Room Picnic

BLACK BREAD MUFFULETTAS

ROBERT REDFORD RED POTATO SALAD

HOT 'N' BOTHERED STEAMY VEGETABLES

CENTRAL PARK SORBET

CHARDONNAY

S E R V E S   4

A living room picnic is a great way for two couples to enjoy a classic movie. If you prefer, use low-fat meats and cheeses for a menu even fitness guru Jane Fonda would enjoy.

Black Bread Muffulettas

4	dark wheat or pumpernickel sub rolls	½	cup pitted green olives
8	ounces hard salami slices	1	clove garlic
8	ounces Provolone slices	1	tablespoon capers
8	ounces ham slices	2	tablespoons olive oil
¼	cup pitted black olives	1	teaspoon lime juice

Easy • Prep time: 20 minutes
Split sub rolls down the center and arrange layers of salami, provolone, and ham on top. Pulse the remaining ingredients in a food processor or blender until just smooth enough to spread (do not overblend). Spread the olive mixture over meat and cheese and close the sandwiches.
Yields 4 servings

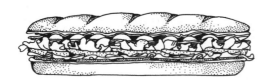

Spread a blanket and oversized pillows on the floor for your living room picnic.

Robert Redford Red Potato Salad

½ cup olive oil
¼ cup red wine vinegar
2 tablespoons chopped
   fresh parsley
1 teaspoon garlic salt
1 teaspoon black pepper

½ teaspoon dried basil
1½ pounds small red potatoes,
   boiled until firm-tender with
   the skins, cooled, and cut
   into quarters

Easy • Prep time: 10 minutes
Combine all ingredients, except potatoes, in a resealable container and
shake well. Pour the dressing over potatoes and toss gently. Serve at
room temperature.
Yields 4 servings

Hot 'n' Bothered Steamy Vegetables

2 teaspoons curry powder
1 lemon, halved
1 cup peeled baby carrots
1 small bunch tender
   asparagus, ends trimmed

2 small yellow squash, sliced
   into disks

Easy • Prep time: 20 minutes
Bring a saucepan one-third full of water to a boil. Pour curry powder
and juice from one half of the lemon in the water. Arrange the vegetables in a steamer over the boiling water. Steam just until crisp-tender.
Drain and squeeze remaining lemon juice over the vegetables. Serve
immediately.
Yields 4 servings

Fresh flowers and wine in
an ice bucket will add to
the romance.

Central Park Sorbet

1 cup sugar
1 cup water

Juice of 1 large or 2 small limes
4 to 6 kiwis, peeled and cubed

Easy • Prep time: 15 minutes • Prepare ahead
Dissolve sugar in water in a saucepan over medium heat. Pour lime juice and kiwi into a blender container. Pour the sugar water into the blender and blend until puréed. Freeze in an ice cream maker, or cover and place in the freezer, stirring every 45 minutes until ready to serve.
Yields about 1 pint

SHOPPING LIST

BAKERY
__ 4 large dark wheat or
  pumpernickel submarine rolls

BUTCHER/DELI
__ ½ pound thinly sliced hard
  salami
__ ½ pound thinly sliced ham

CANNED GOODS
__ 1 can pitted black olives

DAIRY
__ ½ pound thinly sliced Provolone
  cheese

EXTRAS
__ 2 bottles Chardonnay

MISCELLANEOUS
__ 1 small jar Spanish green olives
__ 1 small jar capers

PRODUCE
__ 1 head garlic
__ 3 limes
__ 1 bunch fresh parsley
__ 1½ pounds tiny red potatoes
__ 1 small bag peeled baby carrots
__ 1 small bunch tender asparagus
__ 2 small yellow squash
__ 1 lemon
__ 4 to 6 kiwi fruits

STAPLES/SPICES
__ Curry powder
__ Dried basil
__ Garlic salt
__ Olive oil
__ Pepper
__ Red wine vinegar
__ Sugar

A Working Lunch

ITALIAN HAM STACKS

CRAN-ORANGE SALAD

CRUNCHY GARDEN PEAS

STRAWBERRY REFRESHER

SERVES 8

The next time you need to plan a function for your church or other community organization, prepare this light but satisfying menu for your peers. Good food makes hard work all the more palatable.

Italian Ham Stacks

8 ounces cream cheese, softened	½ teaspoon oregano
½ cup butter, softened	½ teaspoon garlic powder
½ cup grated Parmesan cheese	4 English muffins, split
1 teaspoon paprika	1 pound baked ham, shaved
	8 tomato slices

Easy • Prep time: 20 minutes

In a bowl, combine cream cheese and butter; stir until smooth. Stir in Parmesan cheese, paprika, oregano, and garlic powder. Spread two-thirds of the mixture evenly over cut surfaces of English muffins; top each with shaved ham and a tomato slice. Top each tomato slice with a dollop of remaining cheese mixture. Place on a baking sheet and broil until golden brown. Serve hot.

Yields 8 muffin halves

Cran-Orange Salad

2	3½-ounce packages lemon gelatin		Grated rind of 1 orange
2	cups boiling water	2	oranges, peeled and sectioned
1	16-ounce can whole-berry cranberry sauce	1	cup cottage cheese, optional
1	15½-ounce can crushed pineapple	½	cup pecan pieces
			Romaine lettuce leaves
			Sour Cream Topping

Equal amounts of whipped cream and salad dressing make a smooth dressing.

Easy • Prep time: 20 to 25 minutes • Prepare ahead
Dissolve gelatin in boiling water. Chill until slightly thickened in an 8-inch square dish. Add cranberry sauce, pineapple, orange rind, orange sections, and cottage cheese (if desired). Fold in pecans. Chill until firm. Cut into 8 portions and serve on Romaine lettuce leaves. Garnish with a teaspoon of Sour Cream Topping.
Yields 8 servings

Sour Cream Topping

½	cup sour cream	1	tablespoon poppy seeds
1	cup mayonnaise		

Easy • 5 minutes
Combine ingredients and mix well. Serve over Cran-Orange Salad.
Yields 1½ cups topping

Crunchy Garden Peas

1   17-ounce can petite garden peas
1   4-ounce jar diced pimientos
1   cup grated sharp Cheddar cheese
½   cup finely chopped celery
1   small onion, finely chopped
1   2-ounce package slivered almonds
2   tablespoons cole slaw dressing or mayonnaise
    Lettuce leaves for serving

Easy • Prep time: 15 minutes • Prepare ahead

Drain peas and pimientos. In a medium bowl, combine all ingredients, except cole slaw dressing or mayonnaise and lettuce leaves. Toss ingredients with dressing. Cover and chill for at least 1 hour before serving. Serve in lettuce leaves.

Yields 8 servings

Strawberry Refresher

12   ice cubes
 2   cups fresh strawberries
 1   6-ounce can frozen orange juice concentrate
 3   teaspoons sugar
     White wine to taste, optional

Easy • Prep time: 10 minutes

Wash and hull strawberries, reserving 8 whole berries. In a blender or food processor, crush ice cubes. Add strawberries, orange juice concentrate, sugar, and wine (if desired), blending after each addition until slushy. Pour into chilled wine glasses, top with a fresh strawberry, and serve.

Yields 8 four-ounce servings

SHOPPING LIST _____

BAKERY
__ 1 package English muffins

BUTCHER/DELI
__ 1 pound shaved baked ham

CANNED GOODS
__ 1 14-ounce can petite garden peas
__ 1 16-ounce can whole-berry cranberry sauce
__ 1 15½-ounce can crushed pineapple

DAIRY
__ 1 8-ounce package cream cheese
__ 1 stick butter
__ 1 4-ounce block Parmesan cheese
__ 4 ounces sharp Cheddar cheese
__ ½ pint cottage cheese (optional)
__ ½ pint sour cream

EXTRAS
__ 1 small bottle white wine

MISCELLANEOUS
__ 1 6-ounce container frozen orange juice concentrate
__ 1 4-ounce jar diced pimientos
__ 1 2-ounce package slivered almonds
__ 1 small bottle cole slaw dressing
__ 2 3½-ounce boxes lemon gelatin
__ 1 small package pecan pieces

PRODUCE
__ 1 pint fresh strawberries
__ 2 tomatoes
__ 1 stalk celery
__ 1 small onion
__ 2 heads Romaine lettuce
__ 2 oranges

STAPLES/SPICES
__ Coffee
__ Tea bags
__ Sugar
__ Paprika
__ Oregano
__ Garlic powder
__ Mayonnaise
__ Poppy seeds

ON THE ROAD

- Not only are cookouts fun, they're also versatile. You can host a cookout almost anywhere, from apartment terrace to public campground, with sophisticated or simple appliances and utensils. If you can't use an open campfire, try a hibachi.

- Start the coals well before your plan to grill your food, and allow the briquets to burn until they are white on top. For even heat, avoid adding charcoal after the fire has taken. You need a hot fire in order to cook steaks and hamburgers, so begin with a good many coals and put the meat on the grill when the coals reach their peak heat. For a roast or other larger, longer cooking meat or fowl, you'll need a slow, even-burning fire. So let the coals smolder a while longer or regulate the temperature by raising or lowering the grill.

- Experiment with gas or electric grills before entertaining. Gas and electric heat can be hotter than that produced by charcoal fires, so cooking time may vary.

- Food for your campout should be easy to prepare, easy to transport, and easy to eat. But instead of putting the old tried-and-true in your picnic basket, use your imagination to create some new twists on some old favorites.

AFTERNOON

Teas, showers, and picnics are just some of the events that can be enjoyed during the afternoon. Teas can be formal or casual, traditional or contemporary. Showers have come a long way since the days of overdone bridal games. And picnics don't have to be held on the Fourth of July.

Whether you choose to serve "high tea" at 4 P.M., enjoy a picnic as the sun goes down, gather your peers for a committee meeting, or honor your friend who's having a baby, the menus presented here are easy to prepare and they serve as welcome treats in the middle of a busy day. Whether it's a special occasion like Christmas, or just a cup of tea among friends, these menus will leave you refreshed.

Think of the afternoon as the perfect time for entertaining when you don't want to prepare a formal dinner or casual lunch. Many people have flexible schedules today that allow them the freedom to leave work for a while to visit with friends. If you find that your guest list for your afternoon gathering is full of people who work in traditional work settings, consider hosting your event on the weekend.

Always keep in mind the best atmosphere for your afternoon event. Picnics can be held inside if the weather is bad; clear the floor and throw down some quilts. Teas and showers are lovely on porches or decks. Whatever your choice, remember that the afternoon is a versatile time for entertaining. So consider your purpose, select your location, whip up a few of these delicacies, and share your hospitality with others.

Afternoon Fish Fry

Notes

_____

_____

_____

_____

_____

_____

_____

_____

_____

_____

_____

_____

_____

_____

FRIED FISH WITH HOMEMADE TARTAR SAUCE

POTATO SALAD

ONION RINGS

HUSHPUPPIES

FRUIT CASSEROLE

COOKIES AND BROWNIES

ICED TEA AND BEER

S E R V E S   1 0

There's no need for the old-fashioned fish fry to be a thing of the past. Even in today's health conscious world, surely we all deserve a little fried food every once in a while!

Fried Fish with Homemade Tartar Sauce

20 to 30	*6-ounce fish fillets*
	Salt and pepper to taste
1	*cup prepared mustard*
1	*teaspoon Tabasco sauce*
2	*tablespoons Worcestershire sauce*
3	*cups yellow cornmeal*
5	*quarts oil, or amount needed to fill a 12-quart pot*

Easy • Prep time: 15 minutes
Salt and pepper fillets. Combine mustard with Tabasco and Worcestershire; coat fillets with the mixture and allow to set for about 30 minutes. Put cornmeal in a bag and shake coated fillets in meal. Heat oil in a heavy iron pot to about 380°. Fry fish, one layer deep, in hot oil for 2½ minutes, or until they rise to the top. Drain on paper towels.
Yields 10 servings

Have lots of extra napkins available for guests.

Homemade Tartar Sauce

1	cup mayonnaise	1	tablespoon finely minced onion
⅓	cup dill pickle relish	1	teaspoon garlic salt
1	teaspoon lemon juice	1	tablespoon minced fresh parsley

Easy • Prep time: 15 minutes • Make ahead
Thoroughly mix all ingredients. Cover and refrigerate overnight.
Yields about 1½ cups sauce

Use a 12-quart pot (black iron, if possible) for frying fish.

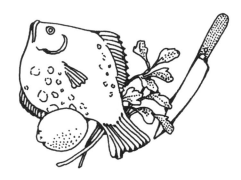

Potato Salad

1	small onion, chopped	1	tablespoon white vinegar
¾	cup mayonnaise	1	teaspoon garlic salt
¼	cup sour cream	2	ribs celery, chopped
¼	cup buttermilk	6	medium potatoes, peeled,
1	tablespoon Dijon mustard		boiled until firm-tender,
1	teaspoon pepper		and cubed

Easy • Prep time: 45 minutes • Prepare a day ahead
Mix onion, mayonnaise, sour cream, buttermilk, mustard, pepper, vinegar, and garlic salt in a large resealable container. Add celery and potatoes and toss gently. Chill overnight.
Yields 10 to 12 servings

If a thermometer isn't available for frying, drop a lemon in the hot oil. When the lemon floats to the top, the oil is ready.

Onion Rings

1½	cups all-purpose flour	Vegetable oil	
1	12-ounce can beer	Salt to taste	
6	onions, sliced and separated into rings		

Easy • Prep time: 15 minutes
In a bowl, combine flour and beer; let set for about 45 minutes. Dip the onion rings in batter and fry in oil heated to 375° until light brown. Drain and salt lightly.
Yields 10 servings

Hushpuppies

4	cups white cornmeal	4	onions, grated
6	tablespoons all-purpose flour	2	eggs, beaten
1	tablespoon salt	2	cups whole milk
8	teaspoons baking powder		Vegetable oil

Easy • Prep time: 10 minutes (including cooking time)
In a bowl, combine the first 4 ingredients; add onions. Combine eggs with milk and stir into cornmeal mixture. Heat oil to 350°, drop batter by teaspoonfuls into hot oil, and fry for about 3 minutes. Turn and cook for an additional 3 to 4 minutes, or until done. Drain on paper towels.
Yields 10 servings (about 2½ hushpuppies per person)

Fruit Casserole

Crust

1	cup butter	½	teaspoon salt
2	cups all-purpose flour	2	egg yolks
2	tablespoons sugar		

Filling

6	cups mixed fresh fruit (cherries, blueberries, peaches, blackberries, raspberries, pears)	1	cup sugar
			Juice of ½ lemon, optional
		½	cup all-purpose flour

Custard

2	eggs	½	cup heavy cream

Moderately easy • Prep time: 25 minutes

Preheat the oven to 350°. In the workbowl of a food processor, combine butter, flour, sugar, and salt. Add egg yolks and process until the dough forms a ball. Press the dough into the bottom of a 9x13-inch pan. Combine the filling ingredients and pour over the crust. Beat the custard ingredients together and pour over the filling. Bake for 45 to 50 minutes. Let cool for 15 minutes before serving.

Yields 10 to 12 servings

SHOPPING LIST _____

BAKERY

__ Assorted cookies and brownies

BUTCHER

__ 20 to 30 fish fillets

DAIRY

__ 1 8-ounce carton sour cream

__ 1 pint buttermilk

__ ½ dozen eggs

__ 1 pint milk

__ 1 pound butter

__ ½ pint heavy cream

EXTRAS

__ 1 12-ounce can beer

__ Keg of beer

MISCELLANEOUS

__ 1 small jar dill pickle relish

__ 1½ gallons oil for frying

__ 1 2-pound bag yellow cornmeal

__ 1 2-pound bag white cornmeal

__ 1 small jar Dijon mustard

PRODUCE

__ 1 lemon

__ 12 onions (10 large, 2 small)

__ 1 small bunch fresh parsley

__ 1 small stalk celery

__ 6 medium potatoes

__ ½ pound cherries

__ ½ pint blueberries

__ 2 peaches

__ ½ pint blackberries

__ ½ pint raspberries

__ 1 pear

STAPLES/SPICES

__ All-purpose flour

__ Baking powder

__ Family-size tea bags

__ Garlic salt

__ Mayonnaise

__ Pepper

__ Prepared mustard

__ Salt

__ Sugar

__ Tabasco sauce

__ Vegetable oil

__ Worcestershire sauce

CHEESE AND CRACKERS

SALAMI WEDGES

TURKEY WITH PESTO IN FRENCH BAGUETTES

COUNTRY COLESLAW

DILLY DEVILED EGGS

SAND TARTS

COLD DRINKS

S E R V E S   8

When you're really in a hurry, this menu allows you to serve good food without any fuss. Most of it can be considered "finger food," so your guests won't need to rest on formality. And because you won't have to, either, you'll have a chance to enjoy yourself along with everyone else.

Salami Wedges

8	ounces cream cheese, softened	Dash of Tabasco sauce
2	tablespoons horseradish	36 thin slices hard Genoa Salami

Moderately easy • Prep time: 15 to 20 minutes • Prepare ahead
Combine cream cheese with horseradish and Tabasco. Make three-decker sandwiches by spreading 1 slice of salami with about 2 teaspoons of the cheese mixture. Top with another slice of salami; spread with cheese and put a final slice of salami on top. Chill for at least 1 hour. Cut into quarters and spear with toothpicks.
Yields 48 appetizers

Consider serving box suppers in small cardboard boxes that have been painted to match the tablecloth.

Use colored picnic baskets with tie-on name tags for each guest.

Turkey with Pesto in French Baguettes

2	bunches fresh basil leaves	2 to 3	tablespoons olive oil
½	cup grated Parmesan cheese	20	4- to 5-inch long French
¼	cup chopped walnuts		baguettes, split
3	cloves garlic, chopped	2	pounds sliced turkey

Easy • Prep time: 25 minutes
Place basil, Parmesan, walnuts, garlic, and olive oil in a food processor. Pulse just until all ingredients are mixed and chopped. Do not form a paste. Spread pesto on baguettes and fill each with turkey.
Yields 20 sandwiches

BASIL

Country Coleslaw

½	head cabbage, shredded	¼	cup mayonnaise
1	onion, shredded	3	tablespoons apple cider vinegar
2	carrots, shredded		Salt and pepper to taste
1	teaspoon sugar		

Easy • Prep time: 10 minutes • Prepare ahead
In a large bowl, combine all ingredients. Mix well and chill for several hours before serving.
Yields 8 servings

Dilly Deviled Eggs

6	hard-boiled eggs	¼	teaspoon freshly chopped
2	tablespoons mayonnaise		dill
2	teaspoons white vinegar		Salt to taste
⅓	teaspoon dry mustard		Paprika for garnish
⅛	teaspoon black pepper		

Easy • Prep time: 20 minutes • Prepare ahead

Halve the eggs. In a small bowl, mash egg yolks and combine with remaining ingredients, except paprika, until blended. Stuff eggs with the yolk mixture and sprinkle with paprika. Refrigerate until ready to serve.

Yields 12 deviled eggs

Sand Tarts

½	cup butter, softened	2	teaspoons baking powder
1	cup sugar	1	egg white, beaten
1	egg, well beaten	1	tablespoon sugar
1¾	cups all-purpose flour	¼	teaspoon ground cinnamon

Moderately easy • Prep time: 20 minutes • Prepare ahead

In a large bowl, cream butter and add sugar slowly. Mix in egg. Sift together flour and baking powder. Add to the butter mixture. Chill overnight. Roll half of the dough at a time on a floured board until ⅛-inch thick. Using cookie cutters, cut into desired shapes. Brush cookies with egg white and sprinkle with sugar and cinnamon. Put on a buttered cookie sheet and bake at 350° for 8 minutes.

Yields 30 cookies.

Serve cold drinks in buckets or tubs of ice.

SHOPPING LIST _____

BAKERY
__ 20 4- to 5-inch-long French
   baguettes

BUTCHER/DELI
__ 36 thin slices Genoa salami
__ 2 pounds thinly sliced turkey

DAIRY
__ 1 dozen eggs
__ 2 sticks butter
__ 8 ounces cream cheese
__ ¼ pound Brie
__ ½ pound Gruyère
__ ½ pound Cheddar cheese
__ 1 4-ounce block Parmesan
   cheese

EXTRAS
__ 2 cases cold drinks
__ 3 cases beer
__ Toothpicks

MISCELLANEOUS
__ 1 small bag chopped
   walnuts
__ Assorted crackers

PRODUCE
__ 2 bunches fresh basil
__ 1 head garlic
__ 1 small head cabbage
__ 2 carrots
__ 1 onion
__ 1 bunch fresh dill

STAPLES/SPICES
__ All-purpose flour
__ Apple cider vinegar
__ Baking powder
__ Cinnamon
__ Dry mustard
__ Horseradish
__ Mayonnaise
__ Olive oil
__ Paprika
__ Pepper
__ Prepared mustard
__ Salt
__ Sugar
__ Tabasco sauce
__ White vinegar

Tailgate Picnic

CHEESE STRAWS

COLD TENDERLOIN

ROLLS OR BISCUITS

ARTICHOKE RICE SALAD

PEANUT BUTTER COOKIES

WINE, BEER, AND SOFT DRINKS

SERVES 8

Football games cry out for tailgating. The next time
you go out to support the home team, prepare a picnic
with a little something extra. The tenderloin adds a
special touch, and the cheese straws and cookies lean
toward the familiar. Throw in some beautiful weather,
a good game, and your closest friends, and you're
sure to come out a winner, no matter the score.

Cheese Straws

1	pound grated New York Cheddar cheese, softened	1½	teaspoons Tabasco sauce
1	cup butter, softened	1	tablespoon paprika
4	cups all-purpose flour	2½	teaspoons salt

Moderately easy • Prep time: 25 minutes • Prepare ahead • Can freeze
In a bowl, cream Cheddar cheese and butter. Blend in flour and seasonings. Chill thoroughly. Preheat the oven to 400°. Roll the dough ¼-inch thick and cut it into strips with a pastry wheel or sharp knife. Place on an ungreased baking sheet. Bake for 15 to 20 minutes.
Yields 36 to 40 straws

Buy a colorful potted mum and set it out with the food. It's easily transportable, and you can plant it later.

When cooking beef, use a meat thermometer in the thickest part of the meat to test for desired doneness: 140° for rare, 160° for medium, and 170° for well done.

Cold Tenderloin

3 to 4   pounds beef tenderloin   Freshly ground pepper

Easy • Prep time: 10 minutes • Prepare ahead
Preheat the oven to 425°. Rub meat with pepper and place on a rack in a pan. Roast for 15 to 20 minutes, or until a meat thermometer inserted in the center registers 170°. Cool, slice thin, and refrigerate.
Yields 8 servings

Artichoke Rice Salad

1   6-ounce box chicken-flavored rice
1   6-ounce jar marinated artichoke bottoms
3   tablespoons chopped green onions
12   large pimiento-stuffed olives, sliced
¼   cup mayonnaise
½   teaspoon curry powder
    Salt and pepper to taste

Moderately easy • Prep time: 20 minutes
Cook rice according to the package directions. Drain and chop artichokes, reserving liquid. Add onions, olives, and artichokes to rice. Combine mayonnaise and curry powder; add to the rice mixture. Slowly add the artichoke marinade until the salad is desired consistency; season. Serve immediately, or refrigerate and serve chilled.
Yields 8 servings

Peanut Butter Cookies

½ cup butter, softened
½ cup sugar
½ cup light brown sugar
½ cup peanut butter
 1 egg, beaten

½ teaspoon vanilla extract
½ teaspoon salt
½ teaspoon baking soda
 1 cup all-purpose flour

If using a quilt or spread for the ground, make sure it's one that can stand the wear and tear.

Moderately easy • Prep time: 15 to 20 minutes • Freezes well
Preheat the oven to 350°. In a large bowl, cream butter and sugars until fluffy; beat in peanut butter. Stir in egg and vanilla. Mix well. In another bowl, sift together salt, soda, and flour. Stir the dry ingredients into the wet ingredients slowly. Drop by teaspoonfuls onto cookie sheets. With a floured fork, press cookies down lightly, making a criss-cross design on the top of each cookie. Bake for 8 to 10 minutes. Cool.
Yields 60 cookies

SHOPPING LIST

BAKERY
__ Assorted rolls or biscuits

BUTCHER
__ 3 to 4 pounds beef tenderloin

EXTRAS
__ 1 case beer
__ ½ case wine

DAIRY
__ 1 pound New York Cheddar cheese
__ 1 pound butter
__ 1 egg

MISCELLANEOUS
__ 1 6-ounce box chicken-flavored rice
__ 1 6-ounce jar marinated artichoke bottoms
__ 1 small jar pimiento-stuffed olives
__ 1 small jar peanut butter
__ 3 six-packs soft drinks

PRODUCE
__ 1 bunch green onions

STAPLES/SPICES
__ All-purpose flour
__ Baking soda
__ Curry powder
__ Light brown sugar
__ Mayonnaise
__ Paprika
__ Peppercorns
__ Salt
__ Sugar
__ Tabasco sauce
__ Vanilla extract

Vegetarian Picnic

CHILLED CANTALOUPE SOUP

BOW TIE PASTA AND SUMMER SQUASH SALAD

CRUSTY ITALIAN BREAD

BUTTER COOKIES

ASSORTED FLAVORS MINERAL WATER

SERVES 8 TO 10

Chances are, even your carniverous friends will enjoy
this menu. But it's meant to celebrate how good food
can be without meat. Try it—you might just like it.

Chilled Cantaloupe Soup

5   cantaloupes
2   tablespoons freshly squeezed
    lime juice
¼   cup Grand Marnier
6   tablespoons heavy cream
    Ground cardamom
    to taste (⅛ teaspoon or less)

Grated nutmeg to taste
(½ teaspoon or less)
Plain lowfat yogurt for garnish
Fresh blueberries for garnish

Easy • Prep time: 25 minutes • Prepare ahead
Cut cantaloupes in half and remove seeds. Cut fruit away from rind; discard rind. Purée fruit in the workbowl of a food processor fitted with a
steel blade. Pour fruit into a large mixing bowl. Add lime juice, Grand
Marnier, cream, and spices. Mix to combine, and refrigerate overnight.
Before transporting or serving, adjust seasonings to taste. Transport to
the picnic site in a large thermos. Serve in clear plastic cups garnished
with a spoonful of plain yogurt and topped with blueberries.
Yields 8 to 10 servings

Bow Tie Pasta and Summer Squash Salad

2	pounds dried bow tie (farfalle) pasta Boiling water (10 to 12 quarts)	8 to 10	cloves garlic, minced
⅔	cup lemon juice	3	14½-ounce cans Italian-style stewed tomatoes, coarsely chopped (with juice)
⅔	cup olive oil, divided	1	bunch fresh basil, finely shredded (reserve a few whole leaves for garnish)
5 or 6	zucchini, diced		
6	yellow summer squash, diced	2	tablespoons sugar Salt to taste

Moderately easy • Prep time: 25 minutes • Prepare ahead

Cook pasta in boiling water until al dente. Drain and rinse with cold water; drain thoroughly. Return pasta to the pot and add lemon juice and half the olive oil; toss. Set aside. Heat remaining olive oil in a large pot. Sauté zucchini and yellow squash until almost tender. Add garlic and cook for another minute. Add stewed tomatoes, basil, sugar, and salt. Cook until heated through. Pour vegetables over pasta; toss until thoroughly combined. Let cool. Refrigerate until chilled, or overnight. Serve chilled or at room temperature. Garnish with whole fresh basil leaves.
Yields 8 to 10 servings

GARLIC

Cook pasta and grains in bouillon for extra flavor.

SHOPPING LIST _____

BAKERY
__ 1 large tin butter cookies
__ 3 loaves crusty Italian bread

CANNED GOODS
__ 3 14½-ounce cans Italian-style
  stewed tomatoes

DAIRY
__ ½ pint heavy cream
__ ½ pint plain lowfat yogurt

EXTRAS
__ 1 small bottle Grand Marnier

MISCELLANEOUS
__ 3 to 4 bottles assorted flavors of
  mineral water
__ 2 pounds dried bow tie (farfalle)
  pasta

PRODUCE
__ 5 cantaloupes
__ 1 lime
__ ½ pint fresh blueberries
__ 6 or 7 lemons
__ 5 or 6 zucchini
__ 6 yellow summer squash
__ 1 head garlic
__ 1 bunch basil

STAPLES/SPICES
__ Ground cardamom
__ Nutmeg
__ Olive oil
__ Salt
__ Sugar

San Francisco Style

MIXED GREENS WITH SHALLOT VINAIGRETTE

ITALIAN TOMATO CHEESE PIE

SOURDOUGH ROLLS

SPICED CALIFORNIA PEARS WITH YOGURT

CHIANTI

S E R V E S   6   T O   8

The easygoing lifestyle of California inspired this easy-to-prepare menu, full of a variety of seasonings and textures. Eat these foods the next time you're inspired to head for the coast and let it all hang out.

"Tomatoes and oregano make it Italian; wine and tarragon make it French. Sour cream makes it Russian; lemon and cinnamon make it Greek. Soy sauce makes it Chinese; garlic makes it good."
—ALICE MAY BROCK,
ALICE'S RESTAURANT COOKBOOK

Notes

Mixed Greens with Shallot Vinaigrette

2 tablespoons balsamic vinegar

2 tablespoons white wine vinegar

1 teaspoon Dijon mustard

1 shallot, finely minced

¾ cup olive oil

Salt and pepper to taste

Mixed salad greens

Easy • Prep time: 10 minutes
Whisk together vinegars and mustard. Stir in shallots. Slowly pour in olive oil, whisking constantly. Add salt and pepper to taste. Pour over mixed salad greens.
Yields 1 cup dressing

Cooking wine may be preserved by adding a few drops of olive oil.

Italian Tomato Cheese Pie

1   9-inch refrigerated pie
    shell, unbaked
¼   cup Dijon mustard
12   ounces Mozzarella cheese,
    thinly sliced
8 or 9   medium tomatoes,
    thinly sliced

2 to 3   tablespoons
    chopped garlic
1   teaspoon dried oregano
1   teaspoon dried basil
    Salt and pepper to taste
2   tablespoons olive oil

Moderately easy • Prep time: 15 to 20 minutes
Preheat the oven to 400°. Spread the bottom and sides of the pie shell with mustard. Top mustard with cheese slices, distributing evenly. Starting at the outer edge of the pie shell, overlap tomatoes around the pie pan to form an outer ring. Make a second ring of overlapping tomatoes just inside the first one. Fill in the center with two or three tomato slices. Sprinkle the top evenly with garlic, oregano, and basil. Season with salt and pepper to taste. Drizzle olive oil over all. Bake for 40 minutes. Remove from the oven, and cool for 10 to12 minutes. Serve warm.
Yields 6 to 8 servings

Spiced California Pears with Yogurt

4 large ripe pears
 (preferably California
 Bartlett)
¾ cup dark brown sugar
½ cup orange juice
 (preferably fresh-squeezed)
 Ground cinnamon to taste

Grated nutmeg to taste
Ground cloves to taste
¾ cup plain yogurt
 Crystallized ginger,
 finely chopped
 Mint for garnish

Moderately easy • Prep time: 20 minutes

Preheat the oven to 350°. Slice each pear in half lengthwise and remove core, taking care to leave stem intact. Sprinkle the bottom of a 9x13-inch glass baking dish with brown sugar. Lay pears, cut side down, on top of sugar. Pour orange juice over pears and sprinkle with spices. Bake for 20 to 25 minutes, basting frequently. Remove from the oven and cool completely.

To serve: Place a pear half, cut side down, in each serving dish. Spoon syrup from the baking dish over pears. Top each serving with a scoop of yogurt. Sprinkle with crystallized ginger and garnish with a mint leaf at the stem end of each pear.

Yields 8 servings

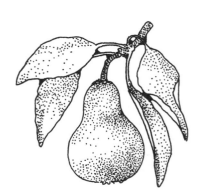

SHOPPING LIST

BAKERY
__ 8 to 10 sourdough rolls

DAIRY
__ 12 ounces sliced Mozzarella
   cheese
__ 1 pint plain yogurt

EXTRAS
__ 2 large bottles Chianti

MISCELLANEOUS
__ 1 9-inch uncooked, refrigerated
   pie shell
__ 1 small jar Dijon mustard
__ 1 bottle balsamic vinegar
__ 1 bottle white wine vinegar

PRODUCE
__ 8 to 9 medium tomatoes
__ 1 head garlic
__ 1 large shallot
__ 1 large bag mixed salad greens
__ 4 large ripe pears (preferably
   California Bartlett)
__ 3 to 4 juice oranges
__ 1 small bunch mint leaves

STAPLES/SPICES
__ Cinnamon
__ Crystallized ginger
__ Dark brown sugar
__ Dried basil
__ Ground cloves
__ Nutmeg
__ Olive oil
__ Oregano
__ Pepper
__ Salt

New England Fireside Lunch

CORN SOUFFLÉ

PUFF PASTRY WRAPPED PORK AND APPLES

MIXED GREENS WITH ROQUEFORT PECAN DRESSING

MAPLE BRANDY MILKSHAKE

SERVES 6

New England winters can be brutal. But they can be lovely as well, blanketing the landscape with white stuff the likes of which many of us have never seen. Don't let harsh weather snuff out your culinary inclinations. This menu was created to satisfy your hunger and chase away your winter blues.

Corn Soufflé

1   can creamed corn
1   can whole kernel corn, drained
1   box Jiffy cornbread mix
½   cup butter, melted
1   cup sour cream, plus extra for garnish

Grated Cheddar cheese for garnish
Chopped chives for garnish

Easy • Prep time: 10 minutes
Preheat the oven to 350°. Combine the first 5 ingredients in a mixing bowl. Turn into a 9x13-inch baking dish. Bake for 50 minutes. Serve warm in individual bowls garnished with a scoop of sour cream and a sprinkling of Cheddar cheese and chives.
Yields 6 servings

Notes

One pound of Cheddar, Swiss, Parmesan, or Romano cheese equals 4 cups grated. One pound of cottage or cream cheese equals 2 cups.

Puff Pastry Wrapped Pork and Apples

1 17¼-ounce package frozen puff pastry dough
½ pound ground pork
½ pound ground pork sausage
1 small apple, peeled, cored, and diced
⅓ cup (3 ounces) diced Cheddar cheese
1 small onion, finely chopped
2 or 3 cloves garlic, minced
¼ cup finely chopped parsley
2 tablespoons finely chopped sage
½ teaspoon salt
⅛ teaspoon pepper
2 eggs, lightly beaten

Moderate • Prep time: 15 minutes

Preheat the oven to 425°. Thaw 2 sheets of puff pastry according to the package directions. In a large mixing bowl, combine pork, apple, cheese, onion, garlic, herbs, and seasonings. Mix thoroughly. Add most of beaten egg (reserve a small amount, about ¼ cup, for brushing over the pastry later). Mix again to integrate. Divide the pork mixture into 2 equal portions and shape into logs about 8 inches long and 2 to 3 inches wide. Place a log down the center of each piece of pastry. Cut the overhanging pastry into ½-inch-wide strips on each side of the pork. Lightly moisten the end of each pastry strip with a little water and wrap the strips up over the pork to create a lattice effect. Press the pastry ends to seal. Wrap the ends of the logs with remaining pastry. Trim, tuck, and fold neatly as necessary. Transfer to baking sheets. Brush pastry logs lightly with remaining beaten egg. Bake for 20 minutes. Reduce the oven temperature to 350° and bake for 20 minutes more. Remove from the oven and let cool for 10 minutes before slicing.

Yields 6 servings

Mixed Greens with Roquefort Pecan Dressing

2	tablespoons lemon juice	⅔	cup crumbled Roquefort cheese
½	teaspoon lemon zest	½	cup chopped pecans,
½	cup plain yogurt		toasted and cooled
¼	cup olive oil		Salt and pepper to taste
¼	cup parsley leaves		Mixed salad greens

Easy • Prep time: 5 minutes
Combine all ingredients in a blender container. Pulse until the mixture reaches a smooth consistency. Serve over mixed salad greens.
Yields 1½ cups dressing

Maple Brandy Milkshake

4½	cups milk	6	shots brandy
⅓	cup maple syrup	6	scoops vanilla ice cream

Easy • Prep time: 5 minutes
Combine all ingredients in a blender container. Pulse until the mixture reaches milkshake consistency. Serve immediately.
Yields 6 servings

SHOPPING LIST _____

BUTCHER
__ ½ pound ground pork
__ ½ pound ground pork sausage

CANNED GOODS
__ 1 17-ounce can creamed corn
__ 1 17-ounce can whole kernel corn

DAIRY
__ 1 4-ounce block Cheddar cheese
__ 2 eggs
__ 1 stick butter
__ 1 16-ounce container sour cream
__ 1 8-ounce container plain yogurt
__ 1 3-ounce block Roquefort
cheese
__ 1 quart milk

EXTRAS
__ 1 ½-liter bottle brandy

MISCELLANEOUS
__ 1 box Jiffy cornbread mix
__ 1 2-ounce package chopped
pecans
__ 1 17¼-ounce box puff pastry
__ 1 quart vanilla ice cream

PRODUCE
__ 1 large bag mixed salad greens
__ 1 small apple
__ 1 small onion
__ 1 head garlic
__ 1 bunch fresh parsley
__ 1 bunch fresh sage
__ 1 bunch fresh chives
__ 1 large lemon

STAPLES /SPICES
__ Maple syrup
__ Olive oil
__ Pepper
__ Salt

SHRIMP AND CASHEW PINEAPPLE BOATS

POLYNESIAN PORK SATAY

COCONUT BREAD

ISLAND ICE CREAM BALLS

MAI TAIS

SERVES 4

Say hello to Hawaii with foods that reflect the Aloha State's bounty. With this cornucopia of flavors, the tropical nature of things comes to life. While savoring the tangy shrimp and cool coconut, you may just find yourself doing the hula.

Shrimp and Cashew Pineapple Boats

1	fresh pineapple	4	cups cooked white rice
2	tablespoons fish sauce	¼	teaspoon white pepper
¼	cup sugar	¼	cup chopped cilantro
2	cups coconut milk	½	cup toasted cashew nuts
1	pound cooked medium shrimp	½	cup golden raisins

Moderately easy • Prep time: 30 minutes

Preheat the oven to 350°. Cut pineapple in half lengthwise, core, and remove the fruit, leaving the shells and leaves intact. Coarsely chop 1 cup of the fruit and set aside. (The rest of the fruit is not needed for this dish.) Combine fish sauce and sugar in a large pan over medium-low heat. Add coconut milk and bring to a simmer. Stir in pineapple, shrimp, rice, and all remaining ingredients. Remove from the heat and mix thoroughly. Stuff the rice mixture into the pineapple shells and place on a baking sheet. Bake until heated through, about 15 minutes.

Yields 4 servings (each pineapple half yields 2 servings)

Polynesian Pork Satay

12	ounces lean pork, cubed	¼	cup brown sugar
4	wooden skewers	1	tablespoon orange juice
1	lime, halved	3	tablespoons teriyaki sauce
2	cloves garlic, crushed	3	tablespoons sesame seeds
1	cup coconut milk		

Moderate • Prep time: 25 minutes • Start about 1½ hours beforehand
Divide pork into 4 three-ounce portions, skewer, and place in a shallow baking dish. Squeeze half of the lime over pork. Spread garlic over pork. Pour coconut milk over top. Cover and refrigerate for 1 hour, turning occasionally.

Preheat the broiler. In a small bowl, combine brown sugar, orange juice, and teriyaki sauce, along with juice from the remaining lime half. Stir well. Lift pork from the marinade and place on a broiling rack. Use a pastry brush to baste pork with the brown sugar sauce. Broil, basting and turning frequently, for 8 to 10 minutes. Sprinkle pork with sesame seeds just before serving.
Yields 4 servings

Coconut Bread

1	egg	3	cups all-purpose flour
1½	cups milk	3	teaspoons baking powder
½	teaspoon vanilla extract	½	teaspoon salt
¼	teaspoon coconut extract	¼	teaspoon ground cinnamon
1	cup flaked coconut	1	cup sugar

Moderate • Prep time: 20 minutes • Prepare ahead
Preheat the oven to 350°. Combine egg, milk, extracts, and coconut in a blender container. Blend for 30 seconds. Sift the dry ingredients together in a bowl. Pour the liquid mixture over the dry ingredients. Stir to combine; do not beat. Pour the batter into a greased 9x5-inch loaf pan. Bake for 1 hour and 10 minutes. Let cool completely. Remove from pan, wrap, and refrigerate. Serve chilled.
Yields 1 loaf of 8 servings

When planning a party, start working on your menu one week in advance.

Island Ice Cream Balls

1 cup diced mango (or use dried if fresh is unavailable)
2 pints vanilla ice cream, softened
½ cup sweetened flaked coconut
½ cup crushed macadamia nuts

Easy • Prep time: 15 minutes • Start at least 3 hours before serving
Carefully fold mango into ice cream. Scoop 4 rounded balls of ice cream onto individual pieces of plastic wrap. Seal the plastic wrap tightly and freeze for at least 2½ hours. Remove the plastic-wrapped ice cream balls from the freezer and let sit at room temperature for 5 to 10 minutes. Unwrap and roll in coconut and macadamia nuts. Serve immediately.
Yields 4 servings

Mai Tais

8 ounces light rum
2 ounces curaçao
64 ounces pineapple juice

Easy • Prep time: 5 minutes
Combine all ingredients and mix well. Serve cold.
Yields 8 servings

Keep a bulletin board or other record keeping device close at hand so you can make note of things you need for your guests.

SHOPPING LIST _____

BUTCHER
__ 1 pound medium cooked shrimp
__ 12 ounces lean pork

CANNED GOODS
__ 2 cans coconut milk (ethnic foods section of grocery store/Asian market)

DAIRY
__ 1 egg
__ 1 pint milk
__ 2 pints vanilla ice cream

EXTRAS
__ Wooden skewers
__ 1 bottle light rum
__ 1 small bottle curaçao

MISCELLANEOUS
__ 1 small bottle fish sauce (ethnic foods section of grocery store/ Asian market)
__ 1 small tin cashew nuts
__ 1 small box golden raisins
__ 1 small bottle teryaki sauce
__ 1 small bottle coconut extract
__ 1 7-ounce package sweetened flaked coconut
__ 1 small jar macadamia nuts
__ 1 64-ounce container fresh pineapple juice

PRODUCE
__ 1 large pineapple
__ 1 bunch fresh cilantro
__ 1 large lime
__ 1 head garlic
__ 1 small orange
__ 1 large mango (or 4 ounces dried mango pieces)

STAPLES/SPICES
__ All-purpose flour
__ Baking powder
__ Brown sugar
__ Cinnamon
__ Salt
__ Sesame seeds
__ Sugar
__ Vanilla extract
__ White pepper
__ White rice

STUFFED MUSHROOM CAPS

PARTY GUACAMOLE

STEAMED BROCCOLI

FRENCH BAGUETTES

RICE WITH ALMONDS

ROASTED CORNISH HENS

RUM PUDDING WITH RASPBERRY SAUCE

CHAMPAGNE

SERVES 12

Here is a casual but elegant way to celebrate a friend's or family member's nuptials. Plan your picnic as best you can, then hope for the best from Mother Nature!

Stuffed Mushroom Caps

3 slices bacon, cooked, drained, and crumbled

⅓ cup grated sharp Cheddar cheese

1 teaspoon chopped chives

⅛ teaspoon salt

⅛ teaspoon each: black pepper, onion powder, and garlic powder

12 medium mushroom caps, washed and drained

¼ cup butter, melted

Easy • Prep time: 10 minutes • Prepare ahead • Recipe enlarges easily
Preheat the broiler. In a small bowl, combine bacon with cheese, chives, and seasonings. Dip mushroom caps in butter and place on a broiler pan. Fill each cap with a rounded teaspoon of the bacon-cheese mixture. Place tops of mushrooms 4 inches from the broiler. Broil for 6 to 8 minutes.
Yields 12 servings

The ideal time for this picnic is early on a spring or summer evening. Stage the setting in a carefully groomed yard among the blooms of the season.

Notes

Party Guacamole

2 cloves garlic
4 medium soft avocados
1 teaspoon lemon juice
4 green onions, chopped
4 medium tomatoes, chopped
2 tablespoons chopped
   green bell pepper

¼ teaspoon Tabasco sauce
   Salt to taste
   Mayonnaise to thicken
   (if needed)
   Boston or baby lettuce
   for serving
   Tortilla chips

Easy • Prep time: 10 minutes
In a large bowl, mash garlic and scrape it out of the bowl. Mash avocados in the same bowl and add lemon juice. Mix in remaining ingredients. Serve on beds of lettuce or in your favorite serving dish with tortilla chips.
Yields 12 to 16 servings

Rice with Almonds

1 cup butter, melted
2 cups raw long-grain white rice
1 cup slivered almonds
2 tablespoons chopped
   green bell pepper

2 tablespoons chopped
   green onion
1 pound mushrooms, sliced
6 cups chicken broth

Easy • Prep time: 15 minutes • Recipe halves easily
Preheat the oven to 350°. In a large heavy skillet or saucepan, combine all ingredients, except chicken broth. Cook until rice turns yellow, stirring constantly. Combine the mixture with chicken broth. Pour into 1 large or 2 medium buttered casserole dishes. Cover tightly and bake for 1 hour, or until firm.
Yields 18 to 20 servings

Give each couple decorated baskets containing splits of champagne or chilled wine, glasses, china, silver, and linen napkins for eating. Serve the food from a beautifully decorated buffet table compatible with the decorated baskets.

Roasted Cornish Hens

1 pound butter, melted
1½ cups lemon juice
2 teaspoons garlic salt
¼ cup paprika
1 tablespoon oregano
1 teaspoon salt
1 teaspoon ground
   black pepper

Lemon pepper and
   seasoned salt to taste
½ cup white wine
1 tablespoon liquid smoke
14 to 16 Cornish game hens

The leg of the Cornish game hen should twist easily from the joint when done.

Easy • Prep time: 10 minutes • Prepare ahead

In a large bowl, combine and mix all ingredients, except Cornish hens. Place hens in 2 shallow dishes and pour the mixture over them. Marinate overnight in the refrigerator. Remove from the marinade. Roast in a 350° oven for 1 hour, basting several times with reserved marinade. These also may be cooked slowly on a grill for 1¼ hours, brushing frequently with the marinade.

Yields 12 to 16 servings

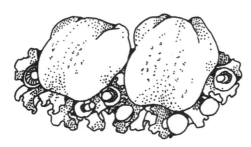

Rum Pudding with Raspberry Sauce

3 packages unflavored gelatin	1 cup sugar
½ cup cold water	1 cup light rum
3 cups boiling water	3 cups heavy cream, whipped
6 egg yolks	

Moderately easy • Prep time: 25 minutes • Prepare ahead • Recipe doubles easily

Soften gelatin in cold water in a bowl. Dissolve this mixture in boiling water. Cool in the refrigerator, stirring occasionally, until the mixture becomes thickened. Beat egg yolks with sugar until lemon colored. Gradually stir into the cooled and slightly thickened gelatin mixture. Stir in rum. Whip cream and fold into mixture. Spray 16 one-half cup molds with nonstick cooking spray for easy removal. Pour the mixture into molds and chill. Top with Raspberry Sauce when ready to serve.
Yields 16 to 20 servings

Raspberry Sauce

4 10-ounce packages frozen raspberries	
2 cups sugar	

Easy • Prepare ahead

In a large saucepan, combine raspberries and sugar. Boil for 5 minutes, pressing the berries to release juices. Strain and chill. Serve over Rum Pudding.
Yields about 4 cups sauce

SHOPPING LIST _____

BAKERY
__ 12 to 24 baguettes

BUTCHER
__ 14 to 16 Cornish game hens
__ ½ pound bacon

CANNED GOODS
__ 3 16-ounce cans chicken broth

DAIRY
__ ½ dozen eggs
__ 1 4-ounce block sharp Cheddar cheese
__ 2 1-pound boxes butter
__ 1 quart heavy cream

EXTRAS
__ 1 small bottle light rum
__ 1 case champagne
__ 1 small bottle white wine

MISCELLANEOUS
__ 2 boxes raw wild rice
__ 1 small bottle liquid smoke
__ 2 boxes unflavored gelatin
__ 1 large bottle fresh lemon juice
__ 1 6-ounce package slivered almonds
__ 1 large bag tortilla chips
__ 4 10-ounce packages frozen raspberries

PRODUCE
__ 3 large bunches broccoli
__ 1 head garlic
__ 4 medium tomatoes
__ 1 bunch green onions
__ 4 medium-soft avocados
__ 2 large green peppers
__ 1 pound mushrooms, plus 12 medium mushroom caps
__ 1 bunch fresh chives

STAPLES/SPICES
__ Black pepper
__ Garlic powder
__ Garlic salt
__ Lemon pepper seasoning
__ Mayonnaise
__ Onion powder
__ Oregano
__ Paprika
__ Salt
__ Seasoned salt
__ Sugar
__ Tabasco sauce

Anchors Away!

Notes

TWICE-BAKED NEW POTATOES

SAUSAGE COINS

GARLIC PUMPERNICKEL FINGER SANDWICHES

BUTTERSCOTCH BROWNIES

BLOODY MARYS (see p. 6)

SERVES 8

A boating excursion can be the perfect setting for a light lunch late in the afternoon. The foods featured here are transportable, and they offer your guests something more than the predictable fried chicken and potato salad one might expect from such a picnic. Hurry, before the boat leaves the dock!

Twice-Baked New Potatoes

12	small new potatoes	½	teaspoon garlic salt
¼	cup butter	½	teaspoon pepper
½	cup grated Cheddar cheese	¼	cup instant potato flakes
¼	cup milk	2	tablespoons freshly grated
1	teaspoon dried basil		Parmesan cheese
1	teaspoon paprika		

Moderately easy • Prep time: 40 minutes • Can serve cold
Preheat the oven to 400°. Bake potatoes with skins on a baking sheet for 20 minutes. Let sit until cool enough to handle. Cut each potato in half and use a melon baller to gently scoop potatoes out to form tiny "bowls" about ¼-inch thick. In a medium bowl, combine the potato pulp with remaining ingredients and use a fork to combine well. Carefully refill each skin with the mixture; they should overflow a little. Sprinkle paprika over top and bake for 10 to 15 minutes, until heated through.
Yields 8 servings

Sausage Coins

3   10-ounce cans crescent
   roll dough
1   small jar Dijon mustard

1   pound smoked Polish
   sausage, sliced into ¼-inch disks

Easy • Prep time: 25 minutes
Preheat the oven to 350°. Roll the crescent dough flat and use a 2-inch biscuit cutter to cut out disks of dough. Press the remaining dough together and reroll to cut out as many disks as possible. Spread a tiny amount of mustard on each disk. Place a slice of sausage between 2 disks (mustard sides facing in) and seal the edges with a fork. Bake for 8 to 10 minutes, or until the pastry is golden.
Yields approximately 48 coins

Garlic Pumpernickel Finger Sandwiches

Pumpernickel bread (or bread of choice), thinly sliced
Garlic butter (softened butter mixed with mashed fresh
clove of garlic to taste)

Easy • Prep time: 15 minutes
Spread garlic butter on bread and cut in delicate shapes.
Yields as many servings as needed

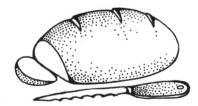

Keep a record of menus, recipes, cooking tips, and brand names that you like. This will save you time when planning future events.

Butterscotch Brownies

1	cup light brown sugar	¾	cup chopped pecans
¼	cup butter	½	teaspoon salt
1	egg, slightly beaten	1	teaspoon vanilla extract
½	cup sifted flour	1	teaspoon baking powder

Easy • Prep time: 10 minutes • Prepare ahead and freeze
Preheat the oven to 350°. In the top of a double boiler or heavy saucepan, melt butter with sugar. Remove from the heat and stir in egg. Add remaining ingredients. Butter and flour a 9-inch pan. Bake for 25 to 30 minutes.
Yields 9 to 12 squares

SHOPPING LIST _____

BAKERY
__ 1 thinly sliced loaf
   pumpernickel or favorite bread

BUTCHER
__ 1 pound smoked Polish sausage

CANNED GOODS
__ 4 32-ounce cans tomato juice

DAIRY
__ 1 10-ounce block sharp Cheddar
   cheese
__ 2 sticks butter
__ ½ pint milk
__ 1 4-ounce block Parmesan
   cheese
__ 1 egg

EXTRAS
__ 1 case beer
__ 1 large bottle vodka

MISCELLANEOUS
__ 1 case soft drinks
__ 1 bag ice
__ 1 envelope instant potato flakes
__ 1 6-ounce package chopped
   pecans
__ 3 10-ounce cans crescent roll
   dough
__ 1 small jar Dijon mustard

PRODUCE
__ 2 large lemons
__ 1 stalk celery
__ 1 head garlic
__ 1½ pounds small new potatoes

STAPLES/SPICES
__ All-purpose flour
__ Baking powder
__ Dried basil
__ Garlic salt
__ Light brown sugar
__ Paprika
__ Peppercorns
__ Salt
__ Tabasco sauce
__ Tea bags
__ Vanilla extract
__ Worcestershire sauce

Tea Time in May

READY RAISIN BISCUITS

ODE TO BRITAIN CRUMPETS

LUSCIOUS LEMON CURD

JAMS

OLD-FASHIONED TEA CAKES

FRESH STRAWBERRIES

VARIETY OF TEAS

S E R V E S   1 2

Spring seems the ideal backdrop for a traditional tea,
but you can serve these delightful delicacies any time.
Combine your favorite treats to offer your guests a
selection they can't refuse.

If your schedule doesn't
allow you time to prepare
this menu, you can
purchase lemon curd,
crumpets, raisin biscuits,
and tea cakes from your
supermarket or bakery.

Ready Raisin Biscuits

2½ cups all-purpose flour
1   tablespoon sugar
1   teaspoon salt
4   teaspoons baking powder
⅓   cup shortening
1   egg, beaten
¾   cup milk
1   cup raisins

Easy • Prep time: 15 minutes
Preheat the oven to 400°. In a large mixing bowl, combine flour, sugar,
salt, and baking powder. Cut in shortening. Combine egg, milk, and raisins in a separate bowl and work into the flour mixture. Turn onto a
well-floured board and knead until smooth. Roll out to ½-inch thickness and cut with a tea biscuit cutter. Bake for 10 to 12 minutes.
Yields 24 to 30 biscuits

Ode to Britain Crumpets

"Tea to the English is really a picnic indoors."—ALICE WALKER

2   eggs
1   cup milk, warmed
1   compressed yeast cake,
    dissolved in ½ cup
    warm water

4   cups all-purpose flour
1   teaspoon salt

Moderately easy • Prep time: 15 minutes

In a large mixing bowl, beat eggs well. Add milk, yeast, and flour to make a stiff batter. Let rise until light in texture, covering the bowl to prevent crusting over top. Pour a large (as large as a batter cake) spoonful of the risen batter on a hot, greased griddle, working carefully. Cook slowly, over medium-low heat, turning when one side has browned. Slice, butter, and serve with Luscious Lemon Curd.

Yields 24 to 30 crumpets

Luscious Lemon Curd

5   egg yolks
1   egg white
¼   cup lemon juice

1   cup sugar
3   tablespoons butter

Easy • Prep time: 5 minutes

Combine all ingredients and cook in the top of a double boiler until thick and clear, stirring constantly. Serve with any of the tea recipes, with gingerbread, or as a tart filling.

Yields 2 cups curd

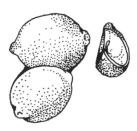

Old-Fashioned Tea Cakes

½ cup butter, softened
¾ cup sugar
2 egg yolks
1 tablespoon cream
½ teaspoon vanilla or
lemon extract

1 ½ cups all-purpose flour
½ teaspoon baking powder
¼ teaspoon salt

Moderately easy • Prep time: 30 minutes • Prepare ahead • Can freeze
In a large mixing bowl, cream butter and sugar until light and fluffy. Add egg yolks and mix well. Add cream and extract. In a separate bowl, sift together flour, baking powder, and salt until well blended. Mix into the creamed mixture. Chill the dough for 1 hour. Preheat the oven to 375°. Roll the dough out about ¼-inch thick on a lightly floured board. Cut with a cookie cutter and bake on a greased cookie sheet for 8 to 10 minutes.
Yields about 3 dozen tea cakes

SHOPPING LIST

DAIRY
__ 1 pint whole milk
__ 2 sticks butter
__ 1 dozen eggs
__ ½ pint cream

MISCELLANEOUS
__ 1 large box raisins
__ 1 .6-ounce compressed yeast cake
__ Assorted English teas
__ Assorted jams and preserves

PRODUCE
__ 6 large lemons (3 for tea)
__ 1 quart fresh strawberries
__ 2 oranges (for tea)

STAPLES/SPICES
__ All-purpose flour
__ Baking powder
__ Salt
__ Sugar
__ Vanilla or lemon extract
__ Vegetable shortening

Afternoon Tea

CURRIED CHICKEN BITES

MINI SHRIMP SANDWICHES

BACON-MARMALADE ROUNDS

LEMON MUFFINS

CANDIED WALNUTS

CHOCOLATE TRUFFLES

APRICOT SPICE CAKE

PARTY CHEESECAKES

CITRUS SHERBET PUNCH AND VARIETY OF TEAS

S E R V E S   2 5

The selections presented here will provide your guests with a full plate indeed. More than sweet stuff, the sandwiches round out the menu nicely.

"Ah, there's nothing like tea in the afternoon. When the British Empire collapses, historians will find that it had made but two invaluable contributions to civilization—this tea ritual and the detective novel."
—AYN RAND

Notes

Curried Chicken Bites

4	ounces cream cheese, softened	1	cup toasted, sliced almonds
2	tablespoons mayonnaise	1	tablespoon chutney
1	cup cooked, diced chicken breasts	½	tablespoon salt
		1	teaspoon curry powder
		1	cup grated coconut

Easy • Prep time: 15 minutes • Prepare ahead
In a large bowl, beat cream cheese and mayonnaise. Add chicken, almonds, chutney, salt, and curry powder. Mix well. Shape into walnut-sized balls. Roll in grated coconut. Chill.
Yields 34 pieces

Be sure to put out cream, along with sugar and sugar substitute, for your guests. As strange as it may sound, some people really do like a spot of milk in their tea!

Mini Shrimp Sandwiches

1 pound fresh, cooked shrimp, peeled	1 tablespoon lemon juice
8 ounces cream cheese, softened	⅛ teaspoon garlic salt
¼ teaspoon onion powder	Mayonnaise
	Whole-wheat bread

Easy • Prep time: 5 to 10 minutes

Grind shrimp in a food processor. Mix in all other ingredients and fold in enough mayonnaise to make a paste. Spread on whole-wheat bread and cut diagonally into 4 triangles.

Yields 2½ cups spread

Bacon-Marmalade Rounds

1 pound sharp Cheddar cheese, grated and softened	½ cup orange marmalade
8 ounces cream cheese, softened	36 Melba rounds (crackers)
3 egg yolks, lightly beaten	½ pound cooked bacon, drained and crumbled

Easy • Prep time: 15 minutes

In a large bowl of an electric mixer, combine cheese and egg yolks. Blend in marmalade. Spread the mixture on Melba rounds. Top with bacon. Broil until hot and bubbly.

Yields 3 dozen rounds

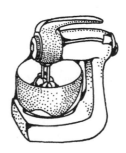

Lemon Muffins

½ cup butter, softened
½ cup sugar
2 egg yolks
   Grated rind and juice
   of 1 lemon

1 cup all-purpose flour
1 teaspoon baking powder
2 egg whites, stiffly beaten
   Confectioners' sugar

Easy • Prep time: 15 minutes • Freezes well
Preheat the oven to 350°. In a large bowl, cream butter and sugar. Mix the next 4 ingredients in order with the creamed mixture. Fold in egg whites last. Fill greased mini-muffin tins and bake for 15 minutes. Roll or dip in confectioners' sugar.
Yields 30 mini-muffins

Candied Walnuts

1½ cups sugar
½ cup water
¼ cup light corn syrup

1 teaspoon vanilla extract
4 cups shelled whole walnuts

Moderately easy • Prep time: 20 minutes
In a heavy saucepan, mix sugar, water, and light corn syrup. Heat to soft-ball stage (240° with a candy thermometer). Remove from the heat and add vanilla. Stir in walnuts and mix until they are coated. Pour onto waxed paper to cool. Break apart. Store in a covered tin.
Yields 1 pound nuts

Chocolate Truffles

½ cup unsalted butter
1⅔ cups heavy cream
1 pound fine grade semisweet chocolate

2 tablespoons Grand Marnier
Dutch process cocoa or confectioners' sugar

Moderately easy • Prep time: 30 minutes • Prepare ahead • Store in refrigerator or freezer indefinitely

Melt butter and cream over medium heat in a heavy saucepan, stirring with a rubber spatula. Increase the heat and bring cream just to a boil. Remove from heat and add chocolate; stir until melted. Continue stirring until the mixture cools and thickens. Stir in Grand Marnier and cover; place in the refrigerator. Allow to thicken for 2 to 3 hours, stirring several times as it cools. After the mixture has hardened, form truffles by scooping portions with a small spoon. Work quickly; dust your hands with cocoa or confectioners' sugar and roll the mixture. These also may be cut into tiny squares and sprinkled with cocoa or confectioners' sugar.
Yields 50 pieces

Apricot Spice Cake

1 cup vegetable oil
2 cups sugar
2 cups self-rising flour
4 eggs
1 teaspoon ground cinnamon

1 cup chopped pecans
1 teaspoon vanilla extract
1 teaspoon ground cloves
2 small jars apricot baby food

Easy • Prep time: 10 minutes

Preheat the oven to 325°. In a large bowl of an electric mixer, blend oil, sugar, and flour. Add eggs, one at a time, and incorporate. Add remaining ingredients and beat well. Pour in a greased and floured tube or bundt pan. Bake for 50 to 60 minutes.
Yields 20 to 24 servings

Party Cheesecakes

1¼ cups graham cracker
    crumbs
3 tablespoons sugar
⅓ cup butter, melted
¾ cup sugar

2 eggs, lightly beaten
2 tablespoons vanilla extract
1 cup sour cream
    Strawberry halves

Moderately easy • Prep time: 25 to 30 minutes • Prepare ahead
Preheat the oven to 350°. To make crust, combine crumbs and sugar. Stir in butter until thoroughly blended. Press the mixture firmly into a 13x9x2-inch pan or individual mini-muffin tins. Bake for 8 minutes. Remove from the oven and cool. Mix remaining ingredients, except sour cream and strawberries, blending until smooth. Pour the filling into the cooled crust and bake for 30 minutes. Remove from the oven and cool for about 3 minutes, then spread with sour cream. Refrigerate overnight. Cut into 1-inch squares and top with strawberry halves.
Yields 48 squares or mini-muffins

Citrus Sherbet Punch

1 6-ounce can frozen orange
    juice concentrate
1 6-ounce can frozen
    lemonade concentrate
1 6-ounce can frozen limeade
    concentrate

4 cups very cold water
1 quart ginger ale, chilled
1 gallon pineapple sherbet

Easy • Prep time: 5 minutes • Prepare ahead
Let juices thaw for about 30 minutes, or until slightly thawed. Mix juices, water, and ginger ale in a large container and refrigerate. When serving, place juice in a punch bowl and float large scoops of sherbet on top. As sherbet melts, stir into punch.
Yields 24 servings

SHOPPING LIST

BAKERY
__ 1 loaf whole-wheat bread

BUTCHER
__ 1 pound boneless, skinless chicken breasts
__ ½ pound bacon
__ 1 pound fresh, cooked shrimp

DAIRY
__ 3 8-ounce packages cream cheese
__ 1 pound sharp Cheddar cheese
__ 1 pint heavy cream
__ 2 dozen eggs
__ 2 sticks butter
__ 1 stick unsalted butter
__ ½ pint sour cream

EXTRAS
__ 1 small bottle Grand Marnier

MISCELLANEOUS
__ 2 small jars apricot baby food
__ 1 small jar chutney
__ 1 small package flaked coconut
__ 1 small jar orange marmalade
__ 2 boxes Melba crackers
__ 1 box graham crackers
__ 1 6-ounce package sliced almonds
__ 1 14-ounce bag whole shelled walnut halves
__ 1 6-ounce package chopped pecans
__ 16 ounces fine grade semisweet chocolate
__ 1 32-ounce bottle ginger ale
__ 1 6-ounce can frozen orange juice concentrate
__ 1 6-ounce can frozen lemonade concentrate
__ 1 6-ounce can frozen limeade concentrate
__ 1 gallon pineapple sherbet
__ 1 small container powdered hot chocolate mix

PRODUCE
__ 1 pint fresh strawberries
__ 2 lemons

STAPLES/SPICES
__ All-purpose flour
__ Baking powder
__ Confectioners' sugar
__ Curry powder
__ Garlic salt
__ Ground cinnamon
__ Ground cloves
__ Light corn syrup
__ Mayonnaise
__ Onion powder
__ Salt
__ Self-rising flour
__ Sugar
__ Vanilla extract
__ Vegetable oil

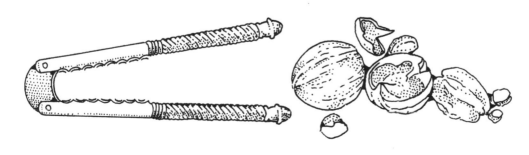
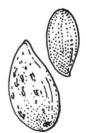

SHRIMP SANDWICHES

BROCCOLI WITH GORGONZOLA DIP

CHEESE TURNOVERS

SCOTTISH SHORTBREAD

PEPPERMINT MERINGUES

RUM CAKE WITH RUM SAUCE

EGGNOG, CHRISTMAS PUNCH, AND VARIETY OF TEAS

SERVES 25

Traditional teas hosted during the holidays don't have to be boring. Combining a few old favorites with some newer offerings makes for a memorable presentation.

Shrimp Sandwiches

2 cups finely diced cooked shrimp
2 tablespoons lemon juice
⅔ cup finely chopped celery

Mayonnaise as needed
Salt and pepper to taste
24 trimmed bread slices, ½ wheat, ½ white

Easy • Prep time: 10 minutes
Sprinkle shrimp with lemon juice. Mix well with celery in a large bowl. Add enough mayonnaise to reach spreading consistency. Add salt and pepper to taste. Spread on bread. Top with slice of opposite flavor, white or wheat, and cut each sandwich into thirds.
Yields about 36 finger sandwiches

Broccoli with Gorgonzola Dip

3 to 4 pounds blanched, chilled broccoli flowerets

Dip
3 cups crumbled white	*3 eggs, at room temperature*
Gorgonzola cheese	*3 egg yolks, at room temperature*
3 tablespoons canola oil	*½ teaspoon salt*
3 tablespoons lemon juice	*Crisp-cooked crumbled*
1 tablespoon lemon zest	*bacon for garnish*

Moderately easy • Prep time: 20 to 25 minutes
Arrange broccoli on a large serving platter, leaving room in the center
for the bowl of dip. Just before serving, combine cheese, oil, lemon
juice, and zest in a blender container. Process to paste consistency.
Add eggs, egg yolks, and salt. Pulse to blend, about 1 minute. Turn the
dip into a serving bowl and sprinkle with crumbled bacon. Serve immediately.
Yields 20 to 25 servings (approximately 3½ cups dip)

Cheese Turnovers

2 jars Old English cheese	*¼ cup cold water*
1 cup butter	*Orange marmalade*
2 cups sifted all-purpose flour	

Easy • Prep time: 15 minutes • Prepare ahead
Preheat the oven to 375°. Cut cheese and butter into flour. Mix with
cold water. Shape into a ball and refrigerate overnight. Roll out the
dough very thin. Cut into 2-inch circles. Put ½ teaspoon of marmalade
in the center of the circles, fold over edges, and mash edges together
with the tines of a fork. Bake for 10 minutes. Cool. Store in covered tins.
Yields 24 turnovers

Scottish Shortbread

  2   *cups butter, softened*
1¼ *cups sugar*
  5   *cups sifted all-purpose flour*

Moderately easy • Prep time: 25 minutes
In a large bowl of an electric mixer, cream butter. Add sugar while creaming. Stir in flour. Mix thoroughly with your hands. Chill. Preheat oven to 375°. Roll out dough between 2 pieces of waxed paper until about ¼-inch thick. Cut with small, fancy cutters. Make designs on tops with the tines of a fork. Place on an ungreased baking sheet and bake for 20 to 25 minutes (cookies will not be brown).
Yields about 48 cookies

Peppermint Meringues

  2 *egg whites*
⅛ *teaspoon salt*
¼ *teaspoon cream of tartar*
¾ *cup sugar*

1 *6-ounce package chocolate chips*
   Peppermint flavoring to taste
   (start with 1 teaspoon)
   Few drops of green food coloring

Moderately easy • Prep time: 30 minutes
Preheat the oven to 350°. Beat egg whites, salt, and cream of tartar until frothy. Gradually add sugar and continue to beat for 15 minutes. Fold in chocolate chips, peppermint flavoring, and green food coloring. Turn off the oven. Put the mixture on ungreased baking sheets by teaspoonfuls and place in the oven for 1½ hours. Do not open the oven door during baking.
Yields 36 meringues

Invite enough people so that you'll have a good crowd. For small parties, two weeks is a standard amount of lead time. For larger parties, consider inviting your guests about a month or so in advance.

Rum Cake with Rum Sauce

1   box yellow cake mix
1   3-ounce package instant
    vanilla pudding
4   eggs

1   cup vegetable oil
1   cup water
1   teaspoon vanilla extract
2   teaspoons rum extract

Easy • Prep time: 12 minutes
Preheat the oven to 350°. In a large bowl of an electric mixer, combine all ingredients and beat for 10 minutes. Pour into a greased tube or bundt cake pan. Bake for 45 minutes. Keep warm and pour Rum Sauce over cake.
Yields 16 servings

Rum Sauce

1   cup sugar
½   cup water

1   teaspoon vanilla extract
2   teaspoons rum extract

In a saucepan, combine sugar and water; boil for 3 minutes. Add flavorings and pour over Rum Cake while cake is still warm.
Yields about ¾ cup sauce

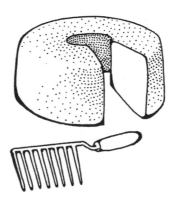

Eggnog

6 large eggs, separated
1 cup sugar, divided
1½ cups bourbon or to taste
1 quart heavy cream
Freshly grated nutmeg
for topping

Easy • Prep time: 20 minutes • Prepare ahead • Keeps in refrigerator for several days • Recipe doubles easily

In a medium mixing bowl, beat egg yolks with ⅔ cup sugar until the mixture is lemon colored. Slowly add bourbon, beating constantly. Beat egg whites with remaining sugar until the mixture is almost stiff. Fold the bourbon mixture into egg whites. Add cream. Grate fresh nutmeg over top.

Yields 20 servings

Christmas Punch

1 large can cranberry juice, chilled
1 quart ginger ale, chilled
1 quart light rum

Easy • Prep time: 2 minutes • Great with an ice ring

In a large punch bowl, combine all ingredients. Serve cold.

Yields 25 servings

SHOPPING LIST _____

_____
_____
_____
_____
_____
_____
_____
_____
_____
_____
_____
_____
_____
_____
_____
_____
_____
_____
_____
_____
_____
_____
_____
_____
_____

BAKERY
__ 1 loaf thinly sliced white bread
__ 1 loaf thinly sliced wheat bread

BUTCHER
__ 1 pound cooked shrimp
__ ½ pound bacon

CANNED GOODS
__ 1 32-ounce can cranberry juice

DAIRY
__ 2 pounds butter
__ 2 dozen eggs
__ 1 quart heavy cream
__ 12 ounces white Gorgonzola
   cheese

EXTRAS
__ 1 quart light rum
__ 1 bottle bourbon

MISCELLANEOUS
__ 2 jars Old English cheese
__ 1 6-ounce package chocolate
   chips
__ 1 small bottle green food coloring
__ 1 32-ounce bottle ginger ale
__ 1 bottle lemon juice
__ 1 bottle peppermint extract
__ 1 bottle rum extract
__ 1 small jar orange marmalade
__ 1 box yellow cake mix
__ 1 3-ounce package instant vanilla
   pudding

PRODUCE
__ 1 stalk celery
__ 4 to 5 pounds fresh broccoli
__ 2 lemons

STAPLES/SPICES
__ All-purpose flour
__ Black pepper
__ Canola oil
__ Cream of tartar
__ Mayonnaise
__ Nutmeg
__ Salt
__ Sugar
__ Vanilla extract
__ Vegetable oil

Three-Way Pizza Party

SEAFOOD AND VEGETABLE LOVERS PIZZA

ROSEMARY, POTATO, AND PROSCIUTTO PIZZA

CLASSIC SAUSAGE AND MUSHROOM COMBO

MIXED GREENS SALAD WITH ITALIAN DRESSING

SOFT DRINKS, RED WINE, AND BEER

SERVES 8 TO 10

Repeat after me: "Pizza's not just for kids." Here is an adult version sure to please your peers' palates. These recipes may even change the way you look at the traditional pie. And they'll certainly keep you from calling your neighborhood pizzeria for delivery.

Seafood and Vegetable Lovers Pizza

4 ounces fresh snow peas
1 yellow summer squash, diced
1 zucchini, diced
1 small onion, chopped
1 clove garlic, minced
1 red bell pepper, diced
1 yellow bell pepper, diced
2 tablespoons butter, melted

½ pound cooked small shrimp
2 teaspoons thyme
  Salt to taste
1 12-inch-diameter baked
  pizza crust (such as Boboli)
1 cup tomato sauce
  Grated Romano cheese
  for topping

Moderately easy • Prep time: 25 to 30 minutes
Preheat the oven to 450°. String snow peas. Sauté vegetables in butter until tender. Pour into a colander to drain liquid. Return vegetables to the pan and mix in shrimp. Add seasonings and stir to blend. Place the pizza crust on a large baking sheet and top with tomato sauce. Spread vegetables and shrimp over sauce, distributing evenly. Sprinkle with cheese. Bake for 8 to 10 minutes.
Yields 6 to 8 servings

Notes

Many people swear by pizza stones, which come in a variety of styles. In reality, any substantial, flat pan will do the trick. And if you don't want to make your own crust, prebaked shells are now common in grocery stores. Or you can use loaves of bread dough from the freezer section.

Rosemary, Potato, and Prosciutto Pizza

2 medium baking potatoes
1 onion, sliced
2 tablespoons olive oil
1 tablespoon rosemary, crushed
¾ cup (6 ounces) basil pesto (homemade or purchased)
1 12-inch-diameter baked pizza crust (such as Boboli)
¼ pound prosciutto, thinly sliced
Grated Parmesan cheese for topping
Crumbled Gorgonzola cheese for topping

Moderately easy • Prep time: 20 to 25 minutes
Microwave or bake potatoes until tender (5 to 6 minutes on high power in the microwave; 1 hour at 375° in the oven). Peel and slice potatoes. Sauté onion in olive oil until limp; add rosemary. Spread pesto on the pizza crust. Top with onions. Layer prosciutto slices and baked potatoes over onions. Sprinkle cheeses over all. Bake at 450° for 8 to 10 minutes.
Yields 6 to 8 servings

Classic Sausage and Mushroom Combo

1 pound fennel sausage, removed from casings
1 onion, chopped
1 pound mushrooms, sliced
Garlic salt to taste
1 cup tomato sauce
1 12-inch-diameter baked pizza crust (such as Boboli)
Shredded Mozzarella cheese

Moderately easy • Prep time: 20 minutes
Preheat the oven to 450°. In a large skillet, cook sausage and onion; drain. Add mushrooms to the skillet and sauté until tender. Return sausage to the skillet and add garlic salt. Mix all ingredients thoroughly. Spread the tomato sauce over the pizza crust. Top with the sausage mixture, distributing evenly. Sprinkle with cheese. Bake on a large baking sheet for 8 to 10 minutes.
Yields 6 to 8 servings

SHOPPING LIST _____

BUTCHER/DELI
__ ½ pound small, cooked shrimp
__ 1 pound fennel sausage
__ ¼ pound prosciutto

CANNED GOODS
__ 1 16-ounce can tomato sauce

DAIRY
__ 1 stick butter
__ 4 ounces Romano cheese
__ 1 4-ounce block Parmesan cheese
__ 4 ounces Gorgonzola cheese
__ 8 ounces Mozzarella cheese

EXTRAS
__ ½ case red wine
__ 1 case beer

MISCELLANEOUS
__ 3 six-packs assorted soft drinks
__ 3 12- to 14-inch precooked pizza
    crusts or focaccia rounds
__ 1 small jar basil pesto
__ 1 bottle Italian salad dressing

PRODUCE
__ Mixed salad greens
__ 4 ounces fresh snow peas
__ 1 yellow summer squash
__ 1 zucchini
__ 3 small onions
__ 1 head garlic
__ 1 red bell pepper
__ 1 yellow bell pepper
__ 1 small bunch fresh thyme
__ 2 medium baking potatoes
__ 1 pound mushrooms

STAPLES/SPICES
__ Dried rosemary
__ Garlic salt
__ Olive oil
__ Salt

THE BASIC PANTRY

Staples
Baking powder
Baking soda
Bread crumbs
Broths, chicken and beef
Chocolate, unsweetened squares,
     semi-sweet morsels
Cocoa, unsweetened
Coconut, shredded (can)
Coffee, beans
Cornstarch
Cream of tartar
Dried fruits: raisins, dates
Extracts: almond, butter, coconut,
     lemon, orange, rum, vanilla
Flour: all-purpose, cake self-rising
Gelatin: powdered and unflavored
Honey
Horseradish
Ketchup
Milk, sweetened condensed,
     evaporated
Meal, white and yellow cornmeal
Mustards, prepared, Dijon
Nuts, pecans, walnuts
Oils, olive, vegetable, safflower,
     canola

Olives, green, black
Pasta, dried: spaghetti, fettucine,
     angel hair, macaroni, penne
Peanut butter
Pickles
Preserves and jellies
Rice, white, long-grain
Soy sauce
Sugars, granulated, confectioners',
     light and dark brown
Syrups, light and dark molasses
Tabasco sauce
Teas, assorted flavors
Tomatoes, whole canned
Tomato sauce
Tomato paste
Vinegars, white wine, red wine,
     cider, balsamic
Rice wine
Worcestershire sauce
Yeast, dry packages

Dry Herbs and Spices
Allspice
Basil
Bay leaves
Curry seeds

Chili powder
Cinnamon, ground and stick
Cloves, ground and whole
Cumin
Curry powder
Dill
Fennel seeds
Ginger, ground and crystallized
Marjoram
Mint
Mustard seeds
Nutmeg, ground and whole
Oregano
Paprika
Pepper, cayenne, dried red flakes,
     hot pepper sauce, ground black
Peppercorns
Pickling spices
Poppy seeds
Rosemary
Sage
Salt, table and kosher
Sesame seeds
Tarragon
Thyme
Turmeric

EVENING

Nothing winds down a busy day—or a hectic week—like a good meal. Whether it's eaten surrounded by friends, joined by family, or in the solitude of one's own company, dinner is often the most appreciated meal of the day. The after five o'clock menus showcased here range from cocktails to late night overtures.

Cocktail parties, to some an anathema to others nirvana, provide great opportunities for socializing, as well as eating and drinking. Keep the number of guests within reason and sprinkle the crowd with new faces.

When something a little more formal is the order of the evening, be sure to invite no more guests than you can seat comfortably. Allow about one foot between each place setting to give your guests adequate elbow room. Set the table early, preferably the day before, so there are no last-minute crises regarding tarnished silver or soiled napkins.

With any party, from casual to elegant, careful planning is the key to success. Prepare ahead of time and freeze as much food as possible. Organize your courses and service.

When organizing a buffet, remember to have a steady surface from which to serve. Provide lap trays, or individual groupings of tables, for your guests.

Don't forget hearty cookouts and light late-night meals as avenues for entertaining your friends and family with flair and taste.

After Caroling Warm-Up Supper

"Beautiful soup! Who cares for fish, game, or any other dish? Who could not give all else for two pennyworth only of beautiful soup?"—LEWIS CARROLL

Notes

_____
_____
_____
_____
_____
_____
_____
_____
_____
_____
_____
_____
_____
_____
_____
_____
_____
_____
_____
_____
_____
_____
_____

BLACK BEAN SOUP

SPEDINI

NUTTY COLESLAW

WARM BANANA MOUSSE

COFFEE WITH CINNAMON SCHNAAPS

SERVES 8

The act of serenading your neighbors with carols seems to have fallen by the wayside. Why not resurrect this lovely tradition during the next holiday season? Afterwards you can serve this festive menu.

Black Bean Soup

1 pound dried black beans	2 cups or less hot chicken broth
2 quarts water	2 tablespoons lemon juice
½ pound salt pork or ham hocks	Salt and pepper to taste
1 yellow onion, quartered	2 tablespoons sherry, optional
¼ cup chopped fresh parsley	8 lemon slices studded with cloves for garnish
4 whole cloves	Sour cream, optional
2 teaspoons Worcestershire sauce	

Easy • Prep time: 15 minutes • Can prepare ahead
In a large pot, combine the first 7 ingredients. Simmer over low heat until tender (about 3 hours). Remove meat and cloves. Dice meat to return to soup later. Purée soup in a blender at low speed; add chicken stock, if thinner soup is desired, and return to the heat. Add remaining seasonings, sherry, and meat. Serve hot, garnished with lemon slices and sour cream, if desired.
Yields 8 to 10 servings

Spedini

2	20-inch loaves French bread	2	tablespoons poppy seeds
½	cup chopped yellow onion	1	pound Swiss cheese, sliced
½	cup butter	16	slices bacon
¼	cup prepared mustard		

Easy • Prep time: 10 minutes • Prepare ahead and freeze
Slice each loaf of bread at 1-inch intervals almost, but not quite, through the bottom crust. Sauté onion in butter; add mustard and poppy seeds. Spoon the mixture into cuts in loaves. Insert slices of Swiss cheese. Arrange bacon over tops of loaves, which may be wrapped and frozen at this point. Preheat the oven to 350°. Bake, uncovered, for 10 to 15 minutes (if frozen, 30 minutes), or until cheese melts and bacon is crisp.
Yields 2 loaves of 14 slices per loaf

Nutty Coleslaw

Dressing

¾	cup mayonnaise	3	tablespoons heavy cream
3	tablespoons lemon juice	1	teaspoon curry powder

Coleslaw

1	medium cabbage, grated	½	15-ounce box golden raisins
½	pound carrots, grated	½	cup salted peanuts

Easy • Prep time: 15 minutes • Prepare dressing ahead of time
The day before serving, combine the dressing ingredients; cover and refrigerate. Combine the coleslaw ingredients and mix with enough dressing to moisten. Serve immediately or slaw will become soggy.
Yields 8 servings

On a rainy day or during a free evening, prepare dishes that can be frozen for later use.

Warm Banana Mousse

3	eggs	3	ripe bananas, mashed
1	cup sugar	1 ½	cups heavy cream,
½	cup light cream, warmed		stiffly beaten
	to room temperature		Vanilla wafers
1	teaspoon vanilla extract		

Moderate • Prep time: 25 minutes (including cooking time)
In the top of a double boiler over hot water (not boiling), beat eggs and sugar until frothy and pale yellow. Beat in light cream and vanilla. Beat in bananas. Allow the mixture to cool slightly and serve with whipped cream and vanilla wafers.
Yields 8 to 12 servings

SHOPPING LIST

BAKERY
__ 2 20-inch loaves French bread

BUTCHER
__ ½ pound bacon
__ ½ pound salt pork or ham hocks

CANNED GOODS
__ 1 16-ounce can chicken broth

DAIRY
__ 1 stick butter
__ 1 pint heavy cream
__ ½ pint light cream
__ 1 pound sliced Swiss cheese
__ ½ dozen eggs
__ 1 8-ounce container sour cream
 (optional)

EXTRAS
__ 1 small bottle sherry
__ 1 small bottle cinnamon
 schnaaps

MISCELLANEOUS
__ 1 16-ounce package dried black
 beans
__ 1 15-ounce box golden raisins
__ 1 small container salted peanuts
__ 1 box vanilla wafers

PRODUCE
__ 3 ripe bananas
__ 1 medium head cabbage
__ ½ pound carrots
__ 2 yellow onions
__ 1 bunch fresh parsley
__ 3 large lemons

STAPLES/SPICES
__ Coffee
__ Curry powder
__ Mayonnaise
__ Pepper
__ Poppy seeds
__ Prepared mustard
__ Salt
__ Sugar
__ Vanilla extract
__ Whole cloves
__ Worcestershire sauce

Poolside Cocktail Party

PARTY CHEESE TRAY

SAUCY MEATBALLS

FRESH FRUIT WITH DIPPING SAUCES

CRUDITÉ PLATTER

NINE-LAYER DIP

CHOCOLATE DELIGHTS

LEMON-GLAZED PECAN BARS

BEER AND SOFT DRINKS

SERVES 25

An elegant, yet casual, cocktail party is a great way to host a big crowd. The next time your entertaining needs call for more than twenty people, consider this menu, which includes both substantial and light offerings.

Party Cheese Tray

1	½-pound wedge Jarlsberg cheese	1	½-pound wedge Brie cheese
1	½-pound wedge Gouda cheese		Assorted crackers
			Approximately 50 thin breadsticks

Easy • Prep time: 15 minutes
Arrange the cheeses, crackers, and breadsticks attractively on a tray.
Yields 25 servings

Saucy Meatballs

Meatballs

2	pounds ground chuck	2	teaspoons salt
1	pound ground hot sausage	½	teaspoon pepper
½	cup chopped onion	1	tablespoon soy sauce
½	cup chopped green bell pepper	2	tablespoons Worcestershire sauce
3	eggs, lightly beaten		
1	package herb-seasoned stuffing mix		

Sauce

1	cup chopped onion	¼	cup Worcestershire sauce
1	cup chopped green bell pepper		Garlic salt to taste
¼	cup butter, melted	1	cup firmly packed brown sugar
4½	cups ketchup	2	tablespoons white vinegar
2	tablespoons mustard		

Easy • Prep time: 20 minutes • Prepare ahead and freeze

Prepare the meatballs by mixing the first 10 ingredients together in a large bowl. Shape into balls and brown in a skillet. Drain. Meatballs can now be frozen for later use.

To prepare the sauce: Sauté onion and green pepper in butter until tender. Add the remaining ingredients; simmer for 20 to 25 minutes. Add meatballs to sauce; simmer for an additional 20 minutes.

Yields 25 servings

Fresh Fruit with Dipping Sauces

1 quart fresh strawberries, rinsed and stems removed

1 large pineapple, peeled and cut into 1-inch cubes

1½ pounds seedless grapes

6 bananas, peeled, cut into disks, and tossed with 3 tablespoons lemon juice

4 Granny Smith apples, cored and sliced

4 Red Delicious apples, cored and sliced

Have plenty of colorful toothpicks on hand for meatballs and for dipping fruit into sauces.

Citrus Yogurt Dip

1 pint vanilla yogurt, drained of most excess liquid

1 tablespoon freshly grated orange zest

3 tablespoons fresh orange juice

1 teaspoon lemon juice

Easy • Prep time: 5 minutes
Combine all ingredients and chill until ready to serve.
Yields 2 cups dip

Chocolate Amaretto Dip

2 tablespoons amaretto or

2 teaspoons almond extract

16 ounces chocolate syrup

Easy • Prep time: 5 minutes
Mix well and serve with fruit.
Yields 2 cups dip

Nine-Layer Dip

4	ripe avocados	4	16-ounce cans refried beans
	Juice of 1 large lemon	4	tomatoes, chopped
½	teaspoon salt	3	cups shredded lettuce
¼	teaspoon pepper	1	4½-ounce can black olives,
2	cups sour cream		chopped
2	1.25-ounce packages taco	1	pound Cheddar cheese, grated
	seasoning mix		Tortilla chips

Easy • Prep time: 20 minutes

Peel, pit, and mash avocados with lemon juice, salt, and pepper. Combine sour cream and taco seasoning mix. To assemble, spread beans on 2 large shallow serving platters; spread the seasoned avocado mixture over beans; spread the sour cream mixture over the avocado mixture. Sprinkle tomatoes, lettuce, and olives over all. Cover with grated cheese. Serve chilled or at room temperature with tortilla chips.

Yields 25 servings

Chocolate Delights

16	ounces semisweet chocolate	2	teaspoons salt
¾	cup butter	2	cups chopped pecans
8	eggs	12	ounces cream cheese, softened
3	cups sugar	½	cup butter, softened
1	tablespoon vanilla extract	1	cup sugar
½	teaspoon almond extract	4	eggs
2	cups all-purpose flour	2	teaspoons vanilla extract
2	teaspoons baking powder	¼	cup all-purpose flour

Moderately easy • Prep time: 30 minutes

Preheat the oven to 350°. Melt chocolate and butter in the top of a double boiler. In a large bowl, beat eggs. Gradually add sugar to eggs until the mixture is thick and light in color. Blend in the chocolate mixture. Add vanilla and almond extracts. Combine flour, baking powder, and salt and stir into the chocolate mixture. Stir in nuts.

To prepare the cream cheese filling: Blend cream cheese and butter; add sugar and mix well. Add eggs one at a time, beating well after each addition. Add vanilla and stir in flour.

Grease two 9x13-inch baking pans. Divide the chocolate mixture between pans, reserving 4 cups for the top layer. Spread the cream cheese mixture evenly between the pans. Top each with 2 cups of the chocolate mixture and marble. Bake for 30 minutes, or until a tester comes out clean.

Yields 8 dozen cookies

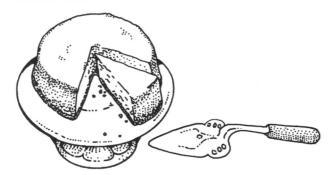

Lemon-Glazed Pecan Bars

1½	cups all-purpose flour	1½	cups flaked coconut
½	cup butter, softened to room temperature	1½	cups chopped pecans
1½	cups brown sugar, divided	½	teaspoon baking powder
2	eggs, beaten	¼	teaspoon salt
2	tablespoons all-purpose flour	½	teaspoon vanilla extract
		1	cup confectioners' sugar
			Juice of 1 large lemon

Moderately easy • Prep time: 20 minutes

Preheat the oven to 275°. Combine 1½ cups flour, butter, and ½ cup brown sugar and press into a 9x13x2-inch glass casserole dish. Bake for 8 to 10 minutes. Cool. Turn the oven temperature to 350°. Combine eggs and 1 cup brown sugar; mix well. Set aside. Combine 2 tablespoons flour, coconut, nuts, baking powder, and salt. Mix well with the egg and brown sugar mixture; stir in vanilla. Spread over the cooled crust. Bake for 18 to 20 minutes. Combine the remaining ingredients and drizzle over the top while hot. Cut into bars when cool.

Yields 54 bars (1x2 inches)

SHOPPING LIST

BAKERY
__ Approximately 50 thin
   breadsticks

CANNED GOODS
__ 4 16-ounce cans refried beans
__ 1 4½-ounce can black olives
__ 1 7-ounce can flaked coconut

BUTCHER
__ 2 pounds ground chuck
__ 1 pound ground hot pork
   sausage

DAIRY
__ 2 dozen eggs
__ 1 pound butter
__ 1 pint lowfat vanilla yogurt
__ 1 16-ounce container sour cream
__ 2 8-ounce packages cream
   cheese
__ 1 pound sharp Cheddar cheese
__ ½ pound wedge Jarlsberg
   cheese
__ ½ pound wedge Gouda
__ ½ pound wedge Brie

EXTRAS
__ 2 or 3 cases beer
__ 1 small bottle amaretto
__ Toothpicks

MISCELLANEOUS
__ 2 or 3 cases soft drinks
__ 1 16-ounce container chocolate
   syrup
__ 2 or 3 boxes assorted crackers
__ 1 8-ounce package herb-
   seasoned stuffing mix
__ 16 ounces semisweet chocolate
__ 2 1.25-ounce packages taco
   seasoning mix
__ 1 large bag tortilla chips
__ 1 16-ounce bag pecan pieces

PRODUCE
__ 1 stalk celery
__ 1 bag carrots
__ 3 or 4 red, yellow, and orange bell
   peppers
__ 2 green bell peppers
__ 1 head cauliflower
__ 1 bunch broccoli
__ 1 quart cherry tomatoes
__ 4 yellow squash
__ 2 onions
__ 1 quart fresh strawberries
__ 1 large pineapple
__ 1½ pounds seedless grapes
__ 6 bananas
__ 4 Granny Smith apples
__ 4 Red Delicious apples
__ 4 large lemons
__ 1 large naval orange
__ 1 head lettuce
__ 4 large tomatoes
__ 4 ripe avocados

STAPLES/SPICES
__ All-purpose flour
__ Almond extract
__ Baking powder
__ Brown sugar
__ Confectioners' sugar
__ Garlic salt
__ Ketchup
__ Pepper
__ Prepared mustard
__ Salt
__ Soy sauce
__ Sugar
__ Vanilla extract
__ White vinegar
__ Worcestershire sauce

Cold Buffet Dinner

VICHYSSOISE

SALMON MOUSSE WITH CUCUMBER DILL SAUCE

SLICED VIRGINIA HAM

CROISSANTS

SOUR CREAM COCONUT CAKE

CHARDONNAY

SERVES 8

You don't need hot foods to call it dinner! Here you find a variety of good foods that are served cold or at room temperature. Try these recipes the next time you find yourself dreading the phrase, "slaving over a hot stove."

Vichyssoise is a thick, creamy potato soup flavored with leeks and onions. The soup, usually served cold, was created in the United States by a French chef from the Bourbonnais. *Vichyssoise* also applies to any cold soup based on potatoes and another vegetable.

Vichyssoise

3 to 4	cups peeled, diced potatoes	1	tablespoon salt, plus additional
2	large yellow onions, thinly sliced	1	cup heavy cream
1	quart water		Fresh chives

Moderately easy • Prep time: 30 minutes • Prepare a day before serving
In a large pot, simmer vegetables, water, and salt together until tender, about 50 to 60 minutes. Strain, reserving liquid, and purée the vegetables in the blender. Add half of the reserved liquid to the puréed vegetables. Stir in heavy cream, over-salt slightly, and chill.
Yields 8 servings

Salmon Mousse with Cucumber Dill Sauce

6	tablespoons all-purpose flour	3	cups milk
6	tablespoons confectioners' sugar	1	cup tarragon vinegar
¼	cup Dijon mustard	6	tablespoons butter, melted
1	tablespoon salt	4	envelopes unflavored gelatin
8	eggs, lightly beaten	½	cup cold water
		6	cups flaked salmon
		2	cups heavy cream, whipped

Moderate • Prep time: 20 minutes • Prepare ahead

Mix flour, sugar, mustard, and salt in the top of a double boiler. Add eggs and whisk until smooth. Add milk. Stir in vinegar slowly, or the mixture will curdle. Mix well. Cook over hot water until thickened, stirring constantly. Add butter. Soften gelatin in cold water; add to the hot mixture. Stir until gelatin is completely dissolved. Add salmon. Mix well. Chill. Stir occasionally. When slightly thickened, fold in whipped cream. Spray two 2-quart fish molds or one very large mold with vegetable cooking spray and pour in the mixture. Chill until firm. Serve with Cucumber Dill Sauce.

Yields 16 servings

Cucumber Dill Sauce

2	medium cucumbers, peeled and seeded	1	teaspoon dill weed
	Salt	1	teaspoon chopped chives
2	tablespoons lemon juice or tarragon vinegar	½	teaspoon white pepper
		2	cups sour cream

Easy • Prep time: 10 minutes • Prepare ahead

Shred cucumber with a coarse grater. Sprinkle with salt and let stand at room temperature for 60 minutes. Drain thoroughly. Combine with remaining ingredients. Chill until ready to serve.

Yields 16 servings

Sour Cream Coconut Cake

2 cups sour cream	½ cup crushed pineapple, drained
2 cups sugar	
2 7-ounce packages flaked coconut	1 box yellow cake mix

Easy • Prep time: 15 minutes • Prepare ahead

The day before baking the cake, combine sour cream, sugar, coconut, and pineapple and let stand in the refrigerator overnight. Bake cake according to the package directions, using two 9-inch round cake pans. When ready to serve, slice the 2 layers of cake in half, making 4 thin layers. Use the sour cream mixture to frost between layers and on top. Keep refrigerated until ready to serve.

Yields 1 cake of 16 slices

SHOPPING LIST

BAKERY

__ 8 to 12 fresh croissants

BUTCHER/DELI

__ 3 pounds cooked salmon (fresh or canned)

__ 2 pounds thinly sliced ham

CANNED GOODS

__ 1 20-ounce can crushed pineapple

DAIRY

__ 1½ pints heavy cream

__ 1 quart milk

__ 2 16-ounce containers sour cream

__ 1 dozen eggs

__ 1 stick butter

EXTRAS

__ 4 bottles chardonnay

MISCELLANEOUS

__ 1 bottle tarragon vinegar

__ 1 box yellow cake mix

__ 2 boxes unflavored gelatin

__ 2 7-ounce packages flaked coconut

__ 1 small jar Dijon mustard

PRODUCE

__ 1 small bag baking potatoes

__ 2 large yellow onions

__ 1 bunch fresh chives

__ 2 medium cucumbers

__ 1 large lemon

STAPLES

__ All-purpose flour

__ Confectioners' sugar

__ Dill weed

__ Salt

__ Sugar

__ Vegetable oil

__ White pepper

Oscar Night Buffet Supper

COCKTAIL SHRIMP

MARINATED FRESH MUSHROOMS

HOT ARTICHOKE DIP

HERB CRUSTED PORK

ASSORTED ROLLS AND CONDIMENTS

PECAN PUFFS

TRIFLE

COFFEE AND CHAMPAGNE

SERVES 8

Nothing brings out the stars like the Academy Awards. If your invitation to the Oscars is lost in the mail, serve this celebratory menu to the stars in your life while watching the awards show on television.

Cocktail Shrimp

4 lemons	2 cups ketchup
1 bay leaf	¼ cup prepared horseradish
1 tablespoon peppercorns	2 tablespoons Worcestershire sauce
2 tablespoons cider vinegar	¼ cup lemon juice
4 pounds raw, unpeeled shrimp	1 tablespoon capers, optional

Easy • Prep time: 30 minutes

Fill a large stock pot with 4 quarts of water and place over high heat. Cut the lemons in half and squeeze the juice into the water. Drop the lemon halves into the water. Add the bay leaf, peppercorns, and vinegar, and bring the mixture to a boil. Carefully drop shrimp into the water and return to a boil. Shrimp are finished cooking when they float. Drain and chill until ready to serve.

Combine the remaining ingredients to form a dipping sauce. Serve shrimp over ice with the sauce available on the side.

Yields 10 servings

Marinated Fresh Mushrooms

1	pound fresh mushrooms	1	teaspoon chopped parsley
¾	cup olive oil	1	teaspoon chopped chives
3	tablespoons tarragon vinegar	½	teaspoon dried tarragon,
½	teaspoon salt		crushed

Easy • Prep time: 10 minutes • Prepare ahead

Wash mushrooms and trim off ends. Slice lengthwise into 2 or 3 pieces, depending on size of mushrooms. Combine all ingredients in a bowl. Mix well. Marinate for at least 3 hours, or overnight.

Yields 10 to 12 servings

Hot Artichoke Dip

1	14-ounce can artichoke hearts, drained and chopped	½	teaspoon Worcestershire sauce
⅛	teaspoon garlic powder	1	cup grated Parmesan cheese
¾	cup mayonnaise		Freshly ground pepper to taste
			Chips and peppered crackers

Easy • Prep time: 5 minutes • Prepare ahead

Combine all ingredients and put in a casserole dish that can be transferred to a chafing dish. Refrigerate until ready to serve. Preheat the oven to 350°. Bake for 20 to 25 minutes. Keep warm in a chafing dish. Serve with large chips and peppered wafers.

Yields 6 to 8 servings

Draw up ballots so your guests can vote on the winners. Have silly prizes for each category.

Herb Crusted Pork

1 5- to 6-pound pork loin
   roast
1 tablespoon garlic salt
1 tablespoon black pepper
½ tablespoon rubbed sage
2 tablespoons Worcestershire
   sauce
½ tablespoon paprika

2 tablespoons dried basil
1 tablespoon dried oregano
1 tablespoon crushed dried
   rosemary leaves
½ tablespoon red pepper flakes,
   optional
½ lemon

Moderate • Prep time: 25 minutes

Preheat the oven to 325°. Carefully rinse pork and pat dry with paper towels. Briskly rub garlic salt all over tenderloin, working it in thoroughly. Repeat, one at a time, with remaining ingredients. Place tenderloin in a baking dish and squeeze lemon over the top. Cover with aluminum foil and bake for 2½ to 3½ hours, or until the internal temperature reaches 170°. Remove the foil for the last 10 to 15 minutes of baking. Allow the meat to sit for 15 minutes before slicing.

Yields 10 to 12 servings

Pecan Puffs

½ cup butter, melted
1 cup all-purpose flour
2 tablespoons sugar

1 teaspoon vanilla extract
1 cup chopped pecans
   Confectioners' sugar

Easy • Prep time: 10 minutes

Preheat the oven to 350°. In a bowl, combine all ingredients, except confectioners' sugar, and shape into quarter-size balls. Bake for 20 to 25 minutes. Remove from the oven, cool slightly, and roll in sifted confectioners' sugar.

Yields 24 puffs

Trifle

1 sponge cake (storebought), cut or torn into 1-inch pieces
2 tablespoons amaretto or Grand Marnier
3 cups prepared vanilla pudding
2 cups diced strawberries, peaches, blueberries, and/or kiwi
½ 10-ounce carton whipped topping or ½ cup heavy cream whipped with 1 tablespoon sugar and ½ teaspoon vanilla extract

Easy • Prep time: 30 minutes (10 minutes if you don't make your pudding) • Prepare ahead

Arrange half of the cake cubes in the bottom of a trifle dish. Sprinkle 1 tablespoon liqueur over the cake. Spread half of the pudding over the cake. Layer half of the fruit over the pudding. Repeat the layers and top with whipped cream. Cover and chill for at least 1 hour before serving.
Yields 10 servings

SHOPPING LIST _____

BAKERY
__ Assorted rolls
__ 1 sponge cake

BUTCHER
__ 4 pounds raw shrimp
__ 1 5- to 6-pound pork loin roast

CANNED GOODS
__ 1 14-ounce can artichoke hearts

DAIRY
__ 1 6-ounce block Parmesan cheese
__ 1 10-ounce container whipped topping
__ 2 sticks butter

EXTRAS
__ 1 case champagne
__ 1 small bottle amaretto or Grand Marnier

MISCELLANEOUS
__ 1 small jar Dijon mustard
__ 1 small jar prepared horseradish
__ 1 small bottle lime juice
__ 1 small jar capers (optional)
__ 1 bottle tarragon vinegar
__ 1 bag chips
__ 1 box peppered crackers
__ 2 3½-ounce boxes instant vanilla pudding
__ 1 small package chopped pecans

PRODUCE
__ 5 lemons
__ 1 pound fresh mushrooms
__ 1 bunch fresh chives
__ 1 bunch fresh parsley
__ Strawberries, peaches, blueberries, and/or kiwi

STAPLES/SPICES
__ All-purpose flour
__ Bay leaf
__ Black pepper
__ Cider vinegar
__ Coffee
__ Confectioners' sugar
__ Dried basil
__ Dried oregano
__ Dried rosemary leaves
__ Dried tarragon
__ Garlic powder
__ Garlic salt
__ Ketchup
__ Mayonnaise
__ Olive oil
__ Paprika
__ Peppercorns
__ Red pepper flakes (optional)
__ Rubbed sage
__ Salt
__ Sugar
__ Vanilla extract
__ Worcestershire sauce

CANTALOUPE WRAPS

SHRIMP AND CRAB RAREBIT

CHEESE POPPY SEED BREAD

BROCCOLI TOSSED WITH LEMON BUTTER

ORANGES IN RED WINE OVER ICE CREAM

CHARDONNAY OR SAUVIGNON BLANC

SERVES 8 TO 10

A night at the opera or symphony can be made all the more elegant and enjoyable with a classy dinner such as the one showcased here. Invite friends who share your love of music, and let the good times roll.

Cantaloupe Wraps

1   medium cantaloupe
20   1x4-inch slices prosciutto
1   lemon

1   lime
    Toothpicks

Easy • Prep time: 20 minutes

Cut cantaloupe in half and clean out seeds. Cut each half into 1-inch thick crescents and peel off the rind. Reserve 10 crescents and use the remainder of the melon for another meal. Cut each of the 10 crescents in half crosswise to form 20 smaller crescents. Squeeze a touch of lemon juice over 10 crescents and a touch of lime juice over the remaining 10 crescents. Peel 10 two-inch slivers of zest from each citrus fruit. Place a sliver of lime zest on top of the crescents flavored with lime juice and lemon zest on those crescents flavored with lemon juice. Wrap a strip of prosciutto around each crescent and secure, puncturing the zest strip, with a toothpick. Arrange on a serving platter with slices of lemon and lime. Serve chilled.

Yields 20 appetizers

Notes

Rarebit is a popular British dish that consists of a melted mixture of Cheddar cheese, beer (sometimes ale or milk), and seasonings served over toast. The cheese mixture can also be toasted on the bread. Because of its British connection, the dish is often referred to as Welsh rarebit or Welsh rabbit.

Shrimp and Crab Rarebit

2 pounds cooked and peeled shrimp, kept warm
2 pounds cooked crab meat, kept warm
1 teaspoon pepper
1 teaspoon garlic salt
1 tablespoon dried, crushed basil
10 thick slices Cheese Poppy Seed Bread, toasted Rarebit Sauce

Moderate • Prep time: 30 minutes

Toss the shrimp and crab with seasonings. Mound the seafood on the bread and pour the sauce over top. Serve immediately.

Yields 10 servings

Rarebit Sauce

3 cups grated sharp Cheddar cheese
1 cup milk
¼ cup light cream
1 tablespoon dry white wine
1½ teaspoons dry mustard
1 teaspoon Worcestershire sauce
1 teaspoon paprika
1 egg, beaten

Combine cheese, milk, cream, wine, mustard, Worcestershire, and paprika in a heavy saucepan over low heat. Stir constantly until cheese melts. Slowly stir about half of the cheese mixture into the egg, then add all to the remaining cheese mixture. Cook and stir over low heat until the sauce thickens. Serve immediately over shrimp and crab.

Yields about 2½ cups sauce

Cheese Poppy Seed Bread

½ cup shortening
2 eggs, beaten
1 cup milk
3 cups biscuit mix (such
    as Bisquick)

2 cups shredded Cheddar
    cheese
2 tablespoons poppy seeds
2 tablespoons minced onions

Easy • Prep time: 15 minutes • Prepare ahead and freeze
Preheat the oven to 375°. In a small saucepan, melt shortening. In a large
bowl, combine eggs, milk, and melted shortening to biscuit mix. Stir in
cheese, poppy seeds, and onion. Mix until the dry ingredients are moistened. Grease and flour two 9x5x3-inch loaf pans. Divide and spread the
dough into the pans. Bake for 25 to 30 minutes, or until browned.
Yields 2 loaves

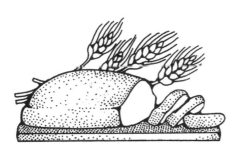

Broccoli Tossed with Lemon Butter

2 10-ounce packages frozen broccoli spears
2 teaspoons lemon juice
¼ cup butter, melted

Easy • Prep time: 10 minutes
Cook broccoli according to the package directions. Stir lemon juice
into butter. Toss with broccoli and serve.
Yields 10 servings

Play some of the music you'll hear at the evening's performance during dinner. Choose selections from the same composers to set the mood.

Oranges in Red Wine over Ice Cream

2	cups water		2	cinnamon sticks
1½	cups sugar		8	lemon slices
2	cups red wine		12	oranges, sectioned
4	whole cloves		1	quart vanilla bean
2	vanilla beans			ice cream

Easy • Prep time: 5 minutes

In a large saucepan, combine water and sugar; bring to a boil. Add red wine, cloves, vanilla beans, cinnamon sticks, and lemon slices. Boil for 20 minutes. Strain and pour the liquid over sections of fruit. Serve immediately as a sauce over ice cream.

Yields 8 to 12 servings

SHOPPING LIST

BUTCHER/DELI
__ ¼ to ½ pound sliced prosciutto
__ 2 pounds cooked and peeled shrimp
__ 2 pounds cooked lump crab meat

DAIRY
__ 20 ounces sharp Cheddar cheese
__ 1 pint milk
__ ½ pint light cream
__ ½ dozen eggs
__ 1 stick butter
__ 1 quart vanilla bean ice cream

EXTRAS
__ 1 case chardonnay or sauvignon blanc
__ 1 bottle red wine
__ Toothpicks

MISCELLANEOUS
__ 1 box biscuit mix
__ 2 10-ounce packages frozen broccoli spears

PRODUCE
__ 1 medium cantaloupe
__ 3 lemons
__ 1 lime
__ 12 oranges
__ 1 small onion

STAPLES/SPICES
__ Cinnamon sticks
__ Dried basil
__ Dry mustard
__ Garlic salt
__ Paprika
__ Pepper
__ Poppy seeds
__ Shortening
__ Sugar
__ Vanilla beans
__ Whole cloves
__ Worcestershire sauce

CHICKEN AND BISCUIT PIE

VEGETABLE MEDLEY SALAD

PEACH MELBA

TEA PUNCH

S E R V E S 6

When you need to create dinner in a hurry, here are
four no-fuss recipes to consider. Now there's no need
to lose your cool when you find you have
to feed six in a flash.

Chicken and Biscuit Pie

1   medium onion, chopped
2   tablespoons melted butter
2   tablespoons all-purpose flour
1   10½-ounce can cream of
     chicken soup, undiluted
1   10½-ounce can chicken
     noodle soup, undiluted

2   cups cooked, chopped chicken
¼   teaspoon salt
¼   teaspoon pepper
1   teaspoon poultry seasoning
1   8- to 10-ounce can
     refrigerated biscuits

Easy • Prep time: 5 minutes • Prepare ahead • Can freeze
Preheat the oven to 400°. Sauté onion in butter; blend in flour and stir
until frothy. Add soups; heat until thickened. Add chicken and seasonings. Mix well. Heat thoroughly. Pour into a greased 3-quart casserole
dish. Arrange biscuits on top. Bake for 10 to 12 minutes, or until biscuits are brown.
Yields 6 servings

Vegetable Medley Salad

1 cup cooked green peas
1 cup cooked diced carrots
1 cup cooked, chopped
   cauliflower
1 cup diced red bell peppers,
   steamed
¼ cup Italian dressing
   Romaine lettuce, for serving

Easy • Prep time: 10 minutes
In a large bowl, combine the first 5 ingredients. Serve on lettuce leaves.
Yields 6 servings

Peach Melba

1 10-ounce package frozen
   raspberries, thawed
   and drained
3 tablespoons sugar
6 cups vanilla ice cream
1 29-ounce can peach halves,
   drained
   Whipped cream

Easy • Prep time: 10 minutes
Purée raspberries and sugar in a blender. Spoon ice cream into dessert cups. Top each portion with a peach half. Cover with raspberry purée. Garnish with whipped cream.
Yields 6 servings

Tea Punch

7	individual tea bags
2	cups sugar
2	6-ounce cans frozen orange juice concentrate
2	6-ounce cans frozen lemonade concentrate

Water (to make a gallon)
Sprigs of fresh mint
1   cup pineapple juice (optional)

Easy • Prep time: 10 minutes • Prepare ahead
Brew tea according to the package directions. Mix the other ingredients in a gallon jug. Add brewed tea and enough water to make a gallon. Refrigerate until ready to serve. Garnish each glass with fresh mint.
Yields 1 gallon

SHOPPING LIST

BUTCHER
__ 1 pound boneless, skinless chicken breast

CANNED GOODS
__ 1 10½-ounce can cream of chicken soup
__ 1 10½-ounce can chicken noodle soup
__ 1 16-ounce can green peas
__ 1 29-ounce can peach halves

DAIRY
__ 1 stick butter
__ ½ gallon vanilla ice cream
__ ½ pint whipping cream

MISCELLANEOUS
__ 1 8- to 10-ounce can refrigerated biscuits
__ 1 small bottle Italian salad dressing
__ 1 10-ounce package frozen raspberries
__ 2 6-ounce containers frozen orange juice concentrate
__ 2 6-ounce containers frozen lemonade concentrate

PRODUCE
__ 1 medium onion
__ 1 bag carrots
__ 1 head cauliflower
__ 2 red bell peppers
__ 1 bunch fresh mint
__ Romaine lettuce

STAPLES/SPICES
__ All purpose flour
__ Pepper
__ Poultry seasoning
__ Salt
__ Sugar
__ Tea bags
__ Vanilla extract

MINT

Porch Supper

HOT SHRIMP COCKTAIL

BARBECUE RIBEYE

MUSHROOM AND TOMATO SALAD

WHITE SQUASH CASSEROLE

FRENCH BAGUETTES

CHOCOLATE POTS DE CRÈME

COFFEE AND BEAUJOLAIS

SERVES 12

Your porch, deck, or veranda provides the perfect backdrop for casual dining. This menu offers a little bit of everything, sure to please each of your guests.

Hot Shrimp Cocktail

¾	cup lemon juice	½	teaspoon Tabasco sauce
2	tablespoons white vinegar	2	cups butter, melted
2	tablespoons Worcestershire	1	teaspoon cornstarch, optional
	sauce	3 or 4	pounds cooked, peeled
¼	cup soy sauce		shrimp

Easy • Prep time: 5 to 10 minutes
In a large saucepan, mix the first 5 ingredients together. Stir in melted butter and heat thoroughly, but do not boil. Add cornstarch dissolved in a small amount of water if a thicker sauce is desired. Serve over shrimp.
Yields 12 servings

Make outside dining easy by having several stations for silverware, napkins, and drinks.

Barbecue Ribeye

2 tablespoons barbecue spice
1 teaspoon hickory
   smoked salt
½ teaspoon garlic powder
⅛ teaspoon celery salt
1 tablespoon cayenne pepper
¼ cup lemon juice

2 tablespoons Worcestershire
   sauce
¼ cup soy sauce
1 cup vegetable oil
   Salt and pepper
1 6-pound ribeye roast

Easy • Prep time: 5 minutes
Combine all ingredients, except meat, to make the marinade. Marinate the roast for at least 1 hour. Cook over low coals in a smoker-type barbecue pit for 1½ hours, or until the desired temperature is reached on a meat thermometer. Turn and baste occasionally with the marinade. Allow to sit for 20 minutes before serving.
Yields 12 servings

Mushroom and Tomato Salad

1½ pounds mushrooms, sliced
6 tomatoes, chopped
2 onions, thinly sliced
1 cup olive oil
½ cup red wine vinegar

½ cup chopped parsley
2 teaspoons salt
2 teaspoons sugar
1 teaspoon garlic powder
½ teaspoon black pepper

Easy • Prep time: 5 minutes
Mix vegetables, cover, and refrigerate. Combine remaining ingredients an hour before serving; mix vegetables with dressing and refrigerate. Use a slotted spoon for serving.
Yields 12 servings

White Squash Casserole

6 to 8	white squash (3 pounds), grated	1	cup grated Monterey Jack cheese
	Salt and pepper	¾	cup heavy cream
1	teaspoon basil	2	cups crushed Ritz crackers
1	teaspoon garlic salt		Butter
1	onion, chopped		

Easy • Prep time: 5 minutes
Preheat the oven to 350°. Mix squash, seasonings, onion, cheese, and cream. In a 3-quart buttered casserole dish, layer the squash mixture and crushed crackers until all are used. Dot with butter. Bake for 45 minutes.
Yields 12 servings

Chocolate Pots de Crème

12	ounces semisweet chocolate morsels	2	cups heavy cream
5	tablespoons sugar	¼	cup Kahlua
¼	teaspoon salt	2	tablespoons brandy
2	eggs		Whipped cream and grated chocolate, for garnish
2	teaspoons vanilla extract		

Moderately easy • Prep time: 25 minutes • Prepare ahead
Put chocolate, sugar, salt, eggs, and vanilla into a blender. Blend for 10 seconds; stop; blend for 10 more seconds. Heat cream to the boiling point and add to the chocolate mixture. Blend for 10 more seconds. Add Kahlua and brandy and blend again for 10 seconds. Pour into demitasse cups. Chill for several hours, or overnight. Top with whipped cream and grated chocolate.
Yields 12 servings

SHOPPING LIST _____

BAKERY
__ 12 or more French baguettes

BUTCHER
__ 3 to 4 pounds cooked, peeled shrimp
__ 1 6-pound ribeye roast

DAIRY
__ 1 pound butter, plus 1 stick
__ 1 quart heavy cream
__ 6 ounces Monterey Jack cheese
__ 2 eggs

EXTRAS
__ 1 case beaujolais
__ 1 small bottle Kahlua
__ 1 small bottle brandy

MISCELLANEOUS
__ 1 8-ounce bottle lemon juice
__ 1 jar hickory smoked salt
__ 1 box Ritz crackers
__ 1 12-ounce bag semisweet chocolate morsels
__ 1 6-ounce box semisweet chocolate squares

PRODUCE
__ 1½ pounds mushrooms
__ 6 tomatoes
__ 3 onions
__ 1 bunch fresh parsley
__ 6 to 8 white squash

STAPLES/SPICES
__ Barbecue spice
__ Black pepper
__ Cayenne pepper
__ Celery salt
__ Coffee
__ Cornstarch
__ Dried basil
__ Garlic powder
__ Garlic salt
__ Olive oil
__ Red wine vinegar
__ Salt
__ Soy sauce
__ Sugar
__ Tabasco sauce
__ Vanilla extract
__ Vegetable oil
__ White vinegar
__ Worcestershire sauce

One-Dish Dinner

QUICK BEEF STROGANOFF

MIXED GREEN SALAD

ASSORTED ROLLS

PECAN PIE

FRUITED TEA AND BURGUNDY

SERVES 6 TO 8

Actually, you have to use more than one dish for this
menu, but it's still easy to prepare and fun to eat.
When time and utensils are at a premium,
these are the recipes for you.

Quick Beef Stroganoff

4	*pounds top round steak*	1	*teaspoon crushed garlic*
	Butter	¼	*teaspoon thyme*
1	*medium onion, chopped*	¼	*teaspoon basil*
1	*can cream of mushroom*	¼	*teaspoon marjoram*
	soup	4 to 5	*cups sliced mushrooms*
1	*cup grated Cheddar cheese*	1	*cup sour cream*
1	*cup burgundy*		*Hot, cooked rice or noodles*

Easy • Prep time: 15 minutes
Preheat the oven to 325°. Cut meat into thin strips and brown in butter in a skillet. Remove meat and sauté onion. Put meat and onion in
a 3-quart casserole dish. Add remaining ingredients, except sour
cream. Stir to blend. Bake, covered, for 2 hours. Add sour cream and
bake for 20 minutes longer. Serve over hot, cooked rice or noodles.
Yields 6 to 8 servings

Mixed Green Salad

1   16-ounce can whole green
    beans, drained
    Oil and vinegar salad
    dressing (storebought
    or homemade)
1   bunch fresh spinach,
    rinsed thoroughly,
    patted dry, and
    stems removed

1   head Romaine lettuce
1   bunch arugula,
    stems removed
1   14-ounce can artichoke
    hearts, drained
1   avocado, sliced
1   red onion, thinly sliced

Easy • Prep time: 15 minutes
Marinate beans in a salad dressing with an oil and vinegar base, using
either your favorite homemade recipe or a commercial brand. Wash,
tear, and crisp greens. When ready to serve, toss all ingredients with
dressing.
Yields 6 to 8 servings

Pecan Pie

3   eggs
1   cup dark brown sugar
¼   cup light corn syrup
3   tablespoons butter, melted

1   teaspoon vanilla extract
½   cup pecan pieces
1   9-inch unbaked pie shell

Easy • Prep time: 5 minutes
Preheat the oven to 350°. In a bowl, beat eggs; add brown sugar, corn
syrup, butter, vanilla, and pecans. Pour into the pie shell and bake for
45 to 50 minutes.
Yields 1 nine-inch pie of 6 to 8 servings

When you're not using a
storebought pastry or pie
shell, chill your pastry
before rolling out. The
same goes for cookie
dough.

Fruited Tea

1   quart water
12 individual tea bags

Juice of 4 lemons
2 cups sugar

Easy • Prep time: 5 to 10 minutes
Boil water in a saucepan; add tea bags, cover, and remove from the heat. Steep for 5 minutes. Remove tea bags. In a ½ gallon jug, add all ingredients and enough water to fill the jug. Refrigerate until ready to serve.
Yields ½ gallon tea

SHOPPING LIST

BAKERY
__ 16 assorted rolls

BUTCHER
__ 4 pounds top round steak

CANNED GOODS
__ 1 10½-ounce can cream of mushroom soup
__ 1 14-ounce can artichoke hearts
__ 1 16-ounce can whole green beans

EXTRAS
__ 3 or 4 bottles burgundy

DAIRY
__ 1 stick butter
__ 6 ounces Cheddar cheese
__ 1 8-ounce container sour cream
__ ½ dozen eggs

MISCELLANEOUS
__ 1 pound uncooked rice or 2 pounds uncooked noodles
__ 1 bottle light corn syrup
__ 1 small package pecan pieces
__ 1 9-inch unbaked pie shell

PRODUCE
__ 1 medium onion
__ 1 red onion
__ 1 head garlic
__ 2 10½-ounce packages fresh mushrooms
__ 1 bunch fresh spinach
__ 1 head Romaine lettuce
__ 1 bunch arugula
__ 1 ripe avocado
__ 4 lemons

STAPLES/SPICES
__ Dark brown sugar
__ Dried basil
__ Marjoram
__ Olive oil
__ Red wine vinegar
__ Sugar
__ Tea bags
__ Thyme
__ Vanilla extract

Grilled Steak Dinner

GRILLED STEAKS

FOIL-BAKED POTATOES

VEGETABLE KABOBS

GRILLED HERB BREAD

FRESH FRUIT AND CHEESE PLATTER

CABERNET SAUVIGNON

S E R V E S   6

Grilling outdoors can be fun for the whole family. And today, many kitchens have grills as well. Either way, inside or out, this menu is sure to draw rave reviews.

Grilled Steaks

2	tablespoons soy sauce	⅛	teaspoon garlic salt
6	tablespoons olive oil	6	steaks (sirloin, T-bone, filet, or ribeye)
1	tablespoon seasoned salt		
½	teaspoon ground black pepper		

Easy • Prep time: 5 minutes
Combine the first 5 ingredients; rub into steaks by hand, on both sides, and allow to marinate at room temperature for at least 2 hours before cooking. Grill over charcoal to desired doneness (gas or electric grill also may be used).
Yields 6 servings

Notes

Grilling is considered a lower-fat method of cooking, because the food is placed above the heat source. The fat drips away from the food, onto the heat source, which creates a smoke that seems to enhance the food's flavor. Many modern stoves come with a grill top.

Foil-Baked Potatoes

3	large russet potatoes	Garlic salt and pepper
¼	cup butter, melted	to taste

Easy • Prep time: 5 minutes

Cut potatoes in half crosswise; brush with melted butter. Sprinkle with garlic salt and pepper. Wrap in aluminum foil and bake at the edge of a hot grill for about 10 minutes, or until soft. Have bowls of selected toppings, such as grated Cheddar cheese, sour cream, butter, chopped cilantro or other fresh herb, and seasoned salt available when serving.

Yields 6 servings

Vegetable Kabobs

2	tablespoons soy sauce	1	red bell pepper, cut
1	teaspoon spicy mustard		into 1½-inch pieces
1	tablespoon water	1	yellow bell pepper, cut
24	mushrooms, cleaned		into 1½-inch pieces
2	purple onions, cut into		
	1½-inch chunks		

Easy • Prep time: 20 minutes

Combine soy sauce, mustard, and water in a small bowl. Skewer vegetables and place on the grill. Use a pastry brush to baste with the sauce during grilling.

Yields 6 servings

Grilled Herb Bread

½ cup butter, softened
1 clove garlic, minced
1 teaspoon dried parsley flakes
¼ teaspoon dried oregano
¼ teaspoon crushed dried dill
1 loaf French bread

Easy • Prep time: 5 minutes • Prepare garlic butter ahead of time
Combine butter, garlic, parsley flakes, oregano, and dill in a bowl. Cover and refrigerate overnight before using. Remove from the refrigerator for 30 to 45 minutes to soften. Cut bread into ¾-inch slices, but do not cut through the bottom crust. Spread the butter mixture between slices. Wrap in aluminum foil and heat on the grill for 15 minutes.
Yields 6 servings

SHOPPING LIST

BAKERY
__ 1 large loaf French bread

BUTCHER
__ 6 6-to 8-ounce steaks (sirloin, T-bone, or ribeye)

DAIRY
__ 1 pound assorted cheeses
__ 1 pound butter
__ 6 ounces Cheddar cheese
__ 1 8-ounce container sour cream

EXTRAS
__ 3 or 4 bottles cabernet sauvignon

MISCELLANEOUS
__ 1 small jar spicy brown mustard

PRODUCE
__ 2 green apples
__ 2 red apples
__ 1 bunch grapes
__ 1 pint strawberries
__ 3 large russet potatoes
__ 1 bunch cilantro or other herb of choice
__ 1½ to 2 pounds mushrooms
__ 2 purple onions
__ 1 red bell pepper
__ 1 yellow bell pepper
__ 1 head garlic

STAPLES/SPICES
__ Dried dill weed
__ Dried oregano
__ Dried parsley flakes
__ Garlic salt
__ Olive oil
__ Peppercorns
__ Seasoned salt
__ Soy sauce

Southwest Buffet

CHILI-RUBBED CHICKEN

PINEAPPLE SALSA

BLACK BEANS IN ORANGE VINAIGRETTE

PEPPERS AND RICE

RIO GRANDE COCKTAILS

MARGARITA PIE

SERVES 6

Venture into the Southwest with this menu full of
flavor. Your tastebuds may never be the same.

Chili-Rubbed Chicken

2 whole chickens (about 3 pounds each)	¼ teaspoon cayenne pepper
	¼ teaspoon ground cumin
1 tablespoon chili powder	2 to 3 tablespoons vegetable oil
1 tablespoon paprika	2 teaspoons Honey Dijon mustard

Easy • Prep time: 15 minutes

Discard chicken necks and giblets. Rinse chickens and pat dry. Cut through both chickens along each side of the backbone. Discard the backbones. Place each chicken, skin side up, on a flat surface (such as a cutting board) and press firmly to flatten. In a small bowl, mix chili powder, paprika, cayenne, and cumin. Add oil and mustard; stir to blend thoroughly. Rub the spice mixture evenly over chicken skin. Grill chickens over medium hot coals until the meat is tender, about 30 to 40 minutes. Serve with Pineapple Salsa.

Yields 6 to 8 servings

Broiling involves cooking the food directly under the heat source.

Pineapple Salsa

1   fresh ripe pineapple
1   medium red onion, finely
    chopped
⅔   cup finely chopped cilantro
1   jalapeño pepper, seeded and
    finely chopped

Easy • Prep time: 15 minutes
Cut the pineapple in half lengthwise (including top). Core and cut fruit from the shell in large chunks. Reserve the shell. Coarsely chop pineapple and place in a colander to drain; reserve the juice for later use. In a mixing bowl, combine drained pineapple with red onion, cilantro, and jalapeño. Chill. When ready to serve, spoon salsa back into the pineapple shell.
Yields 3 to 4 cups salsa

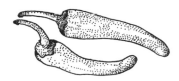

Black Beans in Orange Vinaigrette

½   cup chopped fresh mint
¼   cup fresh orange juice
½   teaspoon orange zest
1 to 2 teaspoons white
        wine vinegar
1   clove garlic, chopped
½   cup vegetable oil
6   cups cooked black beans,
    cooled

Easy • Prep time: 10 minutes • Prepare ahead
Combine all ingredients except beans in a blender container. Pulse until the mixture reaches a smooth consistency. Pour vinaigrette over black beans and toss. Refrigerate until ready to use (can be made 1 to 2 days ahead of time). Serve at room temperature.
Yields 6 servings

Peppers and Rice

1	medium red bell pepper	2	cups cooked long-grain white rice
1	medium yellow bell pepper	1	cup cooked short-grain
1	cup cooked wild rice		brown rice

Vinaigrette

3	tablespoons lemon juice	⅔	cup chopped parsley
½	teaspoon lemon zest	2 to 3	tablespoons
½	cup olive oil		minced chives
	Salt and pepper to taste		

Moderately easy • Prep time: 25 minutes • Prepare ahead
Roast peppers over a gas flame or under a broiler until the skins blister. Place them in a brown paper bag, close, and steam for 15 to 20 minutes. Peel, core, seed, and cut peppers into ¾-inch dice. Combine with cooked rice.

To make the vinaigrette: Thoroughly combine lemon juice, zest, olive oil, salt, and pepper. Pour the vinaigrette over rice salad and toss until well blended. Cover and refrigerate. When ready to serve, stir the parsley and chives into the rice. Adjust seasonings to taste. Serve at room temperature.
Yields 4 to 6 servings

Rio Grande Cocktails

1	cup gold tequila	¼	cup lemon juice
6	cups unfiltered apple juice	⅓	cup crème de Cassis

Easy • Prep time: 15 minutes
Combine all ingredients. Serve chilled.
Yields 6 servings

Margarita Pie

Crust

1	cup finely crushed salted pretzels
2	tablespoons brown sugar
½	cup melted butter

Filling

1	quart vanilla ice cream, softened
¼	cup tequila
⅛	cup Triple Sec
½	6-ounce can frozen lemonade concentrate
2	tablespoons fresh lime juice

Topping

2	egg yolks
¼	cup sugar
¼	cup lime juice
3	tablespoons butter
	Drop of green food coloring, optional
	Lime slices for garnish

To speed up the recipe preparation time of the Margarita Pie, use purchased lime curd or lemon curd mixed with a drop of green food coloring for the topping.

Moderately easy • Prep time: 15 to 20 minutes • Prepare ahead

To make the crust: Combine pretzels, brown sugar, and melted butter. Press into a buttered 9-inch pie plate.

To make the filling: Combine filling ingredients and pour into the pie crust. Cover and freeze while making the topping.

To make the topping: Combine egg yolks and sugar in the top of a double boiler. Slowly add lime juice. Cook, stirring constantly, until the mixture thickens. Add butter and whisk to blend. Remove from the heat. Mix in a drop of green food coloring, if desired. Let cool completely; refrigerate.

Spread lime curd over pie filling just before serving. Garnish with slices of lime.

Yields 6 to 8 servings

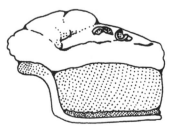

SHOPPING LIST _____

BUTCHER
__ 2 3-pound chickens

DAIRY
__ 2 sticks butter
__ 2 eggs
__ 1 quart vanilla ice cream

EXTRAS
__ 1 bottle gold tequila
__ 1 small bottle crème de cassis
__ 1 small bottle Triple Sec

MISCELLANEOUS
__ 2 quarts unfiltered apple juice
__ 1 8-ounce bottle lemon juice
__ 1 small jar honey Dijon mustard
__ 1 small box wild rice
__ 1 14-ounce package short-grain
   brown rice
__ 1 pound dry black beans
__ 1 small bag pretzels
__ 1 8-ounce bottle lime juice
__ 1 small bottle green food coloring
   (optional)
__ 1 6-ounce can frozen lemonade
   concentrate

PRODUCE
__ 1 lemon
__ 1 orange
__ 1 fresh ripe pineapple
__ 1 medium red onion
__ 1 bunch cilantro
__ 1 jalapeño pepper
__ 1 red bell pepper
__ 1 yellow bell pepper
__ 1 bunch fresh parsley
__ 1 bunch fresh chives
__ 1 bunch fresh mint
__ 1 head garlic
__ 2 limes

STAPLES/SPICES
__ Brown sugar
__ Cayenne pepper
__ Chili powder
__ Ground cumin
__ Long-grain white rice
__ Olive oil
__ Paprika
__ Pepper
__ Salt
__ Sugar
__ Vegetable oil
__ White wine vinegar

Wedding Anniversary Dinner

COUNTRY PÂTÉ

COLD STRAWBERRY SOUP

BUTTER LETTUCE WITH VINAIGRETTE DRESSING

VEAL SCALOPPINI LA MARSALA

FRESH STEAMED ASPARAGUS

ASSORTED ROLLS

ANGEL ALEXANDER

AFTER DINNER COFFEES, CHIANTI, AND CHAMPAGNE

SERVES 6

Hosting a wedding anniversary dinner allows you to include your closest friends and family in a celebration that means so much to you. Add a little love to these recipes and you'll create a night to remember.

"Marriage, as I have often remarked, is not merely sharing one's fettucine but sharing the burden of finding the fettucine restaurant in the first place."
—CALVIN TRILLIN

Notes

Country Pâté

2 cups butter, softened
2 pounds chicken livers
2 medium onions, quartered
1 teaspoon curry powder
1 teaspoon paprika
¼ teaspoon salt
¼ teaspoon freshly ground black pepper
2 tablespoons cognac

Easy • Prep time: 20 minutes • Prepare ahead
Melt ½ cup butter in a saucepan. Add chicken livers, onion, curry powder, paprika, salt, and pepper. Cover and cook over low heat for 8 minutes. Process the mixture in an electric blender until smooth. Add cognac and remaining butter and blend. Press into a mold or loaf pan. Chill until firm.
Yields 5 cups

Show your wedding video to your guests after dinner.

Cold Strawberry Soup

2	cups fresh sliced strawberries	1½	cups cold water
½	cup honey	1	cup dry red wine
½	cup sour cream		Sour cream, for garnish
			Whole strawberries, for garnish

Easy • Prep time: 5 minutes • Prepare ahead
In a blender, combine and mix all ingredients. It is not necessary to strain. Refrigerate. Stir well before serving. Serve in wine glasses or glass bowls. Garnish each serving with a dollop of sour cream and a fresh strawberry.
Yields 6 to 8 servings

Butter Lettuce with Vinaigrette Dressing

½	cup balsamic vinegar	Salt and pepper, to taste
2	teaspoons fresh lemon juice	Butter lettuce
½	cup canola oil	Chopped chives, parsley,
1	teaspoon dry mustard	or garlic, optional

Easy • Prep time: 5 minutes
In a bowl, combine the first 5 ingredients and chill. Bring to room temperature before tossing with butter lettuce. Fresh chopped chives, parsley, or garlic may be added, if desired.
Yields 1¼ cups dressing

Veal Scaloppini La Marsala

2½ pounds veal scallops
    All-purpose flour
1 cup unsalted butter
½ cup olive oil
    Juice of 8 lemons
1½ cups Marsala wine

    Salt and freshly ground
    black pepper to taste
    Sprigs of fresh thyme
1 pound uncooked spinach
    fettuccine

Easy • Prep time: 20 minutes

Very lightly coat each scallop with flour. In a large skillet, heat butter with oil until very hot, but not smoking. Quickly brown veal on both sides. Lower the temperature to medium and add lemon juice and Marsala. Simmer veal for 4 to 5 minutes.

Prepare fettuccine according to the package directions. Sprinkle veal with salt and pepper. Garnish veal with fresh thyme and serve immediately with sauce over fettuccine.

Yields 6 to 8 servings

Fresh Steamed Asparagus

24 to 30 spears fresh asparagus
2 lemons (use twists for garnish)
6 teaspoons butter

Easy • Prep time: 5 minutes

Steam until tender at least 4 to 5 spears per person. Squeeze fresh lemon juice and a teaspoon of butter over each bundle. Garnish with a twist of lemon.

Yields 6 servings (4 to 5 spears per serving)

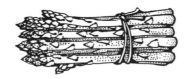

Steaming means that you are cooking foods over boiling water. You can do this with two pans, or by using a separate steamer. Today there are many electric steamers on the market.

Angel Alexander

Ask your guests to share their fondest memories of their own weddings.

2 tablespoons heavy cream
½ cup crème de cacao
1 angel food cake (homemade or storebought)

Sweetened whipped cream
Semisweet chocolate morsels or chocolate shavings

Easy • Prep time: 10 minutes

Combine heavy cream with crème de cacao in a bowl. Using a wooden skewer about 5 inches long, make holes in varying depths in the bottom crust of the cake. Pour half of the mixture into holes. Let stand for 2 hours. Just before serving, invert the cake onto a serving plate, crust side down. Make more holes in the top and pour in the remaining mixture. Frost with whipped cream and decorate with chocolate morsels or shavings.

Yields 8 to 10 servings

SHOPPING LIST

BAKERY
__ 6 to 12 assorted rolls
__ 1 angel food cake

BUTCHER
__ 2 pounds chicken livers
__ 2½ pounds veal scallops

DAIRY
__ 2 pounds butter
__ 2 sticks unsalted butter
__ 1 8-ounce container sour cream
__ ½ pint heavy (whipping) cream

EXTRAS
__ 4 or 5 bottles champagne
__ 4 or 5 bottles Chianti
__ 1 bottle Marsala wine
__ 1 small bottle cognac
__ 1 small bottle crème de cacao

MISCELLANEOUS
__ 1 8-ounce jar honey
__ 1 bottle balsamic vinegar
__ 1 bottle canola oil
__ 1 pound uncooked spinach fettuccine
__ 1 6-ounce bag semisweet chocolate morsels

PRODUCE
__ 2 medium onions
__ 1 pint strawberries
__ 12 lemons
__ 1 head butter lettuce
__ 1 bunch fresh thyme
__ 2 or 3 bunches fresh asparagus

STAPLES/SPICES
__ All-purpose flour
__ Coffee
__ Curry powder
__ Dry mustard
__ Olive oil
__ Paprika
__ Peppercorns
__ Salt
__ Sugar

Dinner at Eight

STANDING RIB ROAST WITH BÉARNAISE SAUCE

BROWNED RICE

OYSTER BISQUE

SPINACH STUFFED SQUASH

FRENCH BAGUETTES

RUM CREAM PIE

CALIFORNIA CABERNET

S E R V E S 1 2

The elegance of serving dinner at eight o'clock in the evening cannot be questioned. When you find that it's time for black tie and tails, these dishes will provide the perfect complement.

Notes

Standing Rib Roast with Béarnaise Sauce

1   *12-pound rib roast, at room temperature*
    Salt, pepper, and garlic powder to taste
    Béarnaise Sauce

Easy • Prep time: 5 minutes
Preheat the oven to 325°. Rub meat with salt, pepper, and garlic powder. Place meat fat side up in a shallow pan; bake, uncovered, until desired degree of doneness is reached.
Yields 12 to 20 servings

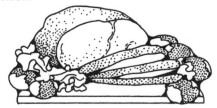

Tenderize a pot roast (or stew meat) by using hot tea for the cooking liquid.

Cook meat 20 minutes per pound for a rare roast, 22 minutes for medium, or 35 minutes for well-done.

Béarnaise Sauce

¼	cup white wine	¼	cup lemon juice
¼	cup tarragon vinegar	½	teaspoon salt
4	teaspoons dried tarragon	½	teaspoon black pepper
4	teaspoons minced green onions	⅛	teaspoon cayenne pepper
6	egg yolks	½	cup butter, melted

Moderately easy • Prep time: 20 to 25 minutes

In a saucepan, combine the first 4 ingredients and heat until the liquid is almost gone. In a blender, mix egg yolks, lemon juice, and seasonings. Pour in butter, a little at a time, turning the blender off and on between additions. Add herbs and blend for 4 seconds.

Yields 2 cups sauce

Browned Rice

½	cup butter	5	cups chicken bouillon
3	cups uncooked rice		

Easy • Prep time: 5 minutes

Melt butter in a large heavy pot. Add rice slowly, and stir over medium heat until rice is dark brown. Pour in bouillon slowly, reduce the heat to low, cover, and cook for 20 to 25 minutes. Turn off the heat and fluff up rice with a fork. Serve immediately or reheat over boiling water.

Yields 12 servings

Oyster Bisque

1½ pints oysters
1 cup water
1 onion, sliced
⅓ cup chopped celery
1 sprig parsley, minced
1 bay leaf
1 teaspoon salt

3 tablespoons butter
3 tablespoons all-purpose flour
  Salt and pepper to taste
2 cups milk
1 cup heavy cream
  Dash of Tabasco sauce

Moderately easy • Prep time: 40 minutes • Prepare ahead

Drain oysters and reserve the liquor. Separate soft portion from hard muscles; chop and refrigerate soft portions. Grind or chop muscles and combine with oyster liquor and the next 5 ingredients; bring to a boil. Reduce heat; cover and simmer for 30 minutes. Press through a sieve; add 1 teaspoon salt. Melt butter over low heat; add flour, salt, and pepper and stir until blended. Gradually add oyster stock and 1 cup milk; cook and stir until thick. Remove from the heat and cool. Refrigerate for several hours to thicken. Before serving, add soft oyster portions, cream, and Tabasco. Heat carefully and remove from the stove. Gradually stir in remaining cup of milk and return to the heat, stirring constantly until thick and smooth.

Yields 48 ounces (12 half-cup servings)

Spinach Stuffed Squash

6	yellow summer squash	1	cup milk, room temperature
2	cups cooked, chopped		Salt and pepper to taste
	spinach, well drained	⅛	teaspoon grated nutmeg
¼	cup butter	⅔	cup shredded Cheddar cheese
¼	cup minced green onion	8	slices bacon, cooked
¼	cup all-purpose flour		and crumbled

Easy • Prep time: 25 minutes • Freezes well
Preheat the oven to 350°. Trim ends off squash. Cook whole in salted boiling water for about 10 minutes, or until barely tender; drain well. Halve lengthwise and scoop out centers. Reserve the shells. Chop pulp and combine with spinach. In a heavy saucepan, melt butter, sauté onions until wilted, and blend in flour. Add milk, stirring constantly, and cook until thick. Add seasonings to the spinach mixture and stir into the sauce. Spoon into squash shells; top with cheese and bacon. Bake for 15 to 20 minutes.
Yields 12 servings

Rum Cream Pie

1 9-inch graham cracker
   pie shell
6 egg yolks
1 cup sugar
1 envelope unflavored gelatin
½ cup cold water

1 pint heavy cream
½ cup rum
   Bittersweet chocolate shavings
   Whipped cream for garnish,
   optional

Moderately easy • Prep time: 30 minutes

Beat egg yolks until light and add 1 cup sugar. Soak gelatin in ½ cup cold water. Put the gelatin and water over low heat and bring to a boil. Pour this over the sugar-egg mixture, stirring briskly. Whip cream until stiff; fold into the egg mixture. Add rum. Cool until the mixture begins to set and then pour into the pie shell. Chill until firm; sprinkle top of pie generously with chocolate shavings and garnish with whipped cream, if desired.

Yields 6 to 8 servings

SHOPPING LIST

BAKERY
__ 12 to 24 French baguettes

BUTCHER
__ 1½ pints shelled oysters
__ 1 12-pound rib roast
__ ½ pound bacon

DAIRY
__ 1 pound butter
__ 1 quart milk
__ 2 pints heavy cream
__ 1 dozen eggs
__ 6 ounces Cheddar cheese

EXTRAS
__ 1 to 1½ cases California cabernet

__ 1 small bottle white wine
__ 1 small bottle rum

MISCELLANEOUS
__ 1 bottle tarragon vinegar
__ 1 8-ounce bottle lemon juice
__ 1 10-ounce package frozen
   chopped spinach
__ 1 9-inch graham cracker pie shell
__ 1 box unflavored gelatin
__ 1 6-ounce box bittersweet
   chocolate squares

PRODUCE
__ 1 onion
__ 1 stalk celery
__ 1 bunch fresh parsley

__ 1 bunch green onions
__ 6 yellow summer squash

STAPLES/SPICES
__ All-purpose flour
__ Bay leaves
__ Cayenne pepper
__ Chicken bouillon cubes
__ Dried tarragon
__ Garlic powder
__ Nutmeg
__ Pepper
__ Salt
__ Sugar
__ Tabasco
__ White rice

End of Winter Dinner

PUMPKIN SOUP

ORANGE AND ONION SALAD WITH CITRUS DRESSING

PORK TENDERLOIN

STEAMED LONG-GRAIN RICE

HARD ROLLS

CRÈME BRÛLÉE

COFFEE AND MERLOT

SERVES 8

Some people are more happy than others to see winter come to a close. Whether you're sad to see it go, or happy that spring is near, your friends will be glad you treated them to the foods on this menu.

Pumpkin Soup

1 onion, finely chopped	Salt and pepper to taste
2 tablespoons butter	½ teaspoon grated nutmeg
3 tablespoons all-purpose flour	2 cups light cream
2 cups milk	½ cup sherry
2 cups cooked pumpkin	1 cup chopped toasted almonds
1 cup chicken broth	

Easy • Prep time: 10 minutes • Prepare ahead • Can refrigerate for several days

In a skillet, sauté onion in butter until tender but not brown; remove from the skillet with a slotted spoon. Stir flour and milk into onions. Purée pumpkin with broth and add to the sauce with seasonings. Add cream and mix well. Refrigerate at this point if desired. Before serving, heat carefully without boiling; stir in sherry and pour into soup bowls or cups. Sprinkle with almonds.

Yields 8 to 10 servings

Orange and Onion Salad with Citrus Dressing

10 navel oranges, peeled and
    sectioned
 2 red onions, sliced into rings

10 Boston lettuce leaves
    Citrus Dressing

Easy • Prep time: 10 minutes • Can refrigerate for several days
Fill each lettuce leaf with sections from 1 orange. Top with onion rings.
Pour Citrus Dressing over the top just before serving.
Yields 8 to 10 servings

Citrus Dressing

 1 cup lemon juice
½ teaspoon salt

 1 cup sugar
 1 cup sherry

Keeps well in refrigerator • Good with any fruit salad
Combine all ingredients in order and refrigerate. Serve over salad.
Yields 2½ cups dressing

Pork Tenderloin

1   4- to 5-pound pork loin,
     at room temperature
     Olive oil
     Salt, pepper, and garlic
     powder to taste

½   cup dry white wine
½   cup chicken or beef broth
¼   cup chopped fresh parsley

Easy • Prep time: 5 minutes

Preheat the oven to 350°. Rub meat with oil and seasonings. Bake, uncovered, in a shallow pan for about 45 minutes, or until a meat thermometer registers 170°. Remove tenderloin and allow it to cool for a few minutes before slicing. Meanwhile, deglaze the baking pan with wine and broth. Add parsley and serve as a sauce over pork medallions.
Yields 8 to 12 servings

Steamed Long-Grain Rice

2½   cups water
1   teaspoon salt

1⅓   cups uncooked long-grain rice
¼   teaspoon vegetable oil

Easy • Prep time: 5 minutes

In a heavy saucepan, bring water and salt to a boil. Stir in rice and oil, cover, reduce heat to low, and simmer for 20 minutes, or until the liquid is absorbed. Place rice in a colander over simmering water, cover with a dish towel, and allow to steam until served.
Yields 6 cups cooked rice

Crème Brûlée

3 cups heavy cream
4½ tablespoons brown sugar
6 egg yolks, beaten

10 tablespoons cream sherry
5 tablespoons brown sugar,
sifted for topping

Moderately easy • Prep time: 30 minutes • Prepare ahead
Scald cream in the top of a double boiler with sugar. Add to egg yolks
very slowly. Return to the double boiler. Stir constantly while cooking
over boiling water, just until the mixture thickens and coats a spoon.
Remove from the heat. Cool. Pour into individual custard cups and add
1 tablespoon sherry to each. Chill thoroughly.

   About 2 hours before serving, sprinkle sifted brown sugar on top of
each custard. Place under the broiler until sugar caramelizes, about 1
to 2 minutes. Chill again before serving.
Yields 10 servings

> To scald milk or cream, bring almost to a boil. Allow bubbles to barely form, but do not boil.

SHOPPING LIST

BAKERY
__ 12 to 24 hard rolls

BUTCHER
__ 1 4- to 5-pound pork loin roast

CANNED GOODS
__ 1 16-ounce can pumpkin
__ 1 16-ounce can chicken broth

DAIRY
__ 1 stick butter
__ 1 pint milk
__ 1 pint light cream
__ 1½ pints heavy cream
__ ½ dozen eggs

EXTRAS
__ 1 case merlot
__ 1 bottle sherry
__ 1 small bottle dry white wine
__ 1 small bottle cream sherry

MISCELLANEOUS
__ 1 6-ounce package slivered
   almonds
__ 1 8-ounce bottle lemon juice

PRODUCE
__ 1 onion
__ 2 red onions
__ 1 bunch fresh parsley
__ 10 naval oranges
__ 1 head Boston lettuce

STAPLES/SPICES
__ All-purpose flour
__ Brown sugar
__ Coffee
__ Garlic powder
__ Long-grain white rice
__ Nutmeg
__ Olive oil
__ Pepper
__ Salt
__ Sugar
__ Vegetable oil

Easy and Elegant

"Poultry is for the cook what canvas is for the painter."

—JEAN-ANTHELME
BRILLAT-SAVARIN

Notes

_____

_____

_____

_____

_____

_____

_____

_____

_____

_____

_____

_____

_____

_____

_____

_____

_____

_____

_____

_____

SHERRIED CRAB SOUP

CORNISH HENS WITH WILD RICE STUFFING

BIBB LETTUCE WITH CAPER AND EGG DRESSING

TOMATOES WITH SPINACH SOUFFLÉ

FRENCH BREAD

LEMON CHARLOTTE RUSSE

COFFEE AND LIGHT RED BORDEAUX

S E R V E S 8

The name of this menu says it all.

Sherried Crab Soup

2 cups cooked crabmeat, fresh or canned	3 cups cream
1 cup sherry	¼ cup chopped parsley
2 10½-ounce cans green pea soup	⅛ teaspoon curry powder
2 10½-ounce cans tomato soup	Salt and pepper to taste

Easy • Prep time: 20 minutes
Soak crabmeat in sherry for 10 minutes. Combine soups and cream in the top of a double boiler. Heat just to simmering, stirring occasionally. Add crabmeat, sherry, parsley, and seasonings. Serve hot.
Yields 8 servings

Cornish Hens with Wild Rice Stuffing

8   Cornish hens
    Salt and pepper to taste

¼   cup butter, melted
    Wild Rice Stuffing

Moderately easy • Prep time: 30 minutes

Preheat the oven to 400°. Season each bird with salt and pepper. Stuff with the wild rice mixture. Close the neck and body cavities with a toothpick. Place hens breast down on a rack in a roasting pan. Brush with melted butter. Bake, covered, for 20 minutes, then reduce the oven temperature to 325° and bake for 30 minutes, or until the breast is fork tender. Uncover the roaster and turn the hens over for the last 10 minutes of baking time to allow the hens to brown. Baste 2 or 3 times while roasting.

Yields 6 to 8 servings

Wild Rice Stuffing

    Giblets out of 4 Cornish hens
¼   cup butter
½   pound chopped
    mushrooms

1   large yellow onion, chopped
1   cup cooked wild rice
    Salt and pepper
1½ teaspoons poultry seasoning

Easy • Prep time: 15 minutes

Cook giblets in water; drain and chop. Add butter, mushrooms, and on-ion. Cook over low heat for 5 minutes. Remove from the stove and stir in drained rice. Add seasonings.

Yields stuffing for 6 to 8 Cornish hens or 2 four-pound chickens

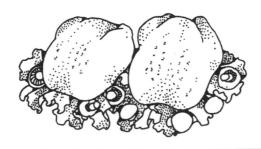

Baking uses dry heat to cook food in an oven. Oven-frying is a lowfat baking technique in which food bakes on a rack, so that all sides will be exposed equally to the heat.

Bibb Lettuce with Caper and Egg Dressing

1	hard-boiled egg	1	tablespoon capers
¼	cup red or white wine vinegar	¼	teaspoon dry mustard
½	teaspoon chopped chives	1	tablespoon lemon juice
¾	cup oil (½ olive, ¼ corn)	¼	teaspoon salt
	Cracked pepper	6 to 8	heads Bibb lettuce

Easy • Prep time: 5 minutes • Can refrigerate dressing for months
Chop egg finely. Combine all ingredients, except lettuce, in a jar and shake well. Wash and tear lettuce. Dry thoroughly and crisp in the refrigerator. Pour dressing over lettuce just before serving.
Yields 8 to 10 servings

Tomatoes with Spinach Soufflé

8	small tomatoes	2	eggs, beaten
2	tablespoons prepared mustard	2	tablespoons milk
8	slices bacon, diced and sautéed	1	teaspoon garlic salt
		1	teaspoon pepper
1	10-ounce package spinach, thawed and drained	¼	cup grated Parmesan cheese
			Parsley sprigs for garnish

Easy • Prep time: 10 minutes
Cut a thin slice from the top of each tomato. Scoop out pulp to make a shell. Drain the shell upside down for 15 minutes. Preheat the oven to 375°. Spread inside of each tomato shell with mustard. Divide bacon evenly between tomatoes. In a blender, mix spinach, eggs, milk, and seasonings. Spoon the spinach mixture into the tomatoes. Sprinkle 1 teaspoon cheese over the top of each. Bake, uncovered, for 20 to 30 minutes, or until golden brown on top. Garnish with parsley sprigs.
Yields 8 servings

Lemon Charlotte Russe

1	tablespoon unflavored gelatin	½	cup fresh lemon juice
			Grated lemon rind
½	cup cold water	24	ladyfingers
4	large eggs, separated	2	cups heavy cream, whipped
1	cup sugar	½	cup toasted almonds

Easy • Prep time: 20 minutes • Prepare ahead

Soften gelatin in cold water and dissolve in a double boiler over hot water. Set aside. Beat egg yolks until thick and lemon colored. Add sugar slowly, while continuing to beat until stiff. Add lemon juice and grated rind. Continue beating. Add gelatin to the egg mixture. Beat egg whites until light and fluffy. Fold into the lemon mixture. Pour into a bowl that is lined on the sides and bottom with ladyfingers. Fill the bowl half full of custard, add another layer of ladyfingers, and fill the rest of the way with custard. Top with whipped cream. Sprinkle top with toasted almonds. Refrigerate overnight.

Yields 10 to 12 servings

SHOPPING LIST _____

BAKERY
__ 2 or 3 loaves French bread

BUTCHER
__ ½ pound cooked lump crabmeat

__ 8 Cornish hens with giblets

__ ½ pound bacon

CANNED GOODS
__ 2 10½-ounce cans green pea soup

__ 2 10½-ounce cans tomato soup

DAIRY
__ 1 quart and ½ pint heavy cream

__ 1 dozen large eggs

__ 1 stick butter

__ ½ pint milk

__ 1 4-ounce block Parmesan
cheese

EXTRAS
__ 4 or 5 bottles light red Bordeaux

__ 1 bottle sherry

MISCELLANEOUS
__ 1 small bottle corn oil

__ 1 small jar capers

__ 1 box wild rice

__ 1 10-ounce package frozen
spinach

__ 1 box unflavored gelatin

__ 2 packages ladyfingers

__ 1 2-ounce package sliced
almonds

PRODUCE
__ 1 bunch fresh parsley

__ 1 bunch fresh chives

__ 6 to 8 heads Bibb lettuce

__ ½ pound fresh mushrooms

__ 1 large yellow onion

__ 8 small tomatoes

__ 4 to 6 lemons

STAPLES/SPICES
__ Coffee

__ Curry powder

__ Dry mustard

__ Garlic salt

__ Olive oil

__ Peppercorns

__ Poultry seasoning

__ Prepared mustard

__ Red or white wine vinegar

__ Salt

__ Sugar

TANGERINE-SAUCED ROASTED DUCKLING

POPOVERS

ENDIVE SALAD

FROZEN GRAND MARNIER SOUFFLÉ

LIQUEURED COFFEE WITH WHIPPED CREAM

SERVES 2

Romance is the order of the day when the fire is crackling and you're eating delicious food. Serve this intimate dinner to someone you love.

Tangerine-Sauced Roasted Duckling

1   *duckling (4½ to 5 pounds), thawed*
2   *small onions, peeled*
1½ *pounds yams, peeled and cut into 2-inch pieces*
Tangerine Sauce

Moderately easy • Prep time: 2 hours (including cooking time)
Preheat the oven to 375°. Remove giblets from the body cavity of the duckling and reserve for sauce. Pull out and discard lumps of fat. Rinse bird with cold water, drain, and pat dry. Fasten neck to back with a skewer. Place duckling breast down on a folding meat rack set in a 12x15-inch roasting pan. Roast for 60 minutes. Continuously spoon out fat from pan while roasting. Turn duckling breast up. Add onions and yam chunks to roasting pan, around or under the roasting rack; turn vegetables to coat with drippings. Continue roasting, turning vegetables several times, until yams are tender when pierced and onions begin falling apart. The duckling skin should be brown and crisp and begin to pull from leg bone (about another 60 to 65 minutes). Lift duckling and vegetables from pan and keep warm. Skim fat from the pan; reserve drippings for the sauce.

To serve: Cut duckling into quarters with poultry shears. Cut onions in quarters or halves and serve with yams. Spoon Tangerine Sauce over each serving.
Yields 2 to 3 servings

Roasting bakes food at a moderate temperature to produce a well-browned exterior and moist interior.

Tangerine Sauce

1½ cups water
    Duck neck and giblets
1 small onion, peeled and
    quartered
1 bay leaf
    Duck drippings from
    roasting pan (see recipe)
1½ teaspoons slivered tangerine
    zest (orange part of peel)

¾ cup tangerine juice (about
    2 or 3 large tangerines)
1½ tablespoons honey
2 teaspoons cornstarch mixed
    with 2 teaspoons water
    Salt and pepper to taste

Easy • Prep time: 15 to 20 minutes

In a small saucepan, combine water, duck neck and giblets, onion, and bay leaf. Cover and simmer for 1 hour. Pour through a wire strainer; discard neck, giblets, onion, and bay leaf, and measure broth. Boil broth to reduce to ¼ cup. Add tangerine peel and juice, broth, and the honey and cornstarch mixture to duck drippings in the roasting pan. Boil over high heat, stirring until the sauce thickens, about 1 minute. Season with salt and pepper to taste.

Yields 2½ to 3 cups sauce

Popovers

1 cup milk
1 cup all-purpose flour
2 eggs

2 tablespoons melted butter,
    cooled
1 teaspoon salt

Easy • Prep time: 5 to 10 minutes

Preheat the oven to 425°. In a blender, mix all ingredients until the batter is just combined. Half fill 6 greased muffin cups with batter. Bake on a preheated baking sheet for 30 minutes until well-puffed and crisp. Serve immediately.

Yields 6 popovers

Endive Salad

Leaves of Belgian endive
Walnut oil

Fresh lemon juice
Walnut halves

Easy • Prep time: 5 minutes
Layer endive leaves on salad plate. Drizzle leaves with a small amount of walnut oil and a squeeze of fresh lemon juice. Sprinkle with walnut halves.
Yields as many servings as needed

"Where the guests at a gathering are well-acquainted, they eat twenty percent more than they otherwise would."—E. W. HOWE

Frozen Grand Marnier Soufflé

4   egg yolks
½   cup sugar
1   cup heavy cream

1   ounce Grand Marnier
½   cup whipped cream
    for garnish

Easy • Prep time: 20 minutes • Prepare ahead and freeze
In a mixing bowl, beat egg yolks until very thick, adding sugar gradually. Whip cream and fold into the yolk mixture; fold in Grand Marnier last. Pour into individual soufflé dishes or parfait or wine glasses. Freeze. Top with whipped cream just before serving.
Yields 4 servings

SHOPPING LIST

BUTCHER
__ 1 4½- to 5-pound duckling with neck and giblets

DAIRY
__ ½ pint milk
__ ½ dozen eggs
__ 1 stick butter
__ 1 pint heavy cream

EXTRAS
__ 1 small bottle Grand Marnier
__ Kahlua or amaretto (for coffee)

MISCELLANEOUS
__ 1 small jar honey
__ 1 small bottle walnut oil
__ 1 small package walnut halves

PRODUCE
__ 3 small onions
__ 1½ pounds yams

__ 3 large tangerines
__ 1 head Belgian endive
__ 1 large lemon

STAPLES/SPICES
__ All-purpose flour
__ Bay leaves
__ Coffee
__ Cornstarch
__ Pepper
__ Salt
__ Sugar

Rib-Stickin' Kansas City Style Dinner

CHEESY POTATO SKINS

KANSAS CITY BARBECUED RIBS

CORN ON THE COB WITH THYME BUTTER

SLOW-SIMMERED BEAN POT

SPINACH SALAD

ICED TEA AND BEER

SERVES 6 TO 8

Use this menu for a down-home cookout. When you stop to think about it, what tastes better than ribs, beans, and cold beer?

Cheesy Potato Skins

5 large russet potatoes	¾ cup shredded Monterey
⅓ cup butter, melted	jack cheese
¾ cup shredded Cheddar cheese	Cilantro for garnish

Easy • Prep time: 20 minutes

Bake potatoes in the oven at 375° for 1 hour, or until tender; or microwave on high power for 6 to 7 minutes, turning once. Let cool. Cut potatoes lengthwise in half, and then quarters. Scoop out most, but not all of the flesh from each quarter and reserve for another use. Brush the shells inside and out with butter. Place on a baking sheet, cut side up. Bake at 500° for 10 to 12 minutes, or until crisp. Remove from the oven. Turn the oven setting to broil. Distribute cheeses among potato skins. Broil for 1 to 2 minutes, or until cheese is bubbly and slightly brown. Let cool slightly. Garnish with cilantro and serve warm.

Yields 20 appetizers

Kansas City Barbecued Ribs

½ cup butter
1 cup dark brown sugar
3 cups tomato ketchup
⅓ cup liquid smoke

2 tablespoons Worcestershire
sauce
2 tablespoons barbecue spice

6 to 8 pounds pork or baby back ribs,
parboiled for 20 to 30 minutes

Easy • Prep time: 10 minutes • Prepare ahead • Can refrigerate sauce for 5 to 6 weeks

To make the barbecue sauce: Melt butter; add brown sugar and stir well. Mix in remaining ingredients and heat to a slow boil. Remove from the heat and use immediately, or refrigerate for later use (yields 5 cups).

Grill ribs (30 to 35 minutes over medium coals) or bake in the oven (375°), turning occasionally and basting frequently with barbecue sauce.
Yields 6 to 8 servings

Corn on the Cob with Thyme Butter

1 cup butter, softened
¼ cup minced fresh thyme

8 to 12 ears fresh corn
on the cob, steamed

Easy • Prep time: 5 minutes • Prepare ahead

Mix butter and thyme until well blended. Cover and refrigerate overnight. Serve at room temperature and spread over fresh steamed corn on the cob.
Yields 1 cup butter

THYME

Sautéing is best done in a sauté pan or a nonstick skillet. When you sauté something, you cook it quickly in a small amount of liquid or fat.

Slow-Simmered Bean Pot

1	15½-ounce can garbanzo beans, drained	1	pound ground pork sausage
1	15-ounce can small red beans	⅓	cup light brown sugar
1	15-ounce can small white beans	1	tablespoon dry mustard
1	15½-ounce can kidney beans, drained	½	cup ketchup
1	large onion, chopped	2	teaspoons cumin
3	cloves garlic, minced or pressed	¼	cup water
		3	tablespoons red wine vinegar
			Salt to taste

Moderately easy • Prep time: 20 minutes

Combine beans in a 3-quart casserole or crock pot. Sauté onion and garlic in a large skillet; add to beans. Brown sausage in the same skillet, drain, and stir in remaining ingredients. Add the sausage mixture to beans and mix thoroughly. Cover and bake the casserole at 325° for 1 hour, or slow-simmer the mixture in a crock pot on low heat for 3 to 4 hours.

Yields 6 to 8 servings

Spinach Salad

2 pounds fresh spinach,
   stemmed, rinsed, and
   patted dry
1 red onion, halved
   and thinly sliced
½ pound fresh mushrooms,
   brushed, stemmed,
   and sliced

   Bottled cheese and
   garlic Italian dressing
8 ounces bacon, cooked crisp,
   drained, and crumbled
2 hard-boiled eggs, finely chopped

Easy • Prep time: 25 minutes
Combine spinach, onion, and mushrooms in a large mixing bowl. Add dressing to taste and toss. Transfer to a serving bowl. Sprinkle top with egg and bacon. Serve immediately.
Yields 6 to 8 servings

SHOPPING LIST

BUTCHER
__ 6 to 8 pounds pork or baby back ribs
__ 1 pound ground pork sausage
__ ½ pound bacon

CANNED GOODS
__ 1 15½-ounce can garbanzo beans
__ 1 15-ounce can small red beans
__ 1 15-ounce can small white beans
__ 1 15½-ounce can kidney beans

DAIRY
__ 1 pound butter
__ 6 ounces Cheddar cheese
__ 6 ounces Monterey Jack cheese
__ 2 eggs

EXTRAS
__ 1 or 2 cases beer

MISCELLANEOUS
__ 1 large bottle tomato ketchup
__ 1 bottle liquid smoke
__ 1 bottle cheese and garlic Italian salad dressing

PRODUCE
__ 5 large russet potatoes
__ 1 bunch fresh cilantro
__ 1 bunch fresh thyme
__ 2 pounds fresh spinach
__ 1 red onion
__ 1 large white or yellow onion
__ 1 head garlic
__ ½ pound fresh mushrooms
__ 8 to 12 ears fresh corn on the cob

STAPLES/SPICES
__ Barbecue spice
__ Cumin
__ Dark brown sugar
__ Dry mustard
__ Light brown sugar
__ Red wine vinegar
__ Salt
__ Sugar
__ Tea bags
__ Worcestershire sauce

Career Kudos

BRANDIED CHICKEN LIVER PÂTÉ

ORANGE SOUP WITH SHERRY

VEAL ROLL-UPS

STEAMED SNOW PEAS

MIXED GREEN SALAD

HARD ROLLS

CHOCOLATE CHEESECAKE

COFFEE AND POUILLY-FUISSÉ

SERVES 8

The next time one of your friends gets a big promotion, why not celebrate with an intimate dinner? All too often we forget to tell our friends that we're proud of their accomplishments. Honoring your friend in this way will demonstrate your support and concern.

Brandied Chicken Liver Pâté

2	pounds chicken livers	¼	teaspoon salt
½	cup butter	¼	teaspoon ground black pepper
2	medium onions, chopped	1	cup butter, softened
1	teaspoon paprika	¼	cup brandy
1	teaspoon curry powder		French bread or crackers

Moderately easy • Prep time: 20 minutes • Prepare ahead
In a saucepan, combine the first 7 ingredients. Cover and cook over low heat for 10 minutes. Purée in a blender or force through a sieve. Stir in softened butter and brandy. Put the pâté in a covered dish; chill until firm. Serve with sliced French bread or crackers.
Yields 8 to 10 servings

Orange Soup with Sherry

1	quart fresh orange juice
¼	teaspoon ground cloves
	Pinch (⅛ teaspoon or less) of grated ginger, nutmeg, and mace
1	whole cinnamon stick
1	tablespoon unflavored gelatin

¼	cup cold water
1	cup pineapple juice
1	cup dry sherry
1	11-ounce can mandarin orange sections
	Fresh mint, for garnish

Easy • Prep time: 10 minutes • Prepare ahead
In a saucepan, bring to boil 1 cup orange juice; add spices. Simmer for 45 minutes. Soak gelatin in cold water; add to hot orange juice. Combine with remaining ingredients and put in a glass container. Cover and refrigerate overnight. Serve cold. Garnish with a mint leaf.
Yields 6 to 8 servings

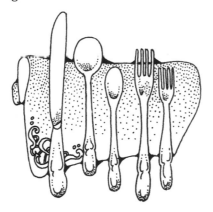

Various herb butters can be made by stirring 2 or more teaspoons dried herbs into 1 small tub softened, whipped butter. These make a different spread for hard rolls and other breads.

Veal Roll-Ups

8	large veal cutlets (or 8 whole chicken breasts)	3	slices bacon, cooked and diced
¾	cup bread crumbs	1	tablespoon minced parsley
⅓	cup milk	2	egg yolks
⅓	pound bulk pork sausage, cooked	3	tablespoons shortening
⅓	cup chopped onion	3	cups consommé
1	teaspoon chopped garlic	1½	tablespoons all-purpose flour
			Parsley for garnish
		8	slices lemon for garnish

Easy • Prep time: 20 minutes
Pound veal until it is ¼ inch thick. Combine crumbs with milk. Mix with sausage, onion, garlic, bacon, parsley, and egg yolks. Put 1 tablespoon filling across the center of each piece of veal; roll up, securing with a wooden toothpick. Heat shortening in a skillet, and sauté the veal rolls until browned. Add consommé and simmer until done, 45 to 60 minutes. Thicken the liquid with flour. Place veal rolls on a platter, cover with sauce, and garnish with parsley and lemon slices.
Yields 8 servings

Mixed Green Salad

Prepare a green salad with escarole, Bibb, romaine, iceberg lettuce, dandelion greens, chives, red onions, green scallions, and watercress. Serve with vinaigrette dressing (homemade by your favorite recipe or storebought).

Chocolate Cheesecake

¾	cup graham cracker crumbs	12	1-ounce squares semisweet chocolate
5	tablespoons melted butter		
2	tablespoons sugar	1	cup sour cream
2	tablespoons cocoa powder	¾	cup butter, softened
3	eggs	1	teaspoon vanilla extract
1	cup sugar	1	cup coarsely chopped pecans
3	8-ounce packages cream cheese		Whipped cream, optional

Moderately easy • Prep time: 30 minutes • Prepare ahead and freeze
Preheat the oven to 325°. In a bowl, combine the first 4 ingredients; press into the bottom of an 8-inch springform pan. Use a mixer to beat the eggs and sugar until pale yellow. In a separate bowl, beat cheese until softened, add to the egg mixture, and mix well. Melt chocolate in a double boiler; stir in sour cream, butter, and vanilla. Stir this mixture into the cheese mixture and fold in nuts. Pour the batter into the pan. Bake for 2 hours, or until center is firm. Cool on a wire rack for 30 minutes; remove from the pan. Chill and serve with whipped cream.
Yields 10 servings

SHOPPING LIST _____

BAKERY
__ 8 to 16 hard rolls

BUTCHER
__ 2 pounds chicken livers
__ 8 large veal cutlets or 8 whole boneless, skinless chicken breasts
__ ⅓ pound bulk pork sausage
__ ¼ pound bacon

CANNED GOODS
__ 1 11-ounce can mandarin oranges
__ 2 16-ounce cans consommé

DAIRY
__ 2 pounds butter
__ ½ pint milk
__ ½ dozen eggs
__ 3 8-ounce packages cream cheese
__ 1 8-ounce container sour cream
__ ½ pint heavy cream (optional)

EXTRAS
__ 4 to 6 bottles pouilly-fuissé
__ 1 small bottle brandy
__ 1 bottle dry sherry
__ Nonstick cooking spray

MISCELLANEOUS
__ 1 quart fresh orange juice
__ 1 8-ounce bottle pineapple juice
__ 1 box unflavored gelatin
__ 1 container bread crumbs
__ 1 box graham crackers or graham cracker crumbs
__ 2 6-ounce boxes semisweet chocolate squares
__ 1 6-ounce package pecan pieces

PRODUCE
__ 2 pounds snow peas
__ 3 medium onions
__ 1 red onion
__ 1 bunch scallions
__ 1 bunch fresh mint
__ 1 head garlic
__ 1 bunch fresh parsley
__ 2 lemons
__ 1 head or bunch each: escarole, Bibb, Romaine, iceberg, dandelion greens, chives, and watercress

STAPLES/SPICES
__ All-purpose flour
__ Cinnamon sticks
__ Cocoa powder
__ Curry powder
__ Ginger
__ Ground cloves
__ Mace
__ Nutmeg
__ Paprika
__ Peppercorns
__ Salt
__ Shortening
__ Sugar
__ Vanilla extract

Lone Star State Reunion

TWO-STEP T-BONES

CHILI-RUBBED POTATOES

COUSIN'S COLESLAW

WATERMELON SLICES

PERFECT PEACH PIE

TEQUILA SHOOTERS AND TEN-GALLON TEA PUNCH

SERVES 10 TO 12

Texas has its own way of doing things, and among its
distinctive approach to life is a deep-seated reverence
for food. The recipes corralled here bear that out.
Loosen your belt and strap on the feedbag!

Notes

Two-Step T-Bones

Marinade

4	cups vegetable oil	8	cloves garlic, minced or pressed
2	cups soy sauce		
1⅓	cups red wine vinegar	5	tablespoons dry mustard
1	cup lemon juice		Salt to taste
¾	cup Worcestershire sauce		Pepper to taste

10 to 12   T-bone steaks

Easy • Prep time: 10 minutes • Prepare ahead
Combine the marinade ingredients and marinate steaks overnight.
Grill or broil steaks to desired degree of doneness.
Yields 10 to 12 servings (9 cups marinade)

Texas has some of the best supermarkets in the country. For some reason, the grocers in the Lone Star state have their pulse on not only what's hot in Texas, but their aisles also bring you the trendy items from Seattle to New York.

Chili-Rubbed Potatoes

10 to 12   *large russet potatoes*
  1   *cup vegetable oil*
  2   *tablespoons honey Dijon mustard*

Chili-Rub Spice
  5   *tablespoons chili powder*   1 ¼   *teaspoons cayenne*
  5   *tablespoons paprika*   1 ¼   *teaspoons ground cumin*

Easy • Prep time: 25 to 30 minutes
Preheat the oven to 375°. Scrub potatoes. Cut into slices or French fries. Transfer to a large pot. Thoroughly combine oil and mustard; pour over potatoes, mixing to coat. In a small bowl, combine spices. Spray baking sheets with vegetable spray. Spread potatoes on baking sheets and sprinkle with the spice mixture. Bake for 50 to 60 minutes.
Yields 10 to 12 servings

Cousin's Coleslaw

  1   *cabbage, quartered and sliced*   1   *green bell pepper, seeded, halved, and sliced*
  2   *onions, halved and sliced*   4   *carrots, peeled and grated*

Dressing
  1⅓   *cups white vinegar*   ½   *cup sugar*
  ⅔   *cup vegetable oil*   *Salt and pepper to taste*

Easy • Prep time: 25 to 30 minutes • Prepare ahead
Combine vegetables in a large mixing bowl. Combine the dressing ingredients in a blender container and process until well blended. Pour over vegetables; toss to combine. Cover and refrigerate overnight. Mix again and drain the excess liquid before serving.
Yields 12 one-cup servings

Perfect Peach Pie

8	cups sliced peaches	½	cup butter, softened
1½	cups sugar	1	cup chopped pecans
¼	cup quick tapioca	2	refrigerated 9-inch pie shells,
1	cup sifted all-purpose flour		unbaked
½	cup firmly packed		Vanilla ice cream, optional
	brown sugar		

When making fruit pies, cut a design from the pastry dough and top the pie with the design.

Moderately easy • Prep time: 25 minutes

Preheat the oven to 450°. Mix peaches, sugar, and tapioca in a large mixing bowl. In a separate bowl, combine flour and brown sugar. Cut in butter until the mixture is crumbly. Stir in nuts. Divide the brown sugar topping mixture in half. Sprinkle one-third of one portion of the brown sugar mixture over the bottom of an unbaked pie shell. Top with half of the peach mixture, then sprinkle the remaining brown sugar mixture (of the first portion) over the top. Repeat the process for the second pie. Bake the pies for 10 minutes. Lower the oven temperature to 350° and bake for another 30 minutes. Remove from the oven and cool on a wire rack before cutting. Serve topped with vanilla ice cream, if desired.

Yields 2 pies of 12 to 16 servings each

Tequila Shooters

Tequila, chilled	Coarse salt
Limes, quartered	

Easy • Prep time: 5 minutes

Serve well chilled shots of tequila with quartered fresh limes. Offer pinches of coarse salt.

Yields as many servings as needed

Ten-Gallon Tea Punch

2 family-size tea bags

1 quart boiling water

½ cup sugar

1 ½-gallon carton lemonade

1 ½-gallon carton pineapple-
    orange juice

Easy • Prep time: 20 minutes

Steep the tea bags in boiling water for 10 minutes, or until the tea is very strong. Remove tea bags and stir in sugar. Pour into a large punch bowl. Pour in lemonade and pineapple-orange juice. Serve over ice.

Yields 20 eight-ounce servings

SHOPPING LIST _____

BUTCHER
__ 10 to 12 T-bone steaks

CANNED GOODS
__ 2 16-ounce cans sliced peaches

DAIRY
__ 1 stick butter
__ 2 quarts vanilla ice cream
  (optional)

EXTRAS
__ 1 liter tequila

PRODUCE
__ 1 large or 2 small watermelons
__ 10 limes
__ 1 head garlic
__ 10 to 12 large russet potatoes
__ 1 head cabbage
__ 2 onions
__ 1 green bell pepper
__ 4 carrots

MISCELLANEOUS
__ 1 box course salt
__ 1 8-ounce bottle lemon juice
__ 1 small jar honey Dijon mustard
__ 1 container nonstick vegetable
  oil spray
__ 1 box quick tapioca
__ 1 6-ounce package chopped
  pecans
__ 2 9-inch refrigerated unbaked
  pie shells
__ 1 ½-gallon carton lemonade
__ 1 ½-gallon carton pineapple-
  orange juice

STAPLES/SPICES
__ All-purpose flour
__ Brown sugar
__ Cayenne pepper
__ Chili powder
__ Dry mustard
__ Family-size tea bags
__ Ground cumin
__ Paprika
__ Pepper
__ Red wine vinegar
__ Salt
__ Soy sauce
__ Sugar
__ Vegetable oil
__ White vinegar
__ Worcestershire sauce

COOKING FOR A CROWD

Use this table when planning and shopping for food for a large group of people. The size of serving has been listed for each item. For heavy eaters, plan approximately 1½ servings per person. Add accordingly for second helpings.

Food	Servings	Unit	Amount
		Beverages	
Coffee	25	1 cup	½ to ¾ pound
Tea, hot	25	1 cup	1 ounce
Tea, iced	25	1 glass	3 ounces
Coffee cream	25	1 tablespoon	1 pint
Milk	24	1 8-ounce glass	1 ½ gallons
		Breads	
Bread	25	1 1-ounce slice	1¼ pounds
Casseroles	25	1 cup	6¼ quarts
Cake	24	1 slice	2 9-inch layers
	24	2½-inch squares	1 15½x10½x1 sheet cake
Pie	24	⅛ pie	3 9-inch pies
Canned fruit	24	½ cup	1 6½- to 7¼- pound can
		Relishes	
Carrot strips	25	2 to 3 strips	1 to 1¼ pounds
Cauliflowerets	25	2 ounces, sliced raw	7 pounds
Celery	25	1 2- to 3-inch piece	1 stalk
Olives	25	3 to 4	1 quart
Pickles	25	2	1 quart
Radishes	25	2	5 bunches
Tomatoes	25	3 ounces, sliced	5 to 6¼ pounds
		Salads	
Cottage cheese	25	⅓ cup	5 pounds
Fruit	24	⅓ cup	2 quarts
Gelatin	25	½ cup liquid	3 quarts
Potato	24	½ cup	3 quarts
Veggie	25	¼ cup	1¼ gallons
		Vegetables	
Canned	25	½ cup	1 6½- to 7½- pound can
Potatoes	25	½ cup mashed	6¾ pounds
	25	1 medium baked	8½ pounds
	25	10 French fries	3¼ pounds
		Frozen	
Beans	25	⅓ cup	5¼ pounds
Carrots	25	⅓ cup	5 pounds
Peas	25	⅓ cup	5 pounds
Pasta	25	4 to 5 ounces	6 to 8 pounds

CELEBRATIONS

Although your specific occasions for celebrating will vary—Super Bowl Sunday, Easter, Mother's Day, Fourth of July, Thanksgiving, anniversaries, graduations—always keep in mind your interests, intent, budget, and schedule. Some will love to create elaborate themes that tie in the food, table decorations, flowers, and invitations, while others will be content simply to call a few friends at the last minute and invite them over, à la "come as you are." Any way you do it, inviting friends and family into your home should be fun for everyone—not just the guests.

There are as many good sites for entertaining as there are personalities. Try placing a table in front of the living room fireplace. Use a corner of your front porch and dress up a table with your best linens. Take advantage of the kitchen counter, draped with dramatic colors and vases filled with tall flowers, to utilize space in a small apartment.

Getting guests to mingle is sometimes a challenge. You can help by providing name tags on a tray near the door. When seating guests for dinner, use place cards. Don't just sit people anywhere. Be creative with the seating of your guests so they will get to know and enjoy someone they haven't been with recently (but try to make sure the guests seated beside each other are compatible with one another!).

Festive occasions call not only for well thought out sites and great menus, but also the best wines. Complimentary wine and food matches are usually achieved when you adopt a "middle of the road" approach.

Whether you are celebrating for two or twenty-four, these fun, event-driven menus will showcase your talents.

Bastille Day Dinner

"One cannot have too large a party."—JANE AUSTEN

Notes

_____

_____

_____

_____

_____

_____

_____

_____

Celebrate classic fine French cuisine by serving your courses in the following order:
- Soup
- Fish
- Palate cleanser (usually sorbet)
- Meat (includes vegetables)
- Salad
- Cheese
- Dessert

SPINACH SOUP

FILLETS PARISIENNE

BERRY SORBET

BEEF TENDERLOIN WITH MARCHAND DE VIN SAUCE

STEAMED HARICOTS VERTS

WILD RICE

FRENCH BREAD

WATERCRESS SALAD

ECLAIRS OR OTHER FRENCH PASTRIES

PINOT NOIR

SERVES 10

Bastille Day is observed in France on July 14, to commemorate the 1789 storming of the Paris Bastille prison. Use this famous date in history as a reason to salute the French.

Spinach Soup

1 onion, finely chopped
2 tablespoons butter, melted
3 tablespoons all-purpose flour
2 cups milk
2 cups cooked spinach, well-drained
1 cup consommé
Salt and pepper to taste
2 cups light cream
½ cup sherry
1 cup chopped toasted almonds

Easy • Prep time: 20 minutes
Sauté onion in butter until tender; remove from the skillet with a slotted spoon. Stir in flour, then milk. Purée spinach with consommé; add the mixture to the sauce. Add seasonings. Stir in cream; mix well. Heat just until simmering; stir in sherry. Sprinkle with almonds before serving.
Yields 10 servings

Fillets Parisienne

10	trout fillets	½	cup bread crumbs
	Salt, pepper, and cayenne	½	cup chopped fresh parsley
	pepper to taste	¼	cup butter
2	cups grated sharp		
	Cheddar cheese		

Easy • Prep time: 5 minutes
Preheat the broiler. Place fillets in a shallow, buttered casserole dish. Season with salt, pepper, and cayenne. Sprinkle with a mixture of cheese, bread crumbs, and parsley. Dot with butter. Place the dish about 5 inches below the broiler and cook for 10 to 15 minutes, or until fish flakes easily with a fork and top is browned.
Yields 10 servings

Berry Sorbet

1	pound cranberries	2	cups sugar
3	cups boiling water	⅛	teaspoon salt
1	tablespoon unflavored	1 ¼	cups orange juice
	gelatin	1	tablespoon lemon juice
½	cup cold water		

Moderately easy • Prep time: 25 minutes • Prepare ahead and freeze
Bring berries to a boil; cook until soft. Drain and purée. Soften gelatin in cold water for 5 minutes. Combine purée, sugar, salt, and juices in a large saucepan; bring to a boil. Stir in gelatin; blend until completely dissolved. Remove from heat. Cool. Freeze until almost firm. Beat until light and fluffy. Freeze again until firm.
Yields 10 servings

Beef Tenderloin with Marchand de Vin Sauce

1	5- to 6-pound filet of beef, at room temperature	4	ounces mushrooms, sliced
	Olive oil	¼	cup butter
	Salt, pepper, and garlic powder to taste	1	cup claret
		1	cup consommé
½	cup chopped green onions	3	tablespoons cornstarch
		1	tablespoon lemon juice

Easy • Prep time: 15 minutes
Preheat the oven to 350°. Rub meat with oil and seasonings. Bake in a shallow pan for 45 minutes, or until a meat thermometer registers desired degree of doneness (see p. 134). Sauté onion and mushrooms in butter until tender. Add wine; simmer for 1 hour until reduced by half. Mix consommé and cornstarch and stir into the mixture; simmer until thickened. Add lemon juice and meat drippings from the roasting pan. Serve the sauce over the meat.
Yields 10 servings

Watercress Salad

2	teaspoons salt	½	cup lemon juice
2	teaspoons pepper	1	cup vegetable oil
¼	cup prepared mustard	10	bunches watercress, washed, drained, and stems removed
1	tablespoon Worcestershire sauce		
½	cup ketchup		

Easy • Prep time: 5 minutes
Combine the first 7 ingredients in a blender. Drizzle lightly over watercress.
Yields 10 servings

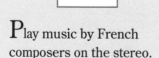

Play music by French composers on the stereo.

SHOPPING LIST

BAKERY
__ 3 loaves French bread
__ 10 eclairs or other French pastries

BUTCHER
__ 10 fillets of trout
__ 1 5- to 6-pound filet of beef

CANNED GOODS
__ 1 16-ounce can consommé

DAIRY
__ 2 sticks butter
__ 1 pint milk
__ 1 pint light cream
__ 8 ounces sharp Cheddar cheese

EXTRAS
__ 1 case pinot noir
__ 1 small bottle sherry
__ 1 bottle claret

MISCELLANEOUS
__ 2 boxes wild rice
__ 1 10-ounce package frozen chopped spinach
__ 1 6-ounce package chopped or slivered almonds
__ 1 container bread crumbs
__ 1 box unflavored gelatin
__ 1 16-ounce bottle orange juice
__ 1 small bottle lemon juice
__ 1 small bottle ketchup

PRODUCE
__ 2 pounds haricots verts or green beans
__ 1 onion
__ 1 bunch fresh parsley
__ 1 16-ounce package cranberries
__ 1 bunch green onions
__ 4 ounces mushrooms
__ 10 bunches watercress

STAPLES/SPICES
__ All-purpose flour
__ Cayenne pepper
__ Cornstarch
__ Garlic powder
__ Olive oil
__ Pepper
__ Prepared mustard
__ Salt
__ Sugar
__ Vegetable oil
__ Worcestershire sauce

Cinco de Mayo

GUACAMOLE SALAD

TACO NACHOS WITH TOMATO-PEPPER RELISH

HOT TAMALES

CHICKEN ENCHILADAS

PINTO BEANS

CARAMEL NUT CANDY

MARGARITAS, ICED TEA, AND BEER

SERVES 24

On the fifth of May, have your friends over for margaritas and such. In 1862, French troops were defeated at the Battle of Puebla in Mexico. Today Cinco de Mayo is acknowledged by Mexicans in Latin America and by Mexican-Americans in the United States.

Guacamole Salad

9 avocados, peeled
   and mashed
3 tomatoes, peeled and
   coarsely chopped
1 onion, finely chopped

6 green chilies, seeded
   and chopped
3 tablespoons lemon juice,
   optional
   Salt and pepper to taste

Easy • Prep time: 20 minutes
Stir tomatoes, onion, chilies, and seasonings into avocados. Mix well. Chill and serve with chips or nachos.
Yields 10 servings

Use sombreros filled with wildflowers as table centerpieces.

Taco Nachos with Tomato-Pepper Relish

2	pounds ground beef	2	tablespoons chili powder
2¼	cups minced onion, divided	1½	teaspoons ground cumin
2	cloves garlic, pressed	2	jalapeño or chili peppers,
5	cups chopped tomatoes,		minced, optional
	divided	2	large bags tortilla chips
4	teaspoons salt	3	cups shredded cheese
	Black and cayenne pepper	3	cups shredded lettuce
	to taste		Tomato-Pepper Relish

Serve Mexican beers, such as Tecate, Dos Equis, and Corona.

Moderately easy • Prep time: 20 to 25 minutes

Sauté ground beef with 1½ cups of the onion and all of the garlic until browned. Add 1½ cups tomatoes, salt, pepper, chili powder, cumin, and jalapeños. Cover and simmer for 10 minutes, adding a little water if the mixture appears dry. Combine remaining tomatoes and onions and refrigerate for at least 30 minutes. At serving time, crisp the tortilla chips in a 350° oven for 5 minutes. Serve with bowls of the meat mixture, remaining tomatoes, remaining onions, cheese, lettuce, and Tomato-Pepper Relish.

Yields 10 servings

Tomato-Pepper Relish

50 to 60	ripe tomatoes	2	cups white vinegar
4	cups juice from the tomatoes	1	cup thinly sliced garlic
5	cups jalapeño and/or chili	1	cup sugar
	peppers, chopped	5	tablespoons salt
5	cups chopped onions	½	teaspoon garlic powder
1	cup tarragon vinegar	2	tablespoons seasoned salt

Moderately easy • Prep time: 30 minutes

Place tomatoes in boiling water until the skins split. Remove and cool. Peel, chop, and drain, reserving juice. Place all the ingredients in a large pot and simmer for 2 to 2½ hours, stirring occasionally. Pack in sterilized pint jars.

Yields 12 pints

Buy small cacti in individual pots. Wrap raffia around the pots and give them as favors when your guests leave.

Chicken Enchiladas

16	boneless, skinless chicken breast halves	4	teaspoons sugar
	Salt	4	teaspoons ground cumin
4	cups chopped onions	2	teaspoons salt
4	cloves garlic, minced	2	teaspoons oregano
½	cup butter, melted	2	teaspoons basil
4	16-ounce cans tomatoes, chopped	4	dozen tortillas
			Vegetable oil
4	cups tomato sauce	10	cups shredded Monterey Jack cheese
1	cup canned, chopped green chili peppers	3	cups sour cream, optional

Moderately easy • Prep time: 30 minutes

Preheat the oven to 375°. Simmer chicken breasts in water until fork tender, about 15 to 20 minutes. Drain. Sprinkle with salt. Cut each piece into 3 strips and set aside. In a large saucepan, sauté onion and garlic in the butter until tender. Add tomatoes, tomato sauce, chilies, sugar, cumin, salt, oregano, and basil. Bring to a boil, reduce heat, and simmer, covered, for 20 minutes.

While the sauce is simmering, soft fry the tortillas in hot oil; drain and set aside. Place 1 strip of chicken and 2 tablespoons of cheese in each tortilla; roll up and place seam side down in four 9x13-inch casserole dishes. Blend sour cream into the sauce, if desired, and pour over tortillas. Sprinkle with remaining cheese and bake, uncovered, for 20 minutes.

Yields 48 enchiladas

Pinto Beans

2 pounds dried pinto beans,
  rinsed and drained
1 10-ounce can Ro-Tel
  chopped tomatoes and
  green chilies
1 16-ounce can tomatoes,
  chopped
1 onion, chopped

1 clove garlic, sliced in half
  and skewered with toothpicks
3 drops of Tabasco sauce
½ pound salt pork or 2 ham hocks
  Freshly ground black pepper
  to taste
  Salt to taste

Easy • Prep time: 10 minutes
In a large heavy kettle, add 5 to 6 quarts of water and the beans; bring
to a boil. Add the remaining ingredients, except salt, reduce heat, and
simmer for at least 6 hours. Remove garlic before serving. Add salt to
taste.
Yields 16 to 20 servings

Caramel Nut Candy

3 cups sugar
1 cup milk
1 teaspoon cornstarch
1 tablespoon butter

1 teaspoon vanilla extract
  Pinch of baking powder
1 cup chopped pecans

Moderately easy • Prep time: 30 minutes (including cooking time)
Over low heat, melt 1 cup of the sugar slowly in a heavy saucepan. Add
milk, bring to a boil, and stir in remaining 2 cups of sugar to which
cornstarch has been added. Continue boiling until soft-ball stage, or
235° on a candy thermometer, is reached. Remove from the heat; add
butter, vanilla, and baking powder. Beat with a wooden spoon until
creamy. Stir in nuts and pour into a buttered 9x13-inch casserole dish.
When nearly cooled, cut into squares.
Yields 24 pieces

Margaritas

2 fifths tequila	1 cup lime juice, optional
1 pint Triple Sec	½ cup lemon juice
3½ quarts water	Coarse salt
8 6-ounce cans frozen limeade	

Easy • Prep time: 5 minutes • Prepare ahead
The day before serving, combine the first 5 ingredients and refrigerate until chilled. Stir well and freeze until 6 hours before serving. Return to the refrigerator. To serve, dip rims of glasses in lemon juice, then in a plate of coarse salt; fill.
Yields 58 four-ounce drinks

SHOPPING LIST

BUTCHER
__ 2 pounds ground beef
__ 4 pounds boneless, skinless
   chicken breasts
__ ½ pound salt pork or 2 ham hocks

CANNED GOODS
__ 5 16-ounce cans tomatoes
__ 4 8-ounce cans tomato sauce
__ 2 4-ounce cans chopped green
   chilies
__ 1 10-ounce can Ro-Tel chopped
   tomatoes and chilies

DAIRY
__ 1 pound Cheddar cheese
__ 2 sticks butter
__ 1½ pounds Monterey Jack
   cheese
__ 2 16 ounce containers sour cream
__ ½ pint milk

EXTRAS
__ 6 pounds fresh tamales (available
   at Hispanic specialty stores)
__ 4 or 5 cases beer
__ 2 fifths tequila
__ 1 16-ounce bottle Triple Sec

MISCELLANEOUS
__ 8 6-ounce cans frozen limeade
__ 1 8-ounce bottle lime juice
   (optional)
__ 2 8-ounce bottles lemon juice
__ 1 or 2 bottles taco sauce
   (optional)
__ 2 large bags tortilla chips
__ 1 bottle tarragon vinegar
__ 4 or 5 packages corn tortillas
__ 2 pounds dried pinto beans
__ 1 6-ounce package chopped
   pecans

PRODUCE
__ 11 large onions
__ 7 heads garlic
__ 68 large tomatoes
__ 2 pounds jalapeño and/or chili
   peppers
__ 6 green chilies
__ 1 head lettuce
__ 9 ripe avocados

STAPLES/SPICES
__ Baking powder
__ Basil
__ Cayenne pepper
__ Chili powder
__ Cornstarch
__ Garlic powder
__ Ground cumin
__ Oregano
__ Peppercorns
__ Salt
__ Seasoned salt
__ Sugar
__ Tabasco sauce
__ Tea bags
__ Vanilla extract
__ Vegetable oil
__ White vinegar

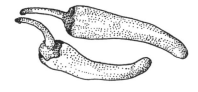

Super Bowl Sunday

GLAZED BEEF BRISKET

SLICED TURKEY BREAST

LAYERED SHRIMP SPREAD

SPINACH FETA PUFFS

VEGGIES WITH DIP

HARD ROLLS AND SLICED DARK BREADS

CHOCOLATE LACED FRUIT

BEER

SERVES 20 TO 25

Some people revere this day as if it were a national holiday. This game, which pits the National Football Conference champion against the American Football Conference champion for the National Football League title, usually occurs each January. Even if you're not a big football fan, it makes a great excuse for having a bunch of people over for food and fun.

Use team logos and colors in your decorations.

For the true fans in your group, or for those who love to toss around a pigskin, have a football handy for half-time pursuits in the backyard.

Glazed Beef Brisket

1 8-pound beef brisket	4 onions, sliced
2 lemons, sliced	2 tablespoons pickling spices
4 oranges, sliced	⅔ cup brown sugar, firmly packed

Easy • Prep time: 10 minutes
Place brisket or other desired roast in a Dutch oven or large pan; cover with cold water. Bring to a boil and skim oil from water. Add lemons, oranges, onion, and spices. Simmer for 4 hours, or until tender. Remove to the roasting pan. Preheat the oven to 350°. Sprinkle meat with brown sugar and bake until sugar melts. Slice and serve with spicy mustard and bread or rolls.
Yields 25 servings

Layered Shrimp Spread

8 ounces cream cheese, softened
1 tablespoon mayonnaise
¼ teaspoon Worcestershire sauce
Juice of 1 lemon
½ teaspoon seasoned salt
½ teaspoon lemon pepper
¾ pound shrimp, boiled and peeled

1 12-ounce jar cocktail sauce
½ pound Monterey Jack cheese, grated
3 green onions with tops, chopped
½ green bell pepper, chopped
½ cup sliced black olives
Crackers

Easy • Prep time: 15 minutes

In a large bowl of an electric mixer, mix cream cheese until smooth. Add mayonnaise, Worcestershire, lemon juice, and seasonings. Spread evenly in a circle on a round glass or silver serving platter. Refrigerate while preparing other toppings. Chop half the shrimp. Layer ingredients on top of cream cheese as follows: cocktail sauce, chopped shrimp, cheese, green onions, green pepper, and olives. Arrange whole shrimp on top. This should resemble a pizza. Serve with crackers.

Yields 25 servings

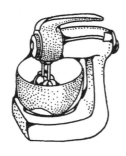

If you have any former football players in your midst, ask them to tell some of their funniest football stories.

Have a collection of visors, pompons, buttons, or other football paraphernalia so guests can show their team loyalty.

Spinach Feta Puffs

2	10-ounce packages frozen chopped spinach		Grated nutmeg to taste
			Salt and pepper to taste
½	cup finely chopped onion	1	cup cottage cheese
¼	cup butter, melted	1	pound feta cheese
¼	cup all-purpose flour	1	pound phyllo pastry
¾	cup milk	1	cup butter, melted

Moderately easy • Prep time: 30 minutes

Preheat the oven to 350°. Thaw spinach; place on paper towels and squeeze until barely moist. Sauté onion in butter until tender. Add spinach and cook over low heat, stirring constantly, for 5 minutes. Add flour and milk; stir until blended. Season to taste with nutmeg, salt, and pepper. Remove vegetables from the skillet; cool. Add cheeses to the spinach mixture; stir well. Cut sheets of phyllo lengthwise into 3½-inch strips. Working with one strip at a time, brush each phyllo strip with melted butter. Keep remaining strips covered, according to the package directions. Place 2 teaspoons of filling at base of phyllo strip, folding the right bottom corner over it into a triangle. Continue folding back and forth into a triangle to the end of the strip. Place the triangles seam side down on buttered baking sheets. Brush tops with melted butter. Bake for about 25 minutes, or until triangles are well browned. Serve immediately.

Yields 60 triangles

Chocolate Laced Fruit

2 cups mandarin orange
   sections
2 cups pineapple chunks

2 pints large strawberries
16 ounces semisweet chocolate

Moderately easy • Prep time: 25 to 30 minutes

Drain canned fruit and pat dry on paper towels. Rinse strawberries, leaving stems intact. For best results, have fruit at room temperature for dipping. Melt chocolate in the top of a double boiler, stirring constantly. Remove chocolate from the heat and add ice cubes to water in the double boiler to bring water temperature to warm. Dip each piece of fruit separately into chocolate, covering half of each fruit piece. Place on waxed paper. Let stand for 10 minutes, until set. Prepare on the day of party and refrigerate until ready to serve. To serve, arrange fruit decoratively on party trays.

Yields 25 servings

SHOPPING LIST _____

BAKERY
__ Assorted hard rolls
__ Sliced dark breads

BUTCHER
__ 1 4-to 5-pound smoked turkey breast
__ 1 8-pound beef brisket
__ ¾ pound shrimp

CANNED GOODS
__ 1 16-ounce can sliced black olives
__ 1 16-ounce can mandarin oranges
__ 1 16-ounce can pineapple chunks

DAIRY
__ 1 8-ounce package cream cheese
__ ½ pound Monterey Jack cheese
__ 1 pound butter
__ ½ pint milk
__ 1 8-ounce container cottage cheese
__ 1 pound feta cheese

EXTRAS
__ 3 to 4 cases beer

MISCELLANEOUS
__ 1 small jar spicy brown mustard
__ 1 small jar Dijon mustard
__ 1 16-ounce container spinach, onion, or dill dip
__ 1 12-ounce jar cocktail sauce
__ 2 boxes salted crackers
__ 2 10-ounce packages frozen chopped spinach

__ 1 16-ounce box phyllo dough
__ 1 16-ounce package semisweet chocolate morsels

PRODUCE
__ 1 stalk celery
__ 1 pint cherry tomatoes
__ 1 head cauliflower
__ 1 bunch broccoli
__ 1 bag carrots
__ ½ pound snow peas
__ 3 or 4 assorted colors of bell peppers
__ 1 green bell pepper
__ 3 lemons
__ 4 oranges
__ 5 onions
__ 1 bunch green onions

STAPLES/SPICES
__ All-purpose flour
__ Brown sugar
__ Lemon pepper seasoning
__ Mayonnaise
__ Nutmeg
__ Pepper
__ Pickling spices
__ Salt
__ Seasoned salt
__ Worcestershire sauce

Mardi Gras Madness

JAMBALAYA

FRENCH QUARTER FRICASSEE

CRAYFISH WITH CAJUN MUSTARD

BOURBON STREET BONBONS

BEER

SERVES 6

Celebrating Mardi Gras is a longstanding tradition in many communities, namely New Orleans. This carnival period, which climaxes the day before Ash Wednesday, brings revelers into the streets and costumes into the mainstream. If you can't lead your own parade or build your own float, you can at least put on a mask and commence the merrymaking.

Ask guests to wear costumes. For those who don't, have festive party hats and/or masks available.

Notes

Jambalaya

1   pound ham, cubed
1   small onion, chopped
2   ribs celery, chopped
¼   cup butter
1   teaspoon cayenne pepper
2   teaspoons pepper
1   teaspoon salt
1   teaspoon oregano
1   teaspoon ground cumin
1   teaspoon thyme
2   cups uncooked white rice
4   cups chicken broth
1   pound cooked, peeled shrimp
2   pounds boneless, skinless chicken breasts, cooked and cut into chunks

Moderately easy • Prep time: 20 minutes
In a Dutch oven, sauté the ham, onion, and celery in the butter until the vegetables are tender. Add the seasonings and heat for 3 to 5 minutes more, stirring constantly. Add the rice, broth, shrimp, and chicken and simmer, covered, for 20 to 30 minutes, or until the rice is tender. Serve hot.
Yields 6 to 8 servings

Use plastic necklaces and trinkets, like those thrown from floats during Mardi Gras parades, as decorations and party favors.

French Quarter Fricassee

10 ounces mushrooms, cleaned and stemmed
2 onions, quartered and then each quarter cut in half crosswise
2 turnips, quartered and then each quarter cut in half crosswise
4 carrots, cut into 2-inch chunks
4 ribs celery, cut into 2-inch chunks
2 large potatoes, peeled and cut into 1½-inch chunks
¼ cup vegetable oil
2 teaspoons salt, or to taste
2 teaspoons pepper, or to taste
⅓ cup all-purpose flour
5 sprigs fresh parsley
2 sprigs fresh thyme
2 fresh bay leaves
Kitchen string
1½ cups dry white wine
2 cups or more chicken broth

Moderate • Prep time: 30 minutes

In a Dutch oven, sauté the vegetables in the oil for 5 minutes over medium heat. Season the vegetables with salt and pepper. Sprinkle the flour over the vegetables and continue to cook, stirring frequently, for 5 more minutes. Form a bouquet garni by tying the parsley, thyme, and bay leaves together with kitchen string. Add the wine, bouquet garni, and enough broth just to cover the vegetables. Simmer uncovered for 30 to 40 minutes, or until the vegetables are very tender and much of the liquid has evaporated. Remove the bouquet garni and serve hot.

Yields 6 to 8 servings

Crayfish with Cajun Mustard

½	cup Dijon mustard		1	teaspoon thyme
1	tablespoon honey		1	teaspoon paprika
½	teaspoon cayenne pepper		6 to 10	steamed crayfish
½	teaspoon black pepper			Crackers
1	teaspoon ground cumin			

Easy • Prep time: 5 minutes • Prepare ahead
Combine the mustard, honey, and seasonings in a bowl; mix well. Allow the mixture to sit for at least 2 hours in the refrigerator before serving with crayfish and crackers.
Yields 6 to 8 servings

Don't forget to provide your guests with tools to open the crayfish shells if they are not used to doing it with their hands!

Bourbon Street Bonbons

1	cup chopped, toasted pecans	¼ teaspoon salt
2	cups vanilla wafer crumbs	3 tablespoons light corn syrup
1½	cups confectioners' sugar	⅓ cup bourbon
½	cup brown sugar	Confectioners' sugar for garnish

Easy • Prep time: 30 minutes
In a large bowl, combine the pecans, crumbs, sugars, and salt. Add the corn syrup and bourbon. Add more corn syrup or confectioners' sugar if needed to shape the mixture into 1-inch balls. Roll each ball in confectioners' sugar.
Yields 6 to 8 dozen balls

SHOPPING LIST _____

BUTCHER/DELI
___ 1 pound ham
___ 1 pound cooked and peeled
    shrimp
___ 2 pounds boneless, skinless
    chicken breasts
___ 6 to 10 crayfish

CANNED GOODS
___ 4 16-ounce cans chicken broth

DAIRY
___ 1 stick butter

EXTRAS
___ Kitchen string
___ 1 small bottle dry white wine
___ 1 small bottle bourbon

MISCELLANEOUS
___ 1 8-ounce jar Dijon mustard
___ 1 8-ounce jar honey
___ 1 box whole-wheat or sesame
    crackers
___ 1 6-ounce package chopped
    pecans
___ 1 box vanilla wafers
___ 1 bottle light corn syrup

PRODUCE
___ 3 small onions
___ 2 turnips
___ 4 carrots
___ 2 large potatoes
___ 1 stalk celery
___ 1 10-ounce package fresh
    mushrooms
___ 1 bunch fresh parsley
___ 1 bunch fresh thyme
___ 1 small bunch fresh bay leaves

STAPLES/SPICES
___ All-purpose flour
___ Black pepper
___ Brown sugar
___ Cayenne pepper
___ Confectioners' sugar
___ Ground cumin
___ Oregano
___ Paprika
___ Salt
___ Thyme
___ Vegetable oil
___ White rice

St. Patrick's Day Brunch

DUBLIN EGG TOSS

APPLES IN SAUTERNE

YEAST ROLLS

"NOT A SNAKE IN SIGHT" SAUSAGE PATTIES

CRÈME DE MENTHE CAKE

IRISH COFFEE

SERVES 6

Observed on March 17, this day pays homage to St. Patrick, the patron saint of Ireland. Although some of us can trace our roots back to Ireland, some of us aren't so lucky. Either way, it's a great excuse to wear something green.

Dublin Egg Toss

1	small onion, diced
3	tablespoons olive oil
1	teaspoon pepper
1	teaspoon salt
2	teaspoons crushed dried rosemary leaves
2	teaspoons crushed dried basil leaves
4	large potatoes, scrubbed and cut into small cubes
2	tablespoons milk
5	large eggs, beaten

Easy • Prep time: 20 minutes

In a large skillet or Dutch oven, sauté the onion in the olive oil over medium-high heat. Add the seasonings and mix well. Add the potatoes and cook, stirring frequently, until the potatoes are cooked through and browned. Whisk the milk into the eggs and pour the mixture into the potatoes. Stir and flip constantly to coat the potatoes and cook the eggs. Serve warm.

Yields 6 servings

Naturally, green is the order of the day. Use green paper plates and napkins.

Apples in Sauterne

7 medium apples, peeled and cored
½ cup sauterne
1 tablespoon chopped, candied orange peel
½ teaspoon grated nutmeg
2 tablespoons orange juice
1 tablespoon lemon juice
Whipped cream, optional

Easy • Prep time: 20 minutes
In a baking dish, combine apples, wine, orange peel, nutmeg, and juices; poach until apples are soft. Take half of an apple and combine with pan juices in a blender. Use as a sauce for remaining whole apples. Serve with whipped cream, if desired.
Yields 6 servings

"Not a Snake in Sight" Sausage Patties

1 pound bulk sausage
1 small onion, minced
½ teaspoon ground cinnamon
1 small Granny Smith apple, cored, peeled, and minced

Easy • Prep time: 10 minutes
Mix all ingredients well. Shape into 3-inch patties and cook in a skillet over medium heat.
Yields 6 servings

St. Patrick is said to have used the word of God to banish all snakes from Ireland.

Crème de Menthe Cake

1	box white pudding cake mix	1	16-ounce jar hot fudge
⅓	cup crème de menthe	½	pint heavy cream, whipped

Easy • Prep time: 20 minutes

Prepare the cake according to the package directions, substituting 3 tablespoons crème de menthe for water. Bake in a 13x9x2-inch pan. Cool. Heat fudge topping and smooth over cake. Cool. Fold remaining crème de menthe into whipped cream and frost the cake.

Yields 24 servings

Irish Coffee

Irish whiskey	Hot coffee
Sugar	Heavy cream

Easy • Prep time: 2 minutes

Pour 1½ ounces whiskey into a large mug. Add sugar to taste. Fill hot coffee to within ½ inch of the top. Add cream; do not stir.

Yields 1 serving

Ask your guests to wear something green in honor of the day.

SHOPPING LIST _____

BAKERY
__ 1 dozen yeast rolls

DAIRY
__ ½ pint milk
__ ½ dozen eggs
__ 1 pint heavy cream

EXTRAS
__ 1 bottle sauterne
__ 1 bottle crème de menthe
__ 1 bottle Irish whiskey

MISCELLANEOUS
__ 1 package candied orange peel
__ 1 box white pudding cake mix
__ 1 16-ounce container hot fudge

PRODUCE
__ 1 small onion
__ 4 large potatoes
__ 7 medium apples
__ 1 orange
__ 1 lemon

STAPLES/SPICES
__ Cinnamon
__ Coffee
__ Dried basil
__ Dried rosemary
__ Nutmeg
__ Pepper
__ Salt
__ Sugar
__ Vegetable oil

HAM WITH APRICOT SAUCE

PINEAPPLE PUDDING

CARROTS IN BOUILLON

KAISER ROLLS

SOUR CREAM COCONUT CAKE (see p. 192)

COFFEE

SERVES 6

Mother's Day is a great time to gather together with family. If you haven't seen yours in a while, plan to have them over in the spring. You'll be glad you did.

Ham with Apricot Sauce

6 slices cooked, boneless ham, cut about ¼-inch thick
2 tablespoons vegetable oil
2 cups sliced onion
1 12-ounce can apricot nectar
1½ teaspoons cornstarch
¼ cup water

Easy • Prep time: 10 minutes • Recipe enlarges easily

Brown ham in hot oil; remove from the skillet. Add onion and cook until tender; stir in nectar. Return ham to the skillet. Cover and simmer for 15 minutes, basting occasionally. Remove ham to a serving platter. Dissolve cornstarch in water; add to the sauce. Cook, stirring constantly, until thickened and translucent. Serve the sauce over warm ham.
Yields 6 servings

Fill a vase with your mother's favorite flowers and use it as a centerpiece.

Pineapple Pudding

½ cup butter, melted
6 slices white bread, cubed and crusts removed
3 eggs, beaten
⅓ cup sugar

1 tablespoon all-purpose flour
⅛ teaspoon salt
1 14-ounce can crushed pineapple
1 teaspoon grated lemon peel

Easy • Prep time: 10 minutes
Preheat the oven to 325°. Mix all ingredients together and pour into a buttered casserole dish. Bake for 1 hour.
Yields 6 servings

Carrots in Bouillon

8 carrots, peeled and trimmed
2 cups water or enough to cover

4 or 5 chicken bouillon cubes

Easy • Prep time: 5 minutes
Coarsely grate carrots. Put in a 1½-quart saucepan and cover with water; add bouillon cubes. Bring to a boil; reduce heat to low and cook gently until carrots are tender and bouillon is dissolved, about 8 to 10 minutes. Do not overcook.
Yields 6 servings

SHOPPING LIST _____

BAKERY
__ 1 loaf white bread
__ 1 dozen small kaiser rolls

BUTCHER/DELI
__ 6 quarter-inch thick slices
    boneless ham

CANNED GOODS
__ 2 14-ounce cans crushed
    pineapple
__ 1 12-ounce can apricot nectar

DAIRY
__ 2 sticks butter
__ ½ dozen eggs
__ 1 pint sour cream

MISCELLANEOUS
__ 2 7-ounce packages flaked
    coconut
__ 1 box yellow cake mix

PRODUCE
__ 1 large onion
__ 1 lemon
__ 1 bag carrots

STAPLES/SPICES
__ All-purpose flour
__ Chicken bouillon cubes
__ Coffee
__ Cornstarch
__ Salt
__ Sugar
__ Vegetable oil

Honor Thy Father

SHRIMP AND ARTICHOKE APPETIZERS

BOSTON LETTUCE WITH BACON

HOT HERB BREAD

FILETS WITH BÉARNAISE SAUCE

STUFFED ZUCCHINI

LEMON SOUR CREAM PIE

ICED TEA AND COFFEE

SERVES 8

Father's Day doesn't have to be in June. Any day is good enough to tell your father how much he means to you and your family. After all he's done for you, surely he deserves a decent meal. Why not be the one to prepare it for him?

Shrimp and Artichoke Appetizers

Shrimp boil
4 pounds medium raw shrimp
4 8½-ounce cans artichoke hearts, drained
Juice of 1 lemon
¼ cup capers
¼ cup chopped basil leaves

¼ cup chopped onion
Black pepper to taste
2 cups mayonnaise
Tabasco to taste
1 teaspoon seasoned salt
Romaine lettuce
Crackers or bread rounds

Easy • Prep time: 30 minutes (including cooking time)
Place shrimp boil in water and boil for 10 minutes. Add shrimp and boil for 7 minutes; drain immediately and cool. Rinse artichoke hearts. Peel shrimp and toss with remaining ingredients, adding artichokes last. Stir to coat. Serve in a shallow bowl or platter lined with lettuce leaves.
Yields 20 to 25 servings

Boston Lettuce with Bacon

2	heads Boston lettuce		2	teaspoons bacon drippings
12	slices bacon, fried crisp and crumbled		2	tablespoons olive oil
3	hard-boiled eggs, sliced		1	tablespoon white vinegar
2	ribs celery, chopped			Salt and pepper to taste
2	green onions, minced		4	drops Tabasco sauce

Easy • Prep time: 20 minutes

Wash and drain lettuce and tear into pieces. Combine the first 5 ingredients shortly before serving time. Combine bacon drippings, olive oil, and vinegar. Add salt, pepper, and Tabasco to the oil mixture and stir well. Pour over salad greens and toss well. Serve immediately.

Yields 8 servings

Hot Herb Bread

2	loaves Italian bread		½	teaspoon oregano
1	cup butter, softened		¼	teaspoon garlic powder
2	teaspoons dried parsley flakes		½	teaspoon dried dill weed
				Grated Parmesan cheese

Easy • Prep time: 10 minutes

Preheat the oven to 400°. Cut bread diagonally into 1-inch-thick slices (do not cut completely through). Combine the next 5 ingredients and spread on bread. Shape aluminum foil around loaf, leaving the top open and twisting the ends. Sprinkle the loaf liberally with cheese and extra parsley flakes. Bake for 10 minutes.

Yields 12 servings

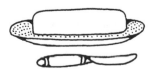

"In my younger and more vulnerable years my father gave me some advice I've been turning over in my mind ever since."

—F. SCOTT FITZGERALD,
THE GREAT GATSBY

To clarify butter, melt whole butter on the stove and carefully skim off the cloudy material that rises to the top. The clear liquid remaining is your clarified butter.

Filets with Béarnaise Sauce

8 beef filets, 1¼ inches thick, about 6 ounces each	Freshly ground black pepper
	¼ cup butter

Easy • Prep time: 15 minutes (including cooking time)
Season the steaks with black pepper, pressing in on both sides of meat. In a very large skillet, melt butter and sear steaks over medium-high heat for 3½ to 5 minutes on each side, or until desired doneness is obtained. Serve with Béarnaise Sauce.
Yields 8 servings

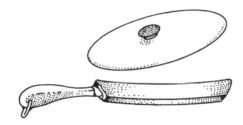

Béarnaise Sauce

¼ cup tarragon vinegar	3 egg yolks, lightly beaten
2 tablespoons minced onion	1 cup clarified butter, cooled
1 tablespoon dried tarragon	Salt and pepper
⅛ teaspoon white pepper	Chopped parsley
1 tablespoon cold water	

Moderate • Prep time: 20 to 25 minutes (including cooking time)
In a heavy saucepan, combine vinegar, onion, tarragon, and pepper. Reduce liquid over high heat to about 1 tablespoon. Remove the pan from the heat and add cold water. Add egg yolks and whisk until the sauce is thick and creamy. Whip in butter, 2 tablespoons at a time, over low heat. Continue to whisk the sauce until it is thick. Season with salt and pepper and garnish with parsley.
Yields 1¼ to 1½ cups sauce

Stuffed Zucchini

4	large zucchini	¾	cup shredded Swiss cheese
	Salt	1	teaspoon onion powder
¾	cup dry bread crumbs	¼	teaspoon grated nutmeg

Easy • Prep time: 15 minutes

Preheat the oven to 350°. Cut zucchini in half. Scoop out pulp and seeds. Sprinkle inside with salt. Place upside down to drain for about 15 minutes. Combine bread crumbs, cheese, onion powder, and nutmeg. Spoon into zucchini shells. Place in a dish and bake until the mixture is firm and toasted on top, about 10 to 15 minutes.

Yields 8 servings

Lemon Sour Cream Pie

1	cup sugar	¼	cup butter
3	tablespoons cornstarch	1	cup sour cream
1	cup milk	1	baked 9-inch pie crust
3	egg yolks, beaten	1	cup heavy cream, whipped
¼	cup lemon juice		and sweetened with
1	tablespoon grated lemon rind		2 tablespoons sugar

Moderately easy • Prep time: 30 minutes • Prepare ahead

In a heavy saucepan, combine sugar and cornstarch. Add milk, egg yolks, lemon juice, rind, and butter. Cook over medium-high heat until thick. Remove from the heat. Cool thoroughly. Add sour cream and pour into a baked pie shell. Top with whipped cream. Refrigerate for several hours.

Yields 6 to 8 servings

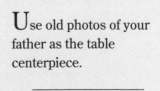

Frame a special photo of you and your father as a gift for him.

Use old photos of your father as the table centerpiece.

Incorporate your father's hobbies into your decorations.

SHOPPING LIST _____

BAKERY
__ 2 loaves Italian bread

BUTCHER
__ 4 pounds medium, raw shrimp
__ 8 beef tenderloin filets (about 6 ounces each)
__ 1 pound bacon

CANNED GOODS
__ 4 8½-ounce cans artichoke hearts

DAIRY
__ 1 dozen eggs
__ 2 pounds butter
__ ½ pint milk
__ ½ pint sour cream
__ 1 6-ounce block Swiss cheese
__ 1 small block Parmesan cheese
__ ½ pint whipping cream

MISCELLANEOUS
__ Shrimp boil
__ 1 container bread crumbs
__ 9-inch pie crust
__ 1 small jar capers

PRODUCE
__ 4 lemons
__ 4 large zucchini
__ 1 bunch fresh basil
__ 2 heads Boston lettuce
__ 1 bunch fresh parsley
__ 1 small bunch green onions
__ 1 stalk celery
__ 1 small onion
__ 1 head Romaine lettuce

STAPLES/SPICES
__ Coffee
__ Cornstarch
__ Dried dill weed
__ Dried parsley flakes
__ Dried tarragon
__ Garlic powder
__ Ground nutmeg
__ Mayonnaise
__ Olive oil
__ Onion powder
__ Oregano
__ Peppercorns
__ Salt
__ Seasoned salt
__ Sugar
__ Tabasco sauce
__ Tarragon vinegar
__ Tea bags
__ White pepper
__ White vinegar

DEVILED HAM DIP

BRAUNSCHWEIGER LOG

REUBEN PIE

HUNGARIAN CABBAGE

APPLE SALAD

FRESH PEACH CRISP

GERMAN BEERS

SERVES 6

October has more to offer than tricks and treats, goblins and ghouls. This autumn celebration, which usually involves lots of food and drink, has its roots in Germany. But you don't have to be German to appreciate good food—and good beer. You just have to host your own Oktoberfest.

Deviled Ham Dip

1½ cups cottage cheese

1 2¼-ounce can deviled ham

2 tablespoons sliced green onions

1 teaspoon paprika
Celery and carrot sticks

Easy • Prep time: 15 minutes

In a large bowl of an electric mixer, combine the cottage cheese, ham, onion, and paprika; beat until smooth. Chill. Serve with celery and carrot sticks.

Yields 1¾ cups dip

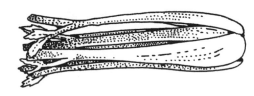

Braunschweiger Log

1	pound Braunschweiger	½	teaspoon basil
2	tablespoons chili sauce	½	cup chopped nuts
2	tablespoons mayonnaise		Crackers

Easy • Prep time: 5 minutes
In a large bowl, combine Braunschweiger, chili sauce, mayonnaise, and basil. Shape the mixture into a 7½-inch long log. Roll in nuts. Serve with assorted crackers.
Yields 2 cups

Reuben Pie

1	9-inch deep-dish pie shell, unbaked	¾	cup sauerkraut, drained
1	tablespoon caraway seeds	1½	cups grated Gruyère cheese
½	pound deli corned beef, shredded	3	eggs, beaten
		1	cup half-and-half
1	tablespoon Dijon mustard	1	tablespoon grated onion
¼	cup Thousand Island dressing	¼	teaspoon dry mustard
		½	teaspoon salt
			Kosher dill spears for garnish

Easy • Prep time: 15 minutes
Preheat the oven to 425°. Sprinkle and press caraway seeds into the unbaked pie crust. With a fork, prick the crust and bake for 7 minutes. Remove the crust and reduce the oven temperature to 350°. Layer corned beef on top of the crust. Combine mustard and dressing and spread over beef. Then layer sauerkraut and cheese. Mix eggs, half-and-half, onion, dry mustard, and salt; pour evenly over the pie. Bake for 40 to 45 minutes. Remove from the oven and allow to set for 5 minutes. Garnish each plate with a dill spear.
Yields 6 servings

Hungarian Cabbage

2 slices bacon
1 pound cabbage, coarsely
  shredded
¾ teaspoon salt

Dash of pepper
2 tablespoons white vinegar
2 tablespoons water

Easy • Prep time: 10 minutes

Cook bacon in a medium-size skillet until crisp; remove from the skillet. Crumble bacon and set aside. Add cabbage, salt, pepper, vinegar, and water to bacon drippings in the skillet. Cover and cook over low heat, stirring occasionally. Cabbage should be tender but crisp. Transfer cabbage to a serving dish and top with bacon. Serve hot.

Yields 6 servings

Apple Salad

2 tart apples, unpeeled
⅓ cup raisins
⅓ cup chopped nuts
½ cup chopped celery

½ cup mayonnaise
½ teaspoon salt
1 avocado
  Romaine lettuce leaves

Easy • Prep time: 5 minutes

Core and dice apples. Combine with the next 5 ingredients in a bowl. Cut avocado lengthwise into halves; remove seed and skin. Dice avocado; fold gently into the salad mixture just before serving in lettuce leaves.

Yields 6 servings

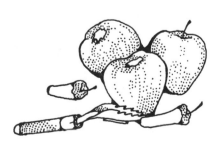

Fresh Peach Crisp

1	cup all-purpose flour	½	cup margarine
½	cup sugar	4	cups sliced fresh peaches
½	cup light brown sugar, firmly packed	¼	teaspoon almond extract
¼	teaspoon salt	2	tablespoons water
½	teaspoon ground cinnamon	¼	teaspoon grated nutmeg
			Whipped cream

Easy • Prep time: 15 minutes

Preheat the oven to 350°. Combine the first 5 ingredients. Cut in margarine with a pastry blender until the mixture resembles coarse cornmeal. Set aside. Combine peaches, almond extract, and water. Spoon into a greased 9-inch square baking dish. Top with the flour-sugar mixture. Sprinkle nutmeg on top. Bake, covered, for 15 minutes. Remove cover and bake for 45 minutes longer, or until the topping is brown. Serve warm with whipped cream.

Yields 6 to 8 servings

SHOPPING LIST _____

BUTCHER/DELI
__ 1 pound Braunschweiger
__ ½ pound shredded corned beef
__ ½ pound bacon

CANNED GOODS
__ 1 2¼-ounce can deviled ham
__ 1 can sauerkraut

DAIRY
__ 6 to 8 ounces Gruyère cheese
__ 1 16-ounce container cottage
    cheese
__ 1 pint half-and-half
__ ½ dozen eggs
__ 1 stick margarine
__ ½ pint heavy cream

EXTRAS
__ 5 or 6 six-packs German beer

MISCELLANEOUS
__ 1 small jar chili sauce
__ 1 6-ounce package chopped nuts
__ 1 box crackers
__ 1 unbaked 9-inch deep-dish pie
    shell
__ 1 small jar Dijon mustard
__ 1 small bottle Thousand Island
    dressing
__ 1 jar kosher dill spears
__ 1 small box raisins

PRODUCE
__ 1 bunch green onions
__ 1 stalk celery
__ 1 bag carrots or carrot sticks
__ 1 small onion
__ 1 pound cabbage
__ 2 tart apples
__ 1 avocado
__ 1 head Romaine lettuce
__ 5 or 6 fresh peaches

STAPLES/SPICES
__ All-purpose flour
__ Almond extract
__ Basil
__ Caraway seeds
__ Cinnamon
__ Dry mustard
__ Light brown sugar
__ Mayonnaise
__ Nutmeg
__ Paprika
__ Pepper
__ Salt
__ White vinegar

No Tricks, Just Treats, Dessert Buffet

Notes

_____

_____

_____

_____

_____

_____

_____

_____

_____

_____

_____

_____

_____

_____

_____

_____

_____

_____

_____

_____

ORANGE AND BLACK SPIDER WEB CUPCAKES

WHITE-AS-A-GHOST CHOCOLATE FONDUE

CARAMEL CORN BAGS

CHOCOLATE ORANGE BURSTS

BOB-FOR-APPLES PUNCH

SERVES 15 TO 20

Sure, Halloween is for kids. But adults can enjoy it, too. Young and old alike will find something sweet that suits them in this menu. Invite the kids from your neighborhood, certainly, but don't forget to include the young at heart.

White-as-a-Ghost Chocolate Fondue

2 packages (six 1-ounce squares; 12 squares total) white baking chocolate

1½ cups milk

½ cup sugar

Marshmallows
Angel food cake, torn in chunks
Banana slices
Fresh strawberries (if available)

Easy • Prep time: 15 minutes
Combine white chocolate, milk, and sugar in a fondue pot. Place over low heat and stir until chocolate melts and the mixture is smoothly blended. Serve with marshmallows, angel food cake, banana slices, and strawberries.
Yields 12 to 15 servings (3 cups dip)

Caramel Corn Bags

6   quarts popped popcorn

Syrup

1   cup butter, melted

2   cups light brown sugar

½   cup white corn syrup

1   teaspoon salt

1   teaspoon baking soda

1   teaspoon vanilla extract

Moderately easy • Prep time: 25 to 30 minutes • Prepare ahead
Preheat the oven to 250°. Put popped corn in a big roasting pan. In a large saucepan, combine butter, brown sugar, and syrup. Bring to a boil; boil for 5 minutes. Remove from the heat. Add salt, soda, and vanilla. Mix well and slowly pour over popcorn. Blend and coat all of the popcorn. Bake for 40 minutes, stirring every 10 minutes. Remove from the oven and pour out onto waxed paper. Let cool completely. Fill individual clear cellophane bags with caramel corn (or use clear cellophane sheets); tie up top with orange and black curling ribbon or store in airtight containers until ready to use.
Yields 6 quarts

Chocolate Orange Bursts

3 to 4   pints tangerine sorbet or orange sherbet

2   jars hardening chocolate ice cream topping

Easy • Prep time: 15 minutes • Prepare ahead and freeze
Using a small ice cream scoop, scoop rounded balls of sorbet and place on a wire rack with a sheet of waxed paper underneath. Pour hardening chocolate over to coat. Using a spatula, quickly transfer to a baking sheet lined with waxed paper. Freeze for 2 to 3 hours. (You may need to work in batches, moving the baking sheet in and out of the freezer to keep sorbet from melting.) Transfer frozen balls to a waxed-paper-lined, airtight container and store in the freezer until ready to serve.
Yields 30 to 40 balls

Encourage the kids to wear their Halloween costumes. (Okay, the adults can, too.)

Buy small pumpkins for older children and adults to carve. Vote on the most original, scariest, etc., and have prizes ready.

Give the children candy for their trick-or-treat bags. For the adults, have a plastic pumpkin full of small gag gifts.

Bob-for-Apples Punch

	Ice cubes		Lemon juice
1 or 2	apples		Cold water

Punch

1	gallon apple juice	1	quart apricot nectar

Easy • Prep time: 10 minutes • Prepare ahead

Core apples, cut in chunks, and place in a mixing bowl. Squeeze fresh lemon juice over apples and mix well to coat. Place 1 apple chunk in each section of an empty ice cube tray; fill 2 trays. Fill trays with water and freeze until ready to use. Combine apple juice and apricot nectar. Chill. When ready to serve, combine punch and apple ice cubes in a punch bowl.

Yields 25 cups

SHOPPING LIST

BAKERY
__ 2 dozen Halloween cupcakes
__ 1 angel food cake

CANNED GOODS
__ 1 gallon can apple juice
__ 1 32-ounce can apricot nectar

DAIRY
__ 1 pint milk
__ 2 sticks butter

MISCELLANEOUS
__ 2 6-ounce boxes white baking chocolate
__ 2 bags large marshmallows
__ 1 jar unpopped popcorn
__ 1 bottle light corn syrup
__ ½ gallon orange sherbet
__ 2 containers hardening chocolate topping for ice cream

PRODUCE
__ 1 bunch bananas
__ 1 pint fresh strawberries (if available)
__ 1 or 2 apples
__ 1 lemon

STAPLES/SPICES
__ Baking soda
__ Light brown sugar
__ Salt
__ Sugar
__ Vanilla extract

OYSTER STEW

ROAST TURKEY WITH GIBLET GRAVY

CORNBREAD AND PECAN STUFFING

SWEET POTATOES IN ORANGE CUPS

BROCCOLI WITH HOLLANDAISE

CRANBERRY RELISH

ROLLS

PUMPKIN PIE

COFFEE

SERVES 12

Every family has its own set of holiday traditions.
Now that you've got a household of your own,
incorporate some new traditions into your
Thanksgiving festivities. That way you can honor the
past *and* celebrate the present.

"Strange to see how a good dinner and feasting reconciles everybody."
—SAMUEL PEPYS

Notes

Oyster Stew

6   *tablespoons butter, melted*
2   *tablespoons all-purpose flour*
    Salt and pepper

2   *quarts milk, heated*
3   *pints stewing oysters*
    Chopped chives

Easy • Prep time: 15 minutes
In a large pan, add flour to melted butter and cook until bubbly. Add
seasonings to taste. Blend in milk and heat the mixture thoroughly.
Add oysters and cook for about 8 minutes, until edges of oysters curl.
Serve immediately, topped with chives.
Yields 12 servings

Canned oysters and
soups are good substitu-
tions if you don't want to
prepare homemade oyster
stew.

When selecting a holiday turkey, allow 12 to 16 ounces per person. This is enough for second helpings, with some left over for the next day.

Roast Turkey with Giblet Gravy

1	14- to 16-pound turkey	½	teaspoon ground ginger
	Melted butter or margarine	1	teaspoon paprika
1	tablespoon salt	¼	teaspoon cayenne pepper
½	teaspoon black pepper	¼	teaspoon dried basil
1	teaspoon poultry seasoning	1	cup water
1	teaspoon garlic powder		

Moderately easy • Prep time: 30 minutes
Preheat the oven to 350°. Clean and dry turkey; reserve and set aside neck, giblets, and liver. Brush turkey with melted butter. Mix dry seasonings and rub thoroughly into inside and outside of bird. Truss and tie securely; place breast-side up in roaster. Add about 1 cup water. Cover and bake until tender, about 3 to 4 hours. If turkey is not evenly browned, remove cover for last ½ hour and lower temperature to 300°.
Yields 12 to 14 servingss

Giblet Gravy

	Turkey giblets	¼	cup all-purpose flour
½	teaspoon salt	3	cups turkey or giblet stock
⅛	teaspoon black pepper	1	hard-boiled egg, chopped
¼	cup shortening		

Easy • Prep time: 15 minutes
Combine giblets, salt, pepper, and enough water to cover in a saucepan. Simmer for 45 to 60 minutes, or until tender. Drain, reserving stock. Chop giblets and set aside. Melt shortening and stir in flour. Add stock, stirring constantly for 5 minutes, or until thickened. Add giblets and egg; stir to blend.
Yields 3 cups (12 servings)

Cornbread and Pecan Stuffing

8 cups dry crumbled cornbread
   or cornbread stuffing
3 cups milk, heated
1 cup butter, melted

1 cup coarsely broken pecan
   pieces
2 teaspoons salt
¼ teaspoon cayenne pepper

Easy • Prep time: 5 minutes • Freezes well
Combine all ingredients. Mix thoroughly. Stuff bird loosely.
Yields stuffing for a 12- to 16-pound bird

Sweet Potatoes in Orange Cups

6 cups cooked mashed sweet
   potatoes (can use canned
   yams)
1½ cups sugar
1 teaspoon salt
4 eggs, lightly beaten
½ cup butter, melted
1 cup milk

1 teaspoon vanilla extract
12 orange half shells,
   pulp removed
2 cups brown sugar, firmly
   packed
⅔ cup all-purpose flour
2 cups chopped nuts
½ cup butter, melted

Easy • Prep time: 25 minutes
Preheat the oven to 350°. In a large bowl, combine the first 7 ingredients and pour into orange halves, which have the pulp removed. Mix the remaining ingredients and sprinkle over the potato mixture. Bake for 40 minutes.
Yields 12 servings

Ask each guest to speak about something—or someone—he or she is thankful for on this day.

Broccoli with Hollandaise

3   egg yolks
3   tablespoons lemon juice
¾   teaspoon salt

Cayenne pepper to taste
¾   cup butter, melted
2   bunches fresh broccoli

Easy • Prep time: 15 minutes
Place egg yolks, lemon juice, salt, and cayenne pepper in a blender. Cover and mix well. Remove cover and slowly pour in hot butter. Pulse to blend. Steam broccoli. Pour warm sauce over broccoli to serve.
Yields 12 servings

Cranberry Relish

1   pound cranberries
1   orange, peeled, seeded,
    and sectioned

2   cups sugar
½   cup water
1   teaspoon grated orange rind

Easy • Prep time: 10 minutes
Combine all ingredients in a saucepan and simmer for about 10 minutes, or until berries pop open. Skim the foam and cool.
Yields 12 servings

SHOPPING LIST _____

BAKERY
__ 2 or 3 dozen rolls
__ 2 pumpkin pies

BUTCHER
__ 1 8- to 10-pound turkey
__ 3 pints stewing oysters

CANNED GOODS
__ 3 16-ounce cans sweet potatoes
   or yams

DAIRY
__ 2 pounds butter
__ 1 gallon milk
__ 1 dozen eggs

MISCELLANEOUS
__ 2 8-ounce packages Pepperidge
   Farm cornbread stuffing mix
__ 1 16-ounce package pecan
   pieces

PRODUCE
__ 1 bunch fresh chives
__ 7 medium oranges
__ 2 lemons
__ 2 bunches broccoli
__ 1 pound cranberries

STAPLES/SPICES
__ All-purpose flour
__ Brown sugar
__ Cayenne pepper
__ Coffee
__ Pepper
__ Salt
__ Shortening
__ Sugar
__ Vanilla extract

Merry Christmas Morning

Notes

Sausage Coffee Cake

1 pound ground pork or turkey sausage	¼ teaspoon Tabasco sauce
½ cup chopped onions	2 tablespoons chopped parsley
½ cup grated Swiss cheese	2 cups biscuit mix (such as Bisquick)
¼ cup grated Parmesan cheese	¾ cup milk
1 egg, lightly beaten	¼ cup mayonnaise
1 ½ teaspoons salt	1 egg yolk
	1 tablespoon water

Easy • Prep time: 25 minutes

Preheat the oven to 400°. In a skillet, brown sausage and onions; drain. Combine the sausage mixture in a bowl with the next 6 ingredients. In another bowl, combine biscuit mix, milk, and mayonnaise; mix well. In a 9x9x2-inch greased pan, spread half of the biscuit mix batter. Pour in and evenly distribute the sausage mixture, then spread remaining batter on top. Combine egg yolk and water and brush over top. Bake for 25 to 30 minutes. Cool for 5 minutes before cutting into 3-inch squares.
Yields 9 servings

Serve all of the foods in this menu on one big plate. That way your family can get down to the business at hand more quickly, and your clean-up time will be shortened.

Holiday Baked Apples

¾	cup raisins	¼	teaspoon grated lemon peel
1½	cups white wine	¼	cup sugar
8	cooking apples, cored	1½	tablespoons butter

Moderately easy • Prep time: 15 minutes • Prepare ahead
Preheat the oven to 400°. Soak raisins in wine for 30 minutes. Drain, reserving wine. Arrange apples in a 9x13-inch baking dish. Stuff apples with raisins. Sprinkle with lemon peel and sugar. Dot with butter and add reserved wine. Bake for 35 minutes. Serve hot or cold.
Yields 8 servings

Eggnog

10	eggs, separated	1	quart heavy cream
¾	cup sugar		Freshly grated nutmeg
1¼	cups bourbon		

Moderate • Prep time: 25 minutes
In a large bowl, beat egg yolks until thick and creamy. Mix in sugar; add bourbon slowly. Beat egg whites until stiff. Fold the yolk mixture into egg whites. Whip cream until it forms peaks and fold into the egg mixture. Sprinkle with nutmeg.
Yields 8 servings

SHOPPING LIST _____

BUTCHER
__ 1 pound ground pork or turkey
sausage

DAIRY
__ 1 dozen eggs
__ 1 quart heavy cream
__ 1 4-ounce block Swiss cheese
__ 1 4-ounce block Parmesan
cheese
__ ½ pint milk
__ 1 stick butter

EXTRAS
__ 1 bottle bourbon
__ 1 bottle dry white wine

MISCELLANEOUS
__ 1 box biscuit mix (such as
Bisquick)
__ 1 small box raisins

PRODUCE
__ 1 onion
__ 1 bunch fresh parsley
__ 8 cooking apples
__ 1 lemon

STAPLES/SPICES
__ Coffee
__ Mayonnaise
__ Nutmeg
__ Salt
__ Sugar
__ Tabasco sauce

Christmas Goose Dinner

SCALLOPED TOMATO CASSEROLE

ROAST GOOSE WITH WINE SAUCE

PILAF OF LENTILS AND RICE

CRANBERRY BUTTER ON WARM YEAST ROLLS

AMBROSIA

YULETIDE JELLYROLL CAKE

RIESLING AND CALIFORNIA PINOT NOIR

SERVES 8 TO 10

For an especially old-fashioned Christmas dinner,
consider serving roast goose. It will bring to mind
tales of Dickens, and provide your guests with
something a little different.

Scalloped Tomato Casserole

2 cups chopped celery

1 cup minced onion

¼ cup butter, melted

2 tablespoons all-purpose
flour

2 28-ounce cans diced tomatoes

4 cups ½-inch toast cubes

2 tablespoons sugar

2 teaspoons salt

Dash of pepper

1 tablespoon prepared mustard

Moderately easy • Prep time: 10 minutes

Preheat the oven to 350°. In a skillet, cook celery and onion in butter until tender, but not brown. Blend in flour. In a 3½-quart casserole dish, combine the onion-celery mixture with tomatoes, half the toast cubes, sugar, and seasonings. Bake for 30 minutes. Top with remaining toast cubes and bake for 10 minutes more.

Yields 10 to 12 servings

"There never was such a goose. Bob said he didn't believe there ever was such a goose cooked. Its tenderness and flavor, size and cheapness were the themes of universal admiration. Eked out by applesauce and mashed potatoes, it was a sufficient dinner for the whole family; indeed, as Mrs. Cratchit said with great delight (surveying one small atom of a bone upon the dish) they hadn't ate it all at last! Yet every one had had enough, and the youngest Cratchits in particular were steeped in sage and onion to the eyebrows."

—CHARLES DICKENS

Roast Goose with Wine Sauce

1	9- to 10-pound goose	1	large onion, sliced
	Salt and freshly ground	2	apples, cored and chopped, optional
	black pepper to taste		Wine Sauce
½	lemon		

Moderately easy • Prep time: 20 minutes

Preheat the oven to 375°. Wash the goose in cold water, pat dry, and rub bird inside and out with cut side of lemon. Salt and pepper cavity and stuff with onion and apples. Close opening and truss the bird securely. Roast on a rack for 3½ hours. Basting is not necessary. When the juices run clear, the bird is done. Allow to sit, covered, for 15 minutes before carving. Discard stuffing. Serve with Wine Sauce.

Yields 8 to 10 servings

Wine Sauce

½	cup butter	½	cup dry red wine
¼	cup all-purpose flour		Salt and pepper to taste
4	cups broth (get as much	¼	cup minced fresh parsley
	broth from the goose as		
	possible; use chicken broth		
	for the rest)		

Moderately easy • Prep time: 20 minutes

Melt butter in a saucepan; stir in flour and blend well. Gradually add broth, stirring constantly until thickened. Add wine, salt, pepper, and parsley. Keep warm until ready to serve.

Yields 4 cups

Pilaf of Lentils and Rice

2 tablespoons olive oil
1 large onion, chopped fine
¼ cup slivered blanched
   almonds
1 cup lentils

1 cup uncooked long-grain
   white rice
5 to 6 cups chicken broth
2 tablespoons soy sauce
   Pepper to taste

Easy • Prep time: 15 minutes • Freezes well

Heat oil in a saucepan and sauté onion until golden, but not brown. Add nuts and sauté until crisp; remove with a slotted spoon, allowing oil to remain in the pan. Stir in lentils and enough water to cover generously. Cover and simmer for 45 minutes to 1 hour, until lentils are almost soft. Add rice, soup broth, and soy sauce, then half the onion-nut mixture. Check seasonings; add pepper to taste. Bring to a boil; cover and reduce heat to simmer. Cook for about 20 minutes, or until rice is done. Garnish with the remaining onion-nut mixture.

Yields 8 to 10 servings

Cranberry Butter on Warm Yeast Rolls

2 tablespoons jellied cranberry sauce
1 cup butter, softened
2 dozen yeast rolls, heated through

Easy • Prep time: 10 minutes

Mix jellied cranberry sauce in softened butter and remold or shape into desired form. Chill. Serve with warm yeast rolls.

Yields 1 cup butter

"What is sauce for the goose may be sauce for the gander, but it is not necessarily sauce for the chicken, the duck, the turkey, or the Guinea hen."—ALICE B. TOKLAS

Drizzle orange juice over cut bananas to keep them from turning brown so quickly.

Ambrosia

6   large oranges
4   ripe bananas
1   medium apple, cored
½   cup flaked coconut

½   cup maraschino cherries,
     cut in halves
     Pecans, optional

Easy • Prep time: 5 minutes • Prepare the day before serving
Peel and section oranges. Slice bananas and drizzle some orange juice over them to keep them from darkening. Dice apple and combine all ingredients. Toss lightly before serving.
Yields 8 servings

Yuletide Jellyroll Cake

½ cup all-purpose flour	½ teaspoon grated nutmeg
1 teaspoon baking powder	1 cup sugar, divided
4 eggs, separated	Confectioners' sugar
½ teaspoon vanilla extract	¾ cup apricot jam
½ teaspoon ground cinnamon	1 container chocolate frosting

Moderately difficult • Prep time: 30 minutes

Preheat the oven to 375°. Sift together the flour and baking powder. Beat the egg yolks with the vanilla, cinnamon, and nutmeg on high speed until smooth. Gradually add ½ cup of the sugar and continue beating until the sugar has dissolved.

In another bowl, beat the egg whites on medium speed until soft peaks form. Gradually add the remaining ½ cup of sugar and beat until stiff peaks form. Fold the egg yolks into the egg whites. Sprinkle the flour mixture over all and carefully fold in just until incorporated.

Pour the batter evenly into a greased and floured 15x10x1-inch jelly-roll pan. Bake for 10 to 15 minutes, or until the center bounces back when touched. Immediately turn the cake out onto a towel sprinkled generously with confectioners' sugar and roll the cake up in the towel, from short end to short end. Allow the cake to cool for 15 to 20 minutes.

Carefully unroll the cake, removing the towel, and spread the apricot jam over the cake to within ½ inch of the sides. Roll the cake up again and frost with chocolate frosting. Run the tines of a fork along the length of the cake to give the effect of tree bark.

Yields 10 servings.

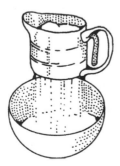

SHOPPING LIST _____

BAKERY
__ 1 loaf bread
__ 2 dozen yeast rolls

BUTCHER
__ 1 9- to 10-pound goose

CANNED GOODS
__ 1 or 2 16-ounce cans chicken
   broth
__ 2 28-ounce cans diced tomatoes
__ 1 small can jellied cranberry
   sauce
__ 3 16-ounce cans chicken broth
__ 1 3½-ounce can flaked coconut

DAIRY
__ 1 pound butter
__ ½ dozen eggs

EXTRAS
__ 1 bottle dry red wine
__ 3 or 4 bottles riesling
__ 3 or 4 bottles California pinot
   noir

MISCELLANEOUS
__ 1 small package slivered
   blanched almonds
__ 1 small box lentils
__ 1 small jar halved
   maraschino cherries
__ 1 small bag pecan pieces
   (optional)
__ 1 small jar apricot jam
__ 1 container chocolate frosting

PRODUCE
__ 1 bunch fresh parsley
__ 1 stalk celery
__ 2 large onions
__ 6 large oranges
__ 4 ripe bananas
__ 1 medium apple

STAPLES/SPICES
__ All-purpose flour
__ Baking powder
__ Cinnamon
__ Confectioners' sugar
__ Long-grain white rice
__ Nutmeg
__ Olive oil
__ Pepper
__ Prepared mustard
__ Salt
__ Soy sauce
__ Sugar
__ Vanilla extract

LIGHTER FARE

Because most of us are watching our weight and paying closer attention to the kinds of food we eat, no cookbook would be complete without a chapter devoted to healthy recipes. Here I offer you several menus that are lower in fat and calories than the other menus in the book. After you try a few of these recipes, you'll find out how easy it is to enjoy food—without the guilt!

With only a little extra effort, you can approach party planning with a new attitude, one infused with low-fat substitutions, fresh produce, and a variety of foods. Don't shy away from entertaining just because you think your guests might expect fat-laden goodies. Most people today prefer healthier options anyway, so why not host them in style and good nutrition?

On these pages you'll find some interesting and filling variations on some old standards, as well as some new offerings. Also included is a chart devoted to ingredient substitutions.

Use this information as inspiration. With a little experimentation, you'll find which spices taste best, what foods you can live without, and any appropriate variations on cooking procedures. Turn old food into new habits!

Celebration Cocktail Party

CRAB AND CHEESE BALL

BAKED PARMESAN CHICKEN STRIPS

HOT ARTICHOKE SPREAD

FRESH FRUIT WITH FRUITY DIP

TOMATO SALSA

LIGHT BEER AND DIET BEVERAGES

SERVES 8

Even people who are watching their weight deserve to celebrate every once in a while. So here's a menu to help you do just that.

Crab and Cheese Ball

4 ounces crab meat, packed in water	1 teaspoon finely chopped fresh chives
1 8-ounce package light cream cheese	¼ teaspoon Worcestershire sauce
1 teaspoon prepared horseradish	Paprika, optional
1 tablespoon lemon juice	Crackers and/or raw veggies
1 teaspoon finely chopped onion	

Easy • Prep time: 5 to 7 minutes
Squeeze excess water from crab meat. In a mixing bowl, combine all ingredients and blend well with a fork. Shape the mixture into a ball and sprinkle with paprika. Refrigerate for at least 1 hour.
Yields 1½ cups or 22 servings of 1 tablespoon each
Calories: 31; Fat: 2 g ; Cholesterol: 12 mg; Sodium: 60 mg;
Carbohydrates: .4 g; Fiber: 0 g; Diabetic Exchange: ½ fat

Keep an assortment of whole grain crackers as well as bite-size fresh veggies ready to eat.

Baked Parmesan Chicken Strips

8   4-ounce skinned, boned
    chicken breast halves
¼   cup skim milk
¼   cup frozen egg substitute,
    thawed
⅔   cup fine dry bread crumbs

1   cup grated Parmesan cheese
1   teaspoon dried basil
¾   teaspoon dried thyme
½   teaspoon onion powder
¼   teaspoon ground black pepper

Such foods as the Baked Parmesan Chicken Strips are great as an appetizer or as a main course.

Easy • Prep time: 10 minutes
Preheat the oven to 400°. Spray a baking sheet with vegetable spray. Cut chicken into 4x1-inch strips. In a small bowl, combine milk and egg substitute, and set aside. In a separate bowl, combine bread crumbs and remaining ingredients, mixing well. Dip chicken into the milk mixture, then the bread crumb mixture. Arrange the strips on the baking sheet. Bake for 15 to 18 minutes, or until golden brown.
Yields 54 strips
Calories: 32; Fat: 1 g; Cholesterol: 11 mg; Sodium: 51 mg;
Carbohydrates: 1 g; Fiber: 1 g; Diabetic Exchange: ½ lower fat meat

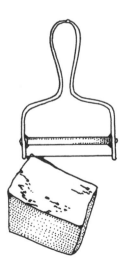

Hot Artichoke Spread

1	cup lowfat cottage cheese	¼	teaspoon hot sauce
½	cup grated Parmesan cheese	1	clove garlic, minced
2	tablespoons plain nonfat yogurt	1	14-ounce can artichoke hearts, drained and finely chopped
2	tablespoons nonfat mayonnaise		Melba rounds or toast points

Easy • Prep time: 5 minutes

Preheat the oven to 350°. Coat a 1-quart baking dish with vegetable spray. In a food processor or blender, combine all ingredients, except artichokes and bread. Mix until smooth. Add artichokes and stir to blend. Pour the mixture into the prepared dish. Bake for 20 minutes. Serve hot with crackers.

Yields 2 cups spread or 16 servings of 2 tablespoons each
Calories: 32; Fat: 1 g; Cholesterol: 3 mg; Sodium: 130 mg
Carbohydrates: 3 g; Fiber: .2 g; Diabetic Exchange: 1 vegetable

Combine two teaspoons garlic powder and 1 teaspoon each of dried basil, oregano, and dehydrated lemon juice for a delicious, no-salt seasoning, which can be used on meats and vegetables.

Fresh Fruit with Fruity Dip

1⅓	cups vanilla lowfat yogurt	⅓	teaspoon ground cinnamon
¼	cup low-sugar orange marmalade		Fresh fruit, cut into chunks, for dipping

Easy • Prep time: 5 minutes

In a serving bowl, combine all ingredients, except cut fruit. Cover and refrigerate. Serve as a dip in the center of your fruit tray.

Yields 1½ cups dip or 24 servings of 1 tablespoon each
Calories: 15; Fat: .1 g; Cholesterol: 1 mg; Sodium: 8 mg;
Carbohydrates: 2 g; Fiber: 0 g; Diabetic Exchange: free

Tomato Salsa

1¼ cups canned Italian plum
    tomatoes, drained

1 rib celery, diced

¼ cup chopped green onions

1 teaspoon minced garlic

1 tablespoon fresh lime juice

2 tablespoons chopped fresh
    cilantro

¼ teaspoon hot red pepper flakes

¼ teaspoon freshly ground black
    pepper

    Baked tortilla chips

Easy • Prep time: 10 minutes • Prepare ahead

Coarsely chop tomatoes. In a large bowl, combine tomatoes and remaining ingredients. Cover and chill. Serve with baked tortilla chips.

Yields 1 ½ cups salsa or 6 servings of 2 to 3 tablespoons each
Calories: 14; Fat: .2 g; Cholesterol: 0 mg; Sodium: 88 mg; Carbohydrates: 3 g; Fiber: .4 g; Diabetic Exchange: free

SHOPPING LIST

BUTCHER
__ 2 pounds boneless, skinless chicken breasts

CANNED GOODS
__ 1 6½-ounce can crabmeat packed in water
__ 1 14-ounce can artichoke hearts
__ 1 16-ounce can Italian plum tomatoes

DAIRY
__ 1 8-ounce package light cream cheese
__ 1 pint skim milk
__ 1 carton egg substitute
__ 1 6- to 8-ounce block Parmesan cheese
__ 1 8-ounce container cottage cheese

__ 1 8-ounce container plain nonfat yogurt
__ 1 16-ounce container vanilla lowfat yogurt

EXTRAS
__ 1 case light beer

MISCELLANEOUS
__ Assorted diet sodas
__ 1 small jar prepared horseradish
__ 1 container bread crumbs
__ 1 box Melba rounds
__ 1 small jar low-sugar orange marmalade
__ 1 large bag baked tortilla chips

PRODUCE
__ 1 lemon
__ 1 small onion

__ 1 bunch fresh chives
__ 1 head garlic
__ 1 stalk celery
__ 1 bunch green onions
__ 2 limes
__ 1 bunch fresh cilantro

STAPLES/SPICES
__ Black peppercorns
__ Dried basil
__ Dried thyme
__ Ground cinnamon
__ Hot sauce
__ Nonfat mayonnaise
__ Onion powder
__ Paprika
__ Red pepper flakes
__ Worcestershire sauce

Holiday Dinner

STEAMED ASPARAGUS WITH FRESH LEMON

CRANBERRY RELISH

TURKEY BREAST

APPLE BREAD STUFFING

SWEET POTATOES IN ORANGE CUPS

GINGERED YOGURT AMBROSIA

PUMPKIN MOUSSE PIE WITH WHIPPED TOPPING

COFFEE

SERVES 6

Celebrating the holidays doesn't have to be a dismal prospect just because you're trying to be health conscious. Instead, by sticking to your exercise program and using menus like this one, it can be fun, satisfying, and free of guilt.

Cranberry Relish

1   medium orange, peeled, sectioned, and seeded
1   medium lemon, peeled, sectioned, and seeded
2   cups fresh cranberries, rinsed
1   8-ounce can unsweetened pineapple chunks, drained
½   cup maple syrup

Easy • Prep time: 5 minutes • Can refrigerate for several weeks
In a food processor or blender, combine orange, lemon, cranberries, pineapple, and maple syrup. Pulse until finely chopped. Transfer to a saucepan and simmer for 5 minutes. Cool and serve.
Yields 1½ cups relish or 6 servings of ¼ cup each
Calories: 108; Fat: .2 g Cholesterol: 0 mg; Sodium: 4 mg;
Carbohydrates: 28 g; Fiber: 1g; Diabetic Exchange: 1 fruit, 1 starch

Apple Bread Stuffing

4 cups whole-wheat bread
   crumbs
1 cup chopped celery
1 cup chopped onion
1 tablespoon chopped fresh
   parsley
1 clove garlic, minced
1 cup defatted turkey or chicken
   broth

2 baking apples, peeled, cored,
   and diced
¼ teaspoon freshly ground black
   pepper
½ teaspoon ground sage
½ teaspoon minced fresh thyme
¼ teaspoon dried basil

Freeze leftover soup or broth in ice cube trays. Remove the cubes and package in resealable freezer bags to store in the freezer and use as needed.

Easy • Prep time: 20 minutes
Preheat the oven to 350°. In a large bowl, combine all ingredients and mix well. Spoon the stuffing into a 2-quart casserole dish. Bake for 40 to 45 minutes.
Yields 8 servings of ½ cup each
Calories: 47; Fat: .5 g; Cholesterol: 0 mg; Sodium: 68 mg;
Carbohydrates: 10 g; Fiber: 2 g; Diabetic Exchange: ½ starch

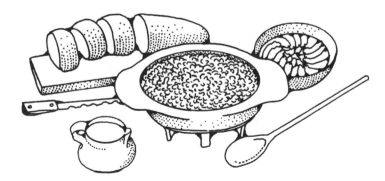

Give mashed potatoes a beautiful whipped cream look by adding hot skim milk to them before you begin mashing.

Sweet Potatoes in Orange Cups

4 medium sweet potatoes	⅛ teaspoon grated nutmeg
¼ cup pineapple juice	3 large oranges, halved
2 tablespoons safflower oil	and pulp removed
1 tablespoon crushed pineapple	Orange slices or fresh mint
⅛ teaspoon ground cinnamon	for garnish

Easy • Prep time: 25 minutes
Preheat the oven to 375°. Spray a baking dish with vegetable spray. In a large pot, boil the potatoes until tender, about 30 minutes. Remove the skins. In a large mixing bowl, mash the potatoes. Add pineapple juice and oil, and whip until fluffy. Add pineapple and spices. Fill each orange cup with the potato mixture and arrange the oranges in the prepared pan. Bake for 20 minutes, or until lightly browned. Garnish with an orange slice or fresh mint.
Yields 6 servings of ½ cup each
Calories: 163; Fat: 5 g; Cholesterol: 0 mg; Sodium: 14 mg;
Carbohydrates: 28g; Fiber: .9g; Diabetic Exchange: 2 bread, 1 fat

Gingered Yogurt Ambrosia

½ cup diced oranges	1 tablespoon grated fresh ginger
½ cup sliced bananas	1 cup nonfat yogurt
½ cup seedless red grapes	6 teaspoons grated coconut

Easy • Prep time: 5 minutes
In a large bowl, mix fruit with ginger and yogurt. When ready to serve, sprinkle each serving with grated coconut.
Yields 6 servings of ½ cup each
Calories: 48; Fat: .6 g; Cholesterol: .8 mg; Sodium: 30 mg;
Carbohydrates: 9 g; Fiber: .3 g; Diabetic Exchange: ½ milk

Pumpkin Mousse Pie with Whipped Topping

10 vanilla wafers, crushed
1 tablespoon margarine, melted
1 package unflavored gelatin
1½ cups evaporated skim milk
½ cup part-skim ricotta cheese

1¼ cups canned pumpkin
10 packages sugar substitute
1 teaspoon vanilla extract
2 teaspoons pumpkin pie spice
1 cup Whipped Topping

Easy • Prep time: 10 minutes • Prepare ahead
In an ungreased 8-inch pie plate, combine crumbs and margarine. Press the mixture into the pie plate and freeze for 1 hour.

In a small saucepan, sprinkle gelatin over ½ cup evaporated milk. Let stand for 10 minutes. Gently heat until gelatin dissolves. In a food processor or blender, process the milk mixture with remaining ingredients except topping. Pour into pie crust and chill. Top each slice with 2 tablespoons Whipped Topping.
Yields 1 eight-inch pie of 8 servings
Calories: 124; Fat: 4 g; Cholesterol: 9 mg; Sodium: 121 mg;
Carbohydrates: 16 g; Fiber: 0 g; Diabetic Exchange: 1 lowfat milk

Whipped Topping

½ cup instant dry milk
⅓ cup cold water
1 tablespoon lemon juice

Dry sugar substitute equal
to ¼ cup sugar
2 teaspoons vanilla extract

Easy • Prep time: 20 minutes
Combine dry milk and water. Chill for 30 minutes. Beat at high speed for 4 minutes. Add lemon juice and beat at high speed for 4 minutes. Gradually stir in sugar substitute while beating. Fold in vanilla. Refrigerate until ready to use.
Yields 3 cups or 24 servings at 2 tablespoons each
Calories: 8; Fat: 0 g; Cholesterol: 3 mg; Sodium: 8 mg;
Carbohydrates: 1 g; Fiber: 0 g; Diabetic Exchange: free

Baked foods in which no sugar is used, such as cakes and cookies, have a short shelf life. Use these within three days, or store in the refrigerator or freezer.

SHOPPING LIST _____

BAKERY
__ 1 loaf whole-wheat bread

BUTCHER
__ 1 5- to 6-pound cooked lowfat turkey breast

CANNED GOODS
__ 1 8-ounce can unsweetened pineapple chunks
__ 1 16-ounce can lowfat turkey or chicken broth
__ 1 small can crushed pineapple
__ 1 12-ounce can evaporated skim milk
__ 1 16-ounce can pumpkin
__ 1 3½-ounce can grated coconut

DAIRY
__ 1 stick margarine
__ 1 8-ounce container part-skim Ricotta cheese
__ 1 8-ounce container vanilla nonfat yogurt

MISCELLANEOUS
__ 1 small jar maple syrup
__ 1 bottle safflower oil
__ 1 box vanilla wafers
__ 1 box unflavored gelatin

__ 1 box sugar substitute packets
__ 1 small box instant dry milk

PRODUCE
__ 1 large bunch fresh asparagus
__ 4 lemons
__ 2 medium and 3 large oranges
__ 1 16-ounce package cranberries
__ 1 stalk celery
__ 1 large onion
__ 1 bunch fresh parsley
__ 1 head garlic
__ 2 baking apples
__ 1 bunch fresh thyme
__ 4 medium sweet potatoes
__ 1 banana
__ 1 small bunch grapes
__ 1 small ginger root

STAPLES/SPICES
__ Coffee
__ Dried basil
__ Ground cinnamon
__ Ground sage
__ Nutmeg
__ Peppercorns
__ Pumpkin pie spice
__ Sugar
__ Vanilla extract

PARTY SPINACH DIP

CRUNCHY BAKED CHICKEN

FESTIVE CORN SALAD

BASIL TOMATOES

APPLE PIE

ICED TEA

SERVES 4

The Fourth of July inspires festivity—and hunger—in most of us. Prepare this picnic for your family and head for the lake. Concentrate on the fireworks and you'll never miss the fat.

Party Spinach Dip

1	10-ounce package frozen chopped spinach	1	8-ounce can chopped water chestnuts
2	tablespoons dry vegetable soup mix	2	tablespoons chopped green onion
1 ½	cups plain nonfat yogurt	⅛	teaspoon dry mustard Raw vegetables for dipping
½	cup reduced-calorie mayonnaise		

Easy • Prep time: 5 to 7 minutes • Recipe halves easily
Thaw, drain, and squeeze spinach until dry. In a serving bowl, combine remaining ingredients and stir in spinach. Serve with raw vegetables.
Yield 4 cups or 32 servings of 2 tablespoons each
Calories: 23; Fat: 1 g; Cholesterol: 2 mg; Sodium: 68 mg;
Carbohydrates: 2 g; Fiber: 1 g; Diabetic Exchange: Free.

Notes

Fresh lemon juice combined with a dash of your favorite herb makes a great calorie-wise sauce for chicken, fish, and vegetables.

Crunchy Baked Chicken

¼ cup plain nonfat yogurt	4 6-ounce skinless, boneless chicken breasts
3 tablespoons chopped fresh parsley	
½ teaspoon poultry seasoning	1 cup cornflakes, crushed
¼ teaspoon Creole seasoning	Fresh parsley sprigs for garnish

Easy • Prep time: 5 minutes
Preheat the oven to 400°. In a small bowl, combine the first 4 ingredients. Brush chicken with the yogurt mixture and dredge each piece in the cereal. Place chicken on a rack in a roasting pan. Bake, uncovered, for 45 to 50 minutes, or until the chicken is tender. Garnish with fresh parsley sprigs.
Yields 4 servings of 5 ounces each
Calories: 304; Fat: 2 g; Cholesterol: 103 mg; Sodium: 550 mg; Carbohydrates: 25 g; Fiber: 1 g; Diabetic Exchange: 6 lower fat meat, 1½ starch

Festive Corn Salad

3 cups frozen whole kernel corn	½ cup chopped green onions
	1 tablespoon sugar substitute
2 4-ounce jars diced pimiento, drained	¼ cup apple cider vinegar
	2 teaspoons celery seeds
1 cup chopped green bell pepper	1 tablespoon safflower oil
	½ teaspoon salt

Easy • Prep time: 10 to 12 minutes • Prepare ahead
Cook corn according to the package directions, omitting salt. Drain and chill. In a serving bowl, combine corn and remaining ingredients, stirring well. Cover and chill for at least 2 hours before serving.
Yields 8 servings of ½ cup each
Calories: 83; Fat 2 g; Cholesterol: 0 mg; Sodium: 145 mg; Carbohydrates: 17 mg; Fiber: 1 g; Diabetic Exchange: 1 starch

Basil Tomatoes

½ teaspoon chopped
  fresh basil
1 teaspoon finely chopped
  garlic

¼ teaspoon salt
⅛ teaspoon black pepper
2 large tomatoes, sliced
  ¼-inch thick

Easy • Prep time: 5 to 7 minutes • Prepare ahead
In a small bowl, combine basil, garlic, salt, and pepper. Spread the mixture evenly on top of tomato slices. Cover and chill.
Yields 4 servings of 2 tomato slices each
Calories: 13; Fat: .2 g; Cholesterol: 0 mg; Sodium: 138 mg;
Carbohydrates: 4 g; Fiber: .5 g; Diabetic Exchange: ½ vegetable

Never-Fail Pie Crust

⅓ cup margarine, softened
1 cup all-purpose flour
¼ cup ice water

¼ teaspoon salt
1 egg white
1½ teaspoons white vinegar

Easy • Prep time: 15 minutes • Prepare ahead
In a small bowl, cut margarine into flour until the mixture resembles coarse meal. In a separate bowl, combine water, salt, egg white, and vinegar. Mix well, then add liquids to the flour mixture. Mix lightly with a fork until the pastry forms a ball. Refrigerate until ready to use.

Preheat the oven to 425°. Roll the crust out on a floured surface to form a circle. Press the pastry into a 9-inch pie tin and prick the bottom with the tines of a fork. Bake for 12 to 15 minutes, or until lightly brown, or fill the unbaked crust with the desired filling and bake according to pie directions.
Yields 1 nine-inch pie crust of 8 servings
Calories: 126; Fat: 8 g; Cholesterol: 0 mg; Sodium: 73 mg;
Carbohydrates: 12 g; Fiber: 0 g; Diabetic Exchange: 1 starch, 1 fat

Apple Pie

4½	cups peeled, sliced apples	¼	cup all-purpose flour
2	tablespoons lemon juice	3	tablespoons brown sugar
⅓	cup sugar	1	tablespoon reduced-calorie
2	tablespoons all-purpose		margarine
	flour	⅛	teaspoon ground cinnamon
½	teaspoon ground cinnamon	1	Never-Fail Pie Crust
¼	teaspoon grated nutmeg		(see page 323)

Easy • Prep time: 15 minutes

Preheat the oven to 375 °. In a large bowl, combine apple slices and lemon juice. Toss gently to coat. In a separate bowl, combine sugar, 2 tablespoons flour, ½ teaspoon cinnamon, and nutmeg; stir to blend. Sprinkle the mixture over apples and toss gently to coat. Spoon the filling into the pastry crust. Set aside.

In a small bowl, combine ¼ cup flour, brown sugar, margarine, and remaining cinnamon. Stir well. Sprinkle the mixture evenly over the apple filling. Bake for 30 minutes. Decrease the oven temperature to 325° and bake for an additional 10 minutes, or until the apples are tender.

Yields 1 nine-inch pie of 10 servings
Calories: 188; Fat: 7 g; Cholesterol: 0 mg; Sodium: 65 mg;
Carbohydrates: 30 g; Fiber: 1g; Diabetic Exchange: 1½ starch, ½ fruit,
1½ fat

SHOPPING LIST _____

BUTCHER
__ 4 6-ounce boneless, skinless
   chicken breasts

CANNED GOODS
__ 1 8-ounce can chopped water
   chestnuts

DAIRY
__ 1 16-ounce container plain
   nonfat yogurt
__ 1 pound reduced-calorie
   margarine
__ 1 egg

MISCELLANEOUS
__ 1 10-ounce package frozen
   chopped spinach
__ 1 box dry vegetable soup mix
__ 1 small box cornflakes
__ 1 16-ounce bag frozen whole
   kernel corn
__ 2 4-ounce jars diced pimiento
__ 1 small container sugar
   substitute
__ 1 bottle safflower oil

PRODUCE
__ 1 stalk celery
__ 1 bag carrots
__ 1 bunch green onions
__ 1 bunch fresh parsley
__ 1 green bell pepper
__ 2 large tomatoes
__ 1 bunch fresh basil
__ 1 head garlic
__ 5 cooking apples
__ 2 lemons

STAPLES/SPICES
__ All-purpose flour
__ Apple cider vinegar
__ Black pepper
__ Brown sugar
__ Celery seeds
__ Cinnamon
__ Creole seasoning
__ Dry mustard
__ Nutmeg
__ Poultry seasoning
__ Reduced calorie mayonnaise
__ Salt
__ Sugar
__ Tea bags
__ White vinegar

Sunday Lunch

SQUASH MEDLEY

TENDERLOIN POT ROAST

MUSHROOM BARLEY CASSEROLE

FRESH FRUIT WITH POPPY SEED DRESSING

FRENCH BREAD

YUMMY CHOCOLATE CAKE

COFFEE AND TEA

SERVES 8

Inviting your family over for lunch doesn't mean you
have to serve them foods that are full of fat and
cholesterol. For a change of pace, and for a change in
your diet, serve this healthy menu the next time your
clan is gathering together.

Squash Medley

1	tablespoon safflower oil	1	medium onion, chopped
2	cups chopped zucchini	¼	teaspoon dried dill
2	cups chopped acorn squash	¼	teaspoon ground black
2	cups chopped crookneck yellow squash		pepper

Easy • Prep time: 15 minutes
In a large sauté pan, heat the oil and sauté remaining ingredients until
tender but still crisp.
Yields 8 servings of ½ cup each
Calories: 38; Fat: 2 g; Cholesterol: 0 mg; Sodium: 3 mg;
Carbohydrates: 5 g; Fiber: 1 g; Diabetic Exchange: 1 vegetable, ½ fat

Tenderloin Pot Roast

1	3-pound beef tenderloin roast	½	pound fresh mushrooms, sliced
¼	cup soy sauce	3	ribs celery, sliced
1	tablespoon Worcestershire sauce	3	carrots, peeled and sliced
1	clove garlic, crushed	¼	cup water
2	onions, quartered	4 to 6	small new potatoes, halved

Easy • Prep time: 10 minutes

Preheat the oven to 325°. Place tenderloin in a bowl. In a separate small bowl, combine soy sauce, Worcestershire, and garlic. Pour the mixture over tenderloin and marinate overnight. In a roasting pan, place marinated tenderloin, onions, mushrooms, celery, and carrots. Cover. Bake for 2 hours and 30 minutes. Add the potatoes and water, and bake for another 30 minutes.

Yields 12 servings of 3 ounces of tenderloin, plus divided vegetables, per person

Calories: 230; Fat: 10 g; Cholesterol: 73 mg; Sodium: 363 mg;

Carbohydrates: 10 g; Fiber: .5 g; Diabetic Exchange: 3 lean meat, ½ starch

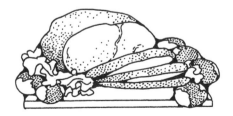

One cup of flavored yogurt combined with two tablespoons of honey makes a great lowfat dressing for fruit salad.

Mushroom Barley Casserole

1 cup chopped onion
10 ounces fresh mushrooms, sliced
¼ cup water
1½ cups barley
3 cups low-sodium beef or chicken broth
½ teaspoon ground black pepper
½ teaspoon ground marjoram

Easy • Prep time: 10 minutes
In a saucepan, sauté onion and mushrooms in water over medium heat until tender. Stir in barley and brown lightly. Add stock and seasoning; mix well. Cover tightly and simmer over low heat for 1 hour, until barley is tender and the liquid absorbed.
Yields 8 servings
Calories: 203; Fat: .8 g; Cholesterol: 0 mg; Sodium: 7 mg;
Carbohydrates: 45 g; Fiber: 1 g; Diabetic Exchange: 2½ starch, 1 vegetable

Fresh Fruit with Poppy Seed Dressing

1 cup vanilla nonfat yogurt
1 tablespoon honey
1 tablespoon lemon juice
1 teaspoon poppy seeds
Assorted fresh fruit, cut into bite-sized pieces

Easy • Prep time: 5 minutes
Combine all ingredients and mix well. Store, covered, in the refrigerator until ready to serve. Toss with fruit just before serving.
Yields 1 cup or 16 servings of 1 tablespoon each
Calories: 12; Fat: .1 g; Cholesterol: .3 mg; Sodium: 10 mg;
Carbohydrates: 2 g; Fiber: 0 g; Diabetic Exchange: free

Yummy Chocolate Cake

¾ cup reduced-calorie
    margarine, softened
¼ cup sugar
½ cup liquid egg substitute,
    at room temperature
    Liquid sugar substitute
    equivalent to ⅓ cup sugar
1 tablespoon vanilla extract

2 cups cake flour
2 teaspoons baking powder
¼ cup instant nonfat dry milk
⅓ cup unsweetened cocoa
1 cup water, at room
    temperature
    Delicious Chocolate Sauce,
    optional (see p. 330)

Easy • Prep time: 20 minutes

Preheat the oven to 350°. Grease a 9-inch square pan with a small amount of reduced-calorie margarine. In a large mixing bowl, cream margarine and sugar until light and fluffy. Add egg substitute, sugar substitute, and vanilla to the creamed mixture and beat at medium speed for 30 seconds. In a separate bowl, combine remaining dry ingredients. Alternately, add the dry mixture and water to the creamed mixture, mixing until smooth. Spread the batter evenly in the prepared pan. Bake for 30 to 35 minutes, or until a toothpick inserted in the center comes out clean. Serve with Delicious Chocolate Sauce, if desired.

Yields 16 servings
Calories: 111; Fat: 5 g; Cholesterol: .3 mg; Sodium: 102 mg;
Carbohydrates: 15 g; Fiber: 0 g; Diabetic Exchange: 1 fat, 1 starch

Delicious Chocolate Sauce

6	tablespoons cocoa powder	2	tablespoons reduced-calorie margarine
2	tablespoons plus 2 teaspoons cornstarch	1	tablespoon vanilla extract
⅔	cup instant nonfat dry milk	20	individual packets sugar substitute
¼	teaspoon salt		
3	cups water		

Easy • Prep time: 20 minutes

In a saucepan, combine cocoa, cornstarch, dry milk, and salt. Stir water into the dry mixture until smooth. Add margarine and cook over low heat, stirring constantly. Bring the mixture to a boil. Reduce the heat and simmer for 2 minutes, stirring constantly. Remove the pan from the heat. Add vanilla and sugar substitute. Stir gently to mix. Store in a glass bowl in the refrigerator until ready to use. Reheat as needed.

Yields 3 cups or 24 servings of 2 tablespoons each
Calories: 21; Fat: 1 g; Cholesterol: 4 mg; Sodium: 37.8 mg;
Carbohydrates: 3 g; Fiber: 0g; Diabetic Exchange: free

SHOPPING LIST _____

BAKERY
__ 3 loaves French bread

BUTCHER
__ 1 3-pound beef tenderloin roast

CANNED GOODS
__ 2 16-ounce cans low-sodium beef or chicken broth

DAIRY
__ 1 8-ounce container nonfat yogurt
__ 1 pound reduced-calorie margarine
__ 1 carton liquid egg substitute

MISCELLANEOUS
__ 1 bottle safflower oil
__ 1 box quick barley
__ 1 small jar honey
__ 1 small bottle liquid sugar substitute
__ 1 small box sugar substitute packets
__ 1 small box instant nonfat dry milk

PRODUCE
__ 1 pint strawberries
__ 1 cantaloupe or honeydew melon
__ 1 bunch grapes
__ 1 head garlic
__ 4 onions
__ 2 10½-ounce packages fresh mushrooms
__ 1 stalk celery
__ 3 carrots
__ 4 to 6 small new potatoes
__ 2 large zucchini
__ 4 large yellow crookneck squash
__ 1 lemon

STAPLES/SPICES
__ Baking powder
__ Cake flour
__ Cocoa powder
__ Coffee
__ Cornstarch
__ Dried dill
__ Ground marjoram
__ Peppercorns
__ Poppy seeds
__ Salt
__ Soy sauce
__ Sugar
__ Tea bags
__ Vanilla extract
__ Worcestershire sauce

Auxiliary Board Brunch

CRAB MORNAY

FESTIVE CRANBERRY SALAD

CHOCOLATE OATMEAL CAKE

COFFEE OR TEA

FRESHLY SQUEEZED ORANGE JUICE

SERVES 8

The stress of planning a fundraiser or improving your
organization's standing in the community is enough;
you don't need to add concern
about what to serve at your next meeting.
Here's the menu that can ease your mind and
get you back to the business at hand.

Enhance the flavor of
vegetables by adding basil,
chives, dill, tarragon, mint,
or pepper.

_____

Drop a few ice cubes into
the pot when making soup.
The fat will cling to the ice
cubes for easy removal.

Crab Mornay

4 green onions, chopped	2 ounces lowfat Swiss cheese, grated
1 cup chopped fresh mushrooms	1 cup fresh crab meat or drained and flaked canned crab meat
2 tablespoons water	
½ cup lowfat milk	
2 teaspoons cornstarch	English muffins, toasted

Easy • Prep time: 20 minutes

In a large skillet, sauté green onions and mushrooms in the water until soft. Set vegetables aside. In a saucepan, combine milk and cornstarch, mixing well. Cook until heated through. Stir in vegetables, cooking until the sauce is thickened. Add cheese and crab, gently stirring until cheese is melted. Serve over English muffins.

Yields 2 cups or 16 servings of 2 tablespoons each
Calories: 30; Fat: .9 g; Cholesterol: 9 mg; Sodium: 165 mg;
Carbohydrates: 1 g; Fiber: 0 g; Diabetic Exchange: ½ lean meat

Festive Cranberry Salad

1   envelope unflavored gelatin
½   cup cold water
1   teaspoon grated orange rind
1   16-ounce can whole-berry
    cranberry sauce

1   8-ounce can crushed
    pineapple, undrained
½   cup finely chopped apple
¼   cup diced celery

Easy • Prep time: 15 minutes • Prepare ahead

In a saucepan, combine gelatin and cold water; let gelatin soften for 1 minute. Cook over low heat, stirring constantly, until gelatin dissolves. Remove the pan from the heat and stir in orange rind. Chill for 30 to 45 minutes. Mix in cranberry sauce, pineapple, apple, and celery. Pour the mixture into a 1½-quart casserole or mold. Cover and chill until firm.

Yields 8 servings of ¾ cup each
Calories: 105; Fat: .1 g; Cholesterol: 0 mg; Sodium: 15 mg;
Carbohydrates: 27 g; Fiber: .4 g; Diabetic Exchange: 2 fruit

Chocolate Oatmeal Cake

½   cup safflower oil
⅓   cup honey
1   large egg
½   cup rolled oats
1   cup whole-wheat flour

1   tablespoon baking powder
½   cup semisweet chocolate
    morsels
¾   cup lowfat milk

Easy • Prep time: 15 minutes

Preheat the oven to 350°. Spray an 8-inch square pan with vegetable spray. In a large mixing bowl, mix oil, honey, and egg. Add oats, flour, baking powder, chocolate chips, and milk. Mix until blended. Pour the batter into the prepared pan. Bake for 35 to 40 minutes, or until the cake tests done.

Yields 12 two-inch squares
Calories: 205; Fat: 13 g; Cholesterol: 23 g; Sodium: 122 mg;
Carbohydrates: 22 g; Fiber: .6 g; Diabetic Exchange: 1½ starch, 2 fat

A quick frosting can be made by adding a spoonful of chocolate syrup to prepared whipped topping.

SHOPPING LIST

BAKERY

__ 2 packages English muffins

BUTCHER

__ ½ pound fresh lump crabmeat

CANNED GOODS

__ 1 16-ounce can whole berry
  cranberry sauce
__ 1 8-ounce can crushed pineapple

DAIRY

__ 1 pint lowfat milk
__ 1 2-ounce block Swiss cheese
__ 1 large egg

MISCELLANEOUS

__ 1 box unflavored gelatin
__ 1 bottle safflower oil
__ 1 small jar honey
__ 1 small container rolled oats
__ 1 small bag semisweet chocolate
  morsels

PRODUCE

__ 24 or more large juice oranges
__ 1 bunch green onions
__ 1 10½-ounce package fresh
  mushrooms
__ 1 large apple
__ 1 stalk celery

STAPLES/SPICES

__ Baking powder
__ Coffee
__ Cornstarch
__ Sugar
__ Tea bags
__ Whole-wheat flour

INGREDIENT SUBSTITUTION

Recipe Listing	Use Instead
American, Cheddar, Swiss, and Monterey Jack cheese	Cheese with 5 grams of fat or less per ounce
Cream cheese	Fat-free cream cheese, Neufchâtel cheese, light cream cheese
Ricotta	Part skim, nonfat, or lite Ricotta
Sour Cream	Nonfat or lowfat sour cream; nonfat or lowfat yogurt
Whole or 2% milk	Skim milk, 1% milk, or nonfat dry milk mixed with water
Whipping cream	Chilled evaporated skim milk, whipped
Half-and-half	Half evaporated skim milk plus half skim milk
1 whole egg	2 egg whites or ¼ cup egg substitute
2 egg yolks	½ cup liquid egg substitute
Margarine	Reduced-calorie margarine, fat-free mayonnaise, unsweetened applesauce with fat-free mayonnaise
Vegetable oil	Reduce amount, using polyunsaturated or monounsaturated oil
Cooking oil for frying	Nonstick cooking spray; Butter Buds for basting or coating
Mayonnaise	Nonfat, reduced calorie, or low-cholesterol mayonnaise
White flour, 1 cup	½ cup whole-wheat plus ½ cup white flour
Salt	Reduce by ½ or eliminate by using herbs or spices or salt-free substitutes
Sugar	For every cup, ½ cup frozen fruit juice concentrate or sugar substitute
Egg noodles	Eggless noodles
White rice	Brown or wild rice
Nuts	Reduce by ½ or use Grape-Nuts cereal
Salad dressings	Fat-free salad dressings
Potato chips	Fat-free potato chips
Butter popcorn	Air-popped popcorn
Sweet rolls	Fat-free cakes and sweet rolls
Cookies	Fat-free cookies
Bacon strips	Turkey bacon or Canadian bacon
Poultry	Skinless poultry
Tuna packed in oil	Tuna packed in water
Ground beef	Lean ground beef or ground turkey
Beef, pork, veal, or lamb	Lean cuts; all visible fat removed

INDEX

338 HOSTING WITHOUT HASSLE